The Politics of Subversion

The Politics of Subversion
A Manifesto for the Twenty-First Century

ANTONIO NEGRI

Translated by James Newell

Polity Press

First published 1989 by Polity Press
in association with Basil Blackwell.

Polity Press
65 Bridge Street
Cambridge, CB2 1UR, UK.

Polity Press
350 Main Street
Malden, MA 02148, USA.

British Library Cataloguing in Publication Data

A CIP catalogue record for this book is available from the British Library.

ISBN 0 7456 0601 6
ISBN 0 7456 3513 X

Typeset in 11 on 13 pt Plantin
by Opus, Oxford and BookEns Ltd, Royston, Herts.
Printed in Great Britain by
MPG Books Ltd, Bodmin, Cornwall

Contents

Acknowledgements

The writings appearing in Part 2 of this work were originally published as follows:

1 'Lettre à Félix Guattari', in: Marie Blanche Tahon and André Corten (1986), *L'Italie: le philosophe et le gendarme. Actes du Colloque de Montréal*, Montréal: vlb editeur, pp. 95–109.

2 'Itinerari nella società civile. In memoria di Peter Brückner', in: Gianni Puglisi and Aurelio Angelini (1986), *Eclisse della società civile*, Palermo: Ediprint, pp. 129–34.

3 'Stato e classe nella fase della sussunzione reale', in: Laura Fiocco (1986), *Per una teoria dello Stato. Contributi all'analisi del potere nella prospettiva della transizione*, Roma: Gangemi editore, pp. 169–84.

4 'Qualche nota sul concetto di "Stato nucleare"', in: Alberto Toniolo *et al.* (1986), *Società nucleare o società civile?*, Palermo: Ila Palma, pp. 57–68.

5 'Postmoderno', in: José Tono Martinez (1986), *La polémica de la postmodernidad*, Madrid: Ediciones Libertarias, pp. 125–36.

6 'Vers de nouvelles valeurs?', in: *Terminal*, no.26, December–January, 1986, Paris, pp. 3–7.

Writings appearing in the Appendix were originally published as follows:

From *Capital: A Critique of Political Economy*, Vol. I by Karl Marx, translated by Ben Fowkes, pp. 1021, 1024, 1034–5, 1039–40. Translation Copyright (c) 1976 by Ben Fowkes. Reprinted by permission of Random House, Inc. and Penguin Books, Ltd. (Harmondsworth, 1976).

From *Grundrisse: Foundations of the Critique of Political* by Karl Marx, pp. 704–5, 705–6, 709. Translation & Foreword (c) 1973 by Martin Nicolaus. Reprinted by permission of Random House, Inc. and Penguin Books, Ltd. (Harmondsworth, 1973).

Preface to the new edition

When, after the first English edition, I published *The Politics of Subversion* in Italian with the title *Fine secolo: Un manifesto per l'operaio sociale*, the review in *Il Manifesto* was entitled 'Unnamed social categories head for conflict'. This was in early 1989, and *Il Manifesto* (whose masthead claims it to be a 'communist newspaper' and which is indeed closely linked to movements of the communist left) did not dare talk of the changes in the composition of the working class that had occurred over the intervening two decades from 1968. It was not yet possible to offend the ears of the older activists by discussing this new reality, even in the case of those who, like *Il Manifesto*'s reviewer, were entirely persuaded. The 'socialized worker' was nobody's child and no one would acknowledge his or her name. Ignorance, ethical and political opportunism, theoretical dogmatism, superficial analysis and trade-union corporatism combined with reality itself to make it impossible to analyse the present. There was a failure to identify the current situation with its irresistible tendency towards the formation of the socialized worker. I myself had already understood some twenty years earlier that the composition of the working class was changing, the period of the 'mass worker' was ending, and an increasingly intangible and cooperative socialized workforce was being gradually formed. For this I was detested and despised by the opportunist and dogmatic leaders of the communist parties, who then let bourgeois judges throw me into jail for ten years. Socialist bureaucrats hate anyone who studies, works, incites the masses and lives among the multitude, and because of this hatred they are capable of exploiting the established powers to destroy the truth. What is upsetting, however, is not this, but the fact that even today the evidence of this tendency (which has dramatically altered the world order) still has not sunk into the heads of activists in the labour movement. As recently as 2003, during a European Forum for the movements in Paris, I had to debate with an English Trotskyist, who spoke of the working class as though we were still in the nineteenth century and, of course, of the revolution, as though the twentieth had never existed. Marx tells us on every page of *Capital* that every law of development and the class struggle is *tendential*. His insistence on this matter even becomes somewhat tiresome: it seems he found his contemporaries (economists and politicians) complete idiots and considered them incapable of understanding the present as something that is always producing new players, and capitalist development as a continuous transformation and adaptation of methods of sub-jugation. Yet no one in the traditional labour movement appears to have listened to Marx. What can we say about his current dogmatic followers? What is there to add about his slavish imitators? It has increasingly become a dialogue of the deaf. However, there is an important minority that has realized that this method of examining tendencies, which was discussed in the 1970s and 1980s, has become established (a method that is moreover genuinely Marxian). Armed with this method, it was impossible not to see the social transformation of work, and the minority understood the significance of the tendency towards the socialized worker. It meant that there was *more exploitation*, even more exploitation (because mental labour and social cooperation have been added to physical labour), but at the same time there is a *greater chance of revolution*.

I re-read *The Politics of Subversion* in order to write this preface (I rarely re-read a book that I have already published, unless I am obliged to do so). It is a great book. The theme of the socialized worker is developed in an empirical manner. In 1984-5 I was far from ideological. It was right at the beginning of my fourteen-year exile following five years of prison: such conditions do not allow you to dream. The socialized worker emerged in relation to a type of work and exploitation from my empirical examination of the new intangible, computer-based, automatic and service production processes, whose rapid spread I had observed in the 1970s and early 1980s. *The Politics of Subversion* was also entirely correct about the periodization of the transition from the 'Taylorite worker' to the socialized worker (who would later be called the 'Fordist' worker and the 'post-Fordist' worker). The chapters on forms of exploitation that followed the transition from the expropriation of relative surplus value to the expropriation of value and/or the cooperative functions of socialized labour are still valid as paradigms for the analysis of the current situation. Finally, the socialized worker (in *The Politics of Subversion*) is part of the ecological machine: the whole environment is consequently included in the process of exploitation. Reflecting on the correctness and extraordinary theoretical significance of those passages, I am stunned by the way in which involvement in the class struggle in those incredible 1960s and 1970s has made it possible for my comrades and myself to make such progress in our empirical knowledge!

The fifth chapter, 'The world economy of the socialized worker', is really important (on re-reading it today). Twenty years later, I published *Empire* (with Michael Hardt), which sold half a million copies around the world, and one wonders why *The Politics of Subversion*, which said the same things as *Empire*, only sold around a thousand copies. This was a pity for my publishers at the time, who are still my publishers today, and agreed with me both then and now. We failed to make use of a great opportunity, because of either bad luck or dereliction.

As I have begun to examine the relationship between this book and *Empire* (and consequently of *Multitude*, which followed on from *Empire*), I will take the argument through to its conclusion. As I have said, there were many similarities with the fifth chapter of *The Politics of Subversion* – the necessary trend towards the globalization of labour and social control was already defined in that work – but it is also a matter of understanding how it differed from *Empire*, and this can usefully throw light on the sources for *Empire* and the process by which it was written. We can now summarize these points as follows:

(a) The philosophical framework of *Empire* is clearly different from that of *The Politics of Subversion*. The latter, which was written in 1985-6, was still very much in the tradition of

Italian workerism, and Foucault's and Deleuze's influence
was still absent. The concept of the socialized worker, the
globalization of the economy and the subsequent capitalist
contradictions did not yet need Foucault and Deleuze for its
formulation. It was simply based on the tendential expansion
of Marxian research into the 'world market'. If anything, it
could be argued that during that period Foucault and Deleuze
needed Italian workerism to create the *mille plateux* for the
production of subjectivity. Here we have the development of a
shared theoretical framework (shared by the Italians and the
French), and it was later taken up creatively by many
sociologists, political scientists and philosophers.

(b) Many of the analytical and theoretical elements that appear in
The Politics of Subversion are absolutely correct, particularly
those that concern and express predictions of a massive spread
of neo-liberal policies (the pace, method and geography of
their introduction). Both *Empire* and *Multitude* would adopt
the same interpretative line, but by then the trend had already
become a reality. It has to be said that the analysis in *The
Politics of Subversion* is occasionally consummate: examples
being chapter 6 on monetarism and more generally the
assessment of the Nixon and Reagan policies, which even then
produced a very close approximation to the way capitalism
would construct its global command and how it would
mutate.

(c) However, discussion of the revolutionary organization of
workers is inadequate in both *The Politics of Subversion* and
the later works. It is certainly the case that chapters 6 and 7 of
The Politics of Subversion examine very precisely some broad
and alternative elements concerning the organization of
socialized workers. But the analysis does not go far enough,
nor does it do so in the later works. Whereas the argument
manages to deal with ontological questions in relation to the
organization of labour and the bio-political contradictions of
social exploitation, it proved much more difficult to determine the relationship between the transformation of labour
and the transformation of organized subversive behaviour.
The analysis of socio-economic historical relations in this
field must be based on the definition of individual phenom-
enologies and theoretical and practical concepts of the active

parties and events. Following *Empire* and *Multitude* (which overturn the Hobbesian point of view put forward in *Leviathan* and *De Cive*), there remains the task of writing a *De Homine* on this theme, or rather to rewrite one just as the great political thinkers of the early modern era did, precisely in order to touch on the ever fundamental and changing link between the anthropological and the political.

The Politics of Subversion belonged entirely to my own experience of the struggle and was inspired by that struggle, particularly in the 1960s and 1970s, but also in 1986 in France, when I was again able to take part in a movement (for the first time since my exile). I discussed this movement in *The Politics of Subversion*: it was a protest movement by secondary-school and university students which made it clear that production was soon to be hegemonized by socialized intellectual labour. That movement was also important because it linked up with the first large organizations for immigrant workers: the flexibility and mobility of the new intellectual and migrant workforce entered the scene. Other phases and episodes in the struggle occurred after writing *The Politics of Subversion*: the French series of struggles in 1995-6 and those important ones in Seattle that provided much material for *Empire* and *Multitude*. Struggles are the great teachers when it comes to our knowledge of social development, and are the engines of revolutionary theory. I do not mean only those struggles in which we have been personally involved, but all the struggles within a period or cycle, which are therefore rooted within a specific class composition. When we consider 1968 as the beginning of the era of the socialized worker, we do not forget the struggles of the mass worker. In accordance with Marxist and Leninist methodology, we are simply considering those episodes of struggle as paradigms of a new configuration that is tendentially hegemonic in the proletariat, and therefore as a new tendentially revolutionary project (to be defined and developed).

My experience of the socialized worker, and his appearance and formation as a social type, is Italian and European. But has the experience of comrades who have analysed the movements and struggles in the United States and former Soviet Union been any different? Recently I had the opportunity to visit China: I was greatly surprised to discover the interpretation of the great contradictory process that led from the Cultural Revolution to the current New Economic Policy by Chinese communists (by which I mean those who still actively support the proletarian cause). They emphasized the transformation of the mass worker into the socialized worker, particularly within the New Economic Policy, and how this occurred amid changing methods of accumulation and socialization of labour. I was also surprised to discover that they increasingly consider the relationship between modernization of life and production, and communist ends as subject to the hegemony, judgement and distinction of a new socially active and anthropologically communist, intellectual worker! In other words, it is quite true that we can often make enormous mistakes when we come to predicting trends, and this has occasionally happened to me; yet we have to construct the *episteme*, the historical truth. We occasionally get it wrong, but we often manage to grasp it: we grab history, the *kairos* and the event by the neck, much as Orlando caught the winged horse to take him to the moon. We discover the materialist *telos* and the revolutionary purpose of development within the workers' struggles and today that is among the global *multitude* of *socialized workers*.

What next? This is perhaps the moment to identify another more advanced task within the cycle of the socialized worker in the twenty-first century – that of organization. Perhaps someone will say, not without irony, that this Negri guy is somewhat comical: he has been trying to show us a new form of organization since 1986 (or rather, since the 1970s). Is he dreaming? Well, just as I was certain that the category of socialized worker would impose himself on globalization, I was equally certain that we were witnessing the birth of a new social monster (not simply an internet worker or creator of cyborgs, but rather someone capable of immediately expressing communist needs), and that the new technical composition of the global workforce was ready for a political transition. While this did not occur then, and we only experienced spontaneous expressions of this political genesis, we did become aware of the tendency through a thousand events and increasing evidence. The margin of error in our prediction was not that great.

One last point, then, on the concept of *tendency*: Marx never tired of reminding us that (1) the form of economic laws is always tendential, but (2) as economic laws are transitory measures of power relations, the tendency is not necessary, but rather a materialist *telos*, a result constructed by struggles, an end produced by wills and desires, and an establishment of the real. (3) The result is that the tendency is not necessarily progress, but can become it. The subjective and the objective encounter each other within it. It is the place where the will to change the world meets up with the power relations that block change. (4) The difficulty with theoretical work is not defining the tendency as a solution to power relations, but defining that tendency as the active component that is open to the adventure of knowledge and the risk of struggle. Indeed the active element in struggles is always the force that changes the world, whether it is victorious or defeated. This is the fundamental argument asserted in *The Politics of Subversion*, and resumed and reinforced in *Empire* and *Multitude*. 5) This last ontological premise is in fact the basis for re-launching the theory of revolutionary organization.

Toni Negri (August 2004)
Translated by Allan Cameron

Introduction

by Yann Moulier
Translated by Philippa Hurd

The history of Marxism's entry into the English language has been fraught with difficulties, sometimes damning, sometimes authoritative, in all cases passionate. It is a repetition, in a more extreme form, of what happened during its translation into French. Whole tracts of thought can remain unknown if they have been conceived in the languages of Goethe, Dante, Cervantes or Pessoa and if they have not been blessed by the 'universalizing' force of translation. For this reason Marx resigned himself to Joseph Roy's French translation of *Capital* in 1872 – it was thought better to have a translation that was imprecise but quickly done, than to wait for a scholarly work which might never become available. It was thus a question of political rather than philological expediency.

More recently, the history of the *Grundrisse* illustrates the same pattern. It took the translation of this text, first published in 1939, for people to realize – albeit very hazily even then – the role that the *Grundrisse* was to play in the rebirth of Marxism in the 1960s and 70s. For behind the return to the Marx of *Capital*, a recurrent theme in the history of Marxism, there lay the amazing discovery of 'another' Marx, causing as great a shock as that provoked by the *Economic and Philosophical Manuscripts* of 1844 and the *Contribution to a Critique of Hegel's Philosophy of Right* of 1843, experienced during the post-war years. It relegated Althusser's thesis of an 'epistemological break' between Marx's ideological texts and his scientific texts to the level of a tactic which had been designed as a rhetorical challenge to Marx's neutralization by existentialist philosophy, a tactic which was convenient but untenable on a theoretical level.

This was Marx who took Hegel's *Logic* seriously, as Lenin had sensed; a Marx who had anticipated a socialized development of capitalism, pursuing this aspect, and bringing out its deepest tendencies, over the long period of the development of techniques such as the category of 'abstract labour'. In short, this was a Marx who was much more at home in the oceans of the twentieth century than in the constricted waters of nineteenth-century Europe, contrary to Foucault's thesis in *The Order of Things*.

We are still waiting for a detailed history of the impact of the *Grundrisse* on Western Marxism. In the context of non-academic Italian Marxism the translation published by La Nuova Italia was the work of a member of the *operaismo* movement, Enzo Grillo. The *Grundrisse*, alongside the unpublished sixth chapter of *Capital*, constitutes the text these 'heretics' referred to the most, taking refuge behind the most monumental of Marx's unpublished works.[1] The *Grundrisse* and Rosdolsky's research[2] continue to dominate problems surrounding the return to Marx. Elsewhere in Europe – with the exception of Germany – the impact of the *Grundrisse* was less direct but by no means negligible. Dangeville's French translation was published in 1968 at the same time as the unpublished sixth chapter of *Capital*; Rubel's translation appeared the same year. Twelve years later the least successful translation by the team led by J.P. Lefébvre[3] bears witness to this mutation of references in serious Marxism.

But it was the appearance of the excellent English translation by Martin Nicolaus[4] which confirmed once and for all the status of this text which even 'scholars' of Marxism had treated with disdain. Negri's seminar at L'Ecole Normale Supérieure in 1978 recaptures the relationship between *operaismo* and the fetishized *Grundrisse*.[5] As a response to Althusser's seminar fourteen years previously, entitled *Reading Capital*, Negri emphasized the freedom of tone in the text, its brilliant methodological insights into science, the development of capitalism, communism, but above all, into the constitution of a revolutionary subjectivity which in *Capital* tends to retreat behind the objectivism of the scientific treatise.[6] He pointed out how in the *Grundrisse* the 'flirtation with Hegelian terminology' is at its greatest, while the rupture with it is more decisive than elsewhere, provided that we realize that it is not so much the dialectic as *instrument*[7] that Marx takes from Hegel as his concept of 'abstract labour'.

It is the *Grundrisse* that initiated a revival of the analysis – already well developed – of large-scale industry, of machinism, of the transformation of absolute surplus-value into relative surplus-value in particular in Mario Tronti's essay of 1966, 'Marx, forza-lavoro, classa operaia', which constitutes the 'first theses' and the previously unpublished section of *Operai e Capitale*. It is also the *Grundrisse*, particularly the chapter on money, that prompted Negri to analyse money (coinage) as a power relation and to deduce from this the formal liberation of capital from the law of value, in 'Crisis of the Planner-State: Communism and Revolutionary Organization', which appeared as a supplement to issue 45 of the journal *Potere Operaio* in September 1971 and appears in English in *Revolution Retrieved*, (Red Notes, London, 1989). This text was to act as preparation for the Third Congress of Potere Operaio, opening up theoretical vistas and allowing a reconstruction of the global structure of the controversies in political economy, from the perspective of a political controversy raging at the time over the organization, and over Leninism. The debate focusing on the interest aroused by *Potere Operaio* between 1970 and 1973 had a considerable intellectual hold over other European militants.

While it might well be said that Negri's *Marx Beyond Marx* is a difficult text, this is all the more reason why the English-speaking world, through *The Politics of Subversion* and other collections of Negri's writings, should have access to the work of one of the rarest of tree-surgeons working on the old trunk of Western Marxism. The tree of Marxism has been pollarded twenty times and more, has been grafted with more or less good will and no longer holds out much hope of recovery. Many see only a stump fit for the bonfire; an impoverished Western Marxism reduced to the level of a respectable burst of critical and 'radical' independence. Soviet Marxism offers equally few perspectives; only the hope of the bitter buds of fifty years of 'real socialism'. From the Lyssenkoist hybrid which is Soviet Marxism, a curious mixture of nineteenth-century revolutionary words and of a twentieth-century state promoted to the rank of a poor religion, nothing could emerge except as a result of a solid class struggle in the Polish style, cleanly breaking through the Bismarkian side of *perestroika*. While waiting for this flowering on the old stump of Western Marxism we could do worse than investigate a few detours and translations.

What can an English-speaking audience find of interest in *The Politics of Subversion*? It provides contact with an 'Italian Marxism' which has been categorized under the label *operaismo*[8] – misleading in its French and English translations; a Marxism which is very often ignored, but which has proved to be of a fecundity equivalent on a formal level to that of the Althusserian movement and of a productivity far superior on the substantial level. The term 'workers' autonomy' which appeared in 1973 is also misleading as it omits the solid Marxist foundation of this school of thought in relation, for example, to the term *autonomia oberera* of the Catalonian CNT.

It is this point above all which demands most explanation and we shall be devoting the first part of our discussion to the genealogy of *operaismo* and its major contributions to the development of Marxist thought. But no current is monolithic – *operaismo* and 'autonomy' even less so than others – so it is equally appropriate for the reader to be able to situate the paradigmatic transformations in relation to the other disciples of this 'cultural and political matrix', notably the adherents of *operaismo* who remained closest to the Italian Communist Party: Mario Tronti, Alberto Asor Rosa and Massimo Cacciari. A discussion of the different forms of *operaismo* and their limitations will form the major theme of the second part of this Introduction. In conclusion we shall look at Antonio Negri's contribution to the ongoing *operaismo* debates, situating the present work with regard to the career of its author and his preceding works.

We shall leave the rest to the readers. It is up to them to decide if this polemical work by a revolutionary philosopher who was expelled from his native Italy, a work which salutes the 1986 student movement in Paris, can provide any assistance in theorizing our twentieth century as an epoch, and motivate us into action for the next century.

I

Knowledge of Italian Marxism in countries to the north of the Alps is limited in general to a few words on Gramsci, a writer who is often quoted but never read,[9] a few words on Della Volpe whose work is often ransacked without acknowledgement, and a few words on Colletti, especially on his work on the history of thought in philosophy.[10] The problem is that there are too many allusions and too little substance. The English-speaking world does not escape this trend either. Perry Anderson, in his classic, honest work *Considerations on Western Marxism*,[11] devotes not a single word to the tradition of *operaismo* which began in 1962 with the *Quaderni Rossi*, and the early groups of the extra-parliamentary left which do not claim any inspiration from the heretical ideologies of the workers' movement (Bordigism, anarchism, Trotskyism or Maoism).[12] Twenty-two years after its publication, Mario Tronti's *Operai e Capitale*, one of the major works in this intellectual tradition, has still not been completely translated into English.[13] Knowledge of Italian Marxism consists primarily of some contributions to the history of the workers' movement in the United Kingdom or United States by the disciples of this current of thought, which have received a small, militant propagation in the collectives *Big Flame* and *Red Notes*, more notably in the United States than in the United Kingdom.[14] Of the works by Antonio Negri the following have appeared: an extract from *Domination and Sabotage*,[15] *Marx Beyond Marx*[16] and *Is there a Marxist Doctrine of the State*.[17] A new collection by Red Notes, published in 1989 and entitled *Revolution Retrieved: Selected Writings by Toni Negri on Marx, Keynes, Capitalist Crisis and New Social Subjects, 1967–83* is a major contribution to the international dissemination of Negri's work.

We still need an anthology of the most important texts as well as a résumé and an examination of the striking development which took place from 1973 onwards. To add to this obstacle there is the problem of the aridity or the obscurity of this form of Marxism which is like no other manifestation we have known.

It should be no surprise that the authors of the Prefaces to *Marx Beyond Marx*, the editor as well as the translators, lay great stress on the difficult and abstract aspects of *operaismo* and the Autonomia movement.[18] The reader cannot remain unmoved in the face of such complicated language, which has been brought into line with the current usage of Marxist terms in Italian itself. The ordinary cultural Marxist is subjected to a veritable conceptual bombardment of terms such as 'refusal of work', 'class composition', 'decomposition', 'recomposition', 'formal subsumption', 'real subsumption', 'social capital', 'state-plan', 'state-crisis', 'mass worker', 'socialized worker', 'political salary', 'auto-valorization', 'large- and small-scale circulation'. In the end, however, so much the better. The facile use of concepts, which are otherwise difficult to master and whose meaning has become imprecise, leads directly to a stereotyped language.

Operaismo too is no stranger to this kind of verbosity, like all political movements which are weighed down by the constant harping of a pure ideology. What counts above all is the operational side of these concepts from the point of view of practical knowledge of the present-day reality of capitalism, or of the reinterpretation of its history: thus we can use 'abstract labour' to mean non-capital labour; 'mass worker' to give a political reading of the social movements of specialized workers; 'capital' when discussing money, in order to interpret the monetary crisis; 'auto-valorization' and 'small-scale circulation' in order to reinterpret the development of the underground economy; 'plan of capital' and 'social capital' in order to understand the meaning of the Keynesian rediscovery of effective demand and of downward rigidity of wages. Henry Cleaver was right to emphasize that it was because of the terrible mediocrity of academic intellectual production that a form of Marxism developing in the heart of the universities in the United States could now be discerned.[19] This illustrates the adage in *operaismo* that knowledge of the system comes from its conflicting forces, and that the plundering of workers' inventiveness goes on all the time.

In the limited scope of this introduction we cannot attempt to overcome the linguistic obstacles which correspond to the particularities of the Italian situation – specifically, an intellectual left which had been the subject of a political and cultural hegemony by the Italian Communist Party in a much more organic way than in France and *a fortiori* than in the English-speaking countries where communist parties have never grown beyond the stage of minority groupings. Such a discussion would require an entire course of seminars. It would equally be impossible to overcome the problem of the very specific character of those references which are available in the English language.

The first problem is an obstacle which will diminish with time and in particular with the evolution of the intellectual production of this current of thought. If it has disseminated many ideas and exerted an undeniable intellectual and political influence since 1975,[20] it has equally extensively borrowed from the political, theoretical and cultural experiences of Europe and the United States. The terrible wave of repression which followed 7 April 1979 in the course of which numerous leaders of the movement were imprisoned or exiled from Italy,[21] helped to bring about a modification of its language and a marked modulation in the themes addressed. The language has become less Italian, less technical and more basic. Its tone is now reminiscent of the great figures of the Enlightenment.

As for the second problem, of a systematic reconstruction of the themes both of the theses of *operaismo* and of autonomous Marxism, this can be tackled properly, if briefly, beginning with what distinguished this school of thought, from its inception, from the great critical and revolutionary movements which ran contemporaneously with it. If the early days of *operaismo* and its manifestation as Autonomia seem to be part of a general renewal of combativity within the social movements throughout their practical translations into politics and culture, its originality remains characterized by its relation to the major currents of Western Marxism and radical, critical thought.

With hindsight, certain features claimed by this theoretical current as specific to its own history appear to us rather more as the common ground it shares with the 'leftism' of the 1960s. The same sort of attention is given to the social demonstrations of dissent which were as much about the regime of Fordist capitalism in the 1950s as about the progressive ossification of the workers' movement in first its socialist then its communist forms. *Operaismo* carries within it the exaltation of the workers' and the students' revolt. It claims to have discovered a new political actor, a third force between the state and the organized working-class movement. The turmoil both on the streets and in people's minds after the division of Germany into two countries and the interminable liquidation of the European and American colonial wars, was general. It was evident all over the world, but it was the small Eurasian peninsula that produced all possible variations. This long experience, of which the events of 1968 and 1969 in West Germany, France and Italy were the climax, was equivalent to the experience of liberation and struggle which the previous generation had gone through against the Nazis.

In the late seventies, when these cultural and political aspirations had not been translated into the sphere of representative democracy, and with the return of the hard face of capitalism in crisis, in the ghettos everywhere an explosive period followed. For some this represented the radicalization of the minorities, for others an attempt to regenerate the old parties of the left and for others a cautious dissent. Between 1970 and 1980 the same rise to extremism could be seen everywhere, which became progressively overdetermined by terrorism, itself becoming a myth worthy of the revolutionary syndicalist Georges Sorel, and which was created as much by repressive bureaucracy as by the reflux of the movement. In any event it was a concrete expression of the delegitimation of the democratic state which had been constructed on the basis of the post-war Pact of Liberation. From 1980–1 onwards in certain countries repression relaxed its grip and the cultural values of 1968 began slowly to penetrate the institutional sphere.

But everywhere in the course of the decade 1965–75 (including Portugal which had seen the only political revolution worthy of the name since the last war in Europe), the revolutionary 'New Left' came up against the same obstacle, the same squared circle: what could be meant by the post-communist organization of a radical, social transformation? What political space was afforded to the masses with an organized spontaneity, at a stage in capitalism's development when the 'Party' could no longer propose the repetition of the events of 1917, much less 'real socialism' (which the Italians with a truly Anglo-Saxon empiricist materialism call *socialismo realizzato,* 'achieved socialism') in its various forms?

Whatever the ideological point of departure, the country, or the size of the 'revolutionary' organizations born of the struggles of the sixties, the years 1972–7 saw the eruption of political forms inherited from the 1920s. As soon as the organizations abandoned their formation as infinitely dividing 'sects', they encountered three major dislocations: (a) the inability to supplant the communist parties which thus created a dramatic absence of institutional space (the only successful breakthrough by the European extra-parliamentary left has been by the German Greens in a country where, by quasi-constitutional definition, the communist party does not exist); (b) a crisis of the *centralist* models of organization, but also a crisis in the whole 'way of doing politics' in the light of feminist critiques of the sexual division of labour, or the appearance on the scene of minority groups (immigrant workers who were, above all else, conducting a struggle against discrimination); (c) the control of the political dimension by violence, manifested in the cancerous growth of armed and highly-professional groups who were resorting to extreme action when faced with the massive appeal of a democratic state which was taking emergency action, and on the grounds of the ineffectiveness of mass movements. This 'affront' to power was inevitably turned to the state's advantage – not because it was better armed but because it was more representative of the power of society as a whole than the four groups who represented bygone struggles or a mythical image of the 'working-class party'.

This idea led Negri in his work on Spinoza[22] to contrast the ineffective, homologous *power* of the individual, and the social power of the state, with the *strength* of the multitude. The question of real socialism (and thus of the Western communist parties who besides their proselytizing or protesting role were still giving voice to a wide-spread dissemination of the socialist model among the social forces), the feminist question and the problem of violence were tackled on all sides to different degrees and in different ways. But these issues sounded the death knell first for the factions, and subsequently for organized workers' autonomy.[23]

Between 1973 and 1976 most formations of the extra-parliamentary left dissolved. But the first-hand accounts by militants, such as Nanni Balestrini's *Vogliamo tutto*, Robert Linhart's *Etabli* and Günter Walraff's *The Lowest of the Low* show clearly the deep similarities between instances of a 'subjectivity' in the process of self-creation, beyond the specifications of situation and formation. It is the same story in the more or less spontaneous accounts of other armed struggles: from 'nationalist minorities' to 'dogmatic leftism' or 'mao-sponti', anarcho-maoists.[24]

Where, then, lies the originality of this new form of Marxism which emerged in Italy and which has coexisted with much better-known forms in other countries, such as different branches of Trotskyism, of Marxist-Leninism in Maoist or pro-Chinese versions? Its originality seems to lie above all in its representation of the first alternative on a theoretical level to the Marxist orthodoxy prevalent in the communist parties, to the critical theories produced

by the Frankfurt School, to Sartrean existentialist humanism and
lastly to the structuralist anti-humanism of Althusser.

In post-war Europe, which was undergoing reconstruction,
capitalism's excellent health was interpreted by those believers in
the ineluctable superiority of the 'socialist cause' as a chance
mishap, like the secondary counter-tendencies against the downward trend of the capitalist mode of production. There was no
doubt that capitalism's days were numbered and sooner or later the
economy's inherent and catastrophic contradictions would emerge.
However, from 1956–60 capitalism's growth rate was maintained,
the internationalization of capital continued unhindered, working-
class households increased their standard of living, technological
innovation flourished – in short, the productive forces developed
very nicely.

In Hungary and Poland, however, the socialist cause became
fragmented and in China and the USSR theoretical revision was the
order of the day. The socialist parties of Northern Europe admired
the virtues of the 'mixed economy' or the 'socially controlled
market economy' which the parties of the old school in Southern
Europe were slower to put into action during the 1970s. Thus
canonical Marxism was abandoned for the sake of the 'socialist
transformation'. In the communist parties the upheaval was even
more dramatic even though this 'revisionism' took on neither the
cynicism of a Bernstein nor the prudence of a Kautsky.

All this was symptomatic of the dissolution of revolutionary
Marxism into the grand humanism of technical progress (as
described by Garaudy); namely a rallying under the bourgeois
democratic themes of expansion; reunification of the working-class
movement into one large party (under Amendola, a leader of the
Italian Communist Party [PCI]); abandonment of the Charter of
Amiens by the *Confédération Générale du Travail* [French
communist-dominated trade union) which advocated the abolition
of wage-labour; and the abandonment of the 'dictatorship of the
proletariat'. On the theoretical level this corresponded to the
doctrine of state monopoly capitalism (known as *Stamokap* in
Germany or as espoused by Boccara in France). Democratic control
of the state would enable the start of a peaceful transition to
socialism. This transformation in socialization was to be effected by
means of a programme of nationalizations (as worked out, for
example, by the Labour Party in the United Kingdom or the

programme of direct state investment in Italy). France had planned for this in its Common Programme and it was carried out in spite of the breakdown of the latter after Mitterrand came to power. Everywhere the union of the left (the Italian 'historical compromise', the post-Franco transition or Salazarism on the Iberian peninsula) were in control. Social struggles which did not fall within this 'political opening-up of structural reforms' were relegated to the sphere of the trades unions where they were likely in some cases to be vigorously opposed. All the more so now that the traditional trade unions bastions were losing their influence, circumvented both by this capitalist restructuring and by the growing weight of unskilled migrant workers from home and abroad. Technical development allowed the communist party theoreticians to establish class allegiances by extending the concept of productive labour to include the work of technicians, engineers, supervisory staff and among the lower orders of the state apparatus, to create and even foster a development even more rapid than that achieved by the 'productive forces'. This theme of a call to structural reform remained on the agenda for the working-class movement after the general upheavals of 1968–9, while the necessary conditions of shop-floor level work, namely an income-based politics and the maintenance of the regular increase in salaries within the scope of gains in productivity, were broken down.

In the face of orthodox structural readings of a crisis of accumulation resulting from under-consumption among the working-classes or from disequilibrium in the cycle of accumulation (over-accumulation), the *operaismo* school of thought saw in the nascent crisis of the Keynesian state a direct effect of the working-class struggle on the economic terrain of wages. The preoccupations of the orthodox Marxists in the Western communist parties were a million miles from this kind of analysis. By contrast, *operaismo* turned more readily to the history of class-struggle in America under the New Deal. While Tronti was writing provocatively that the sun of the revolution rose in the American West, the dominant viewpoint was oriented towards Khrushchev's Russia.

There was undeniably a degree of similarity between this political vision and the often sincere support for Khrushchev's early form of *perestroika* which used an identical language. It spoke of the convergence of ways of life on both sides of the Iron Curtain, the reduction in international tensions, a reduction in violations of

'socialist legality' with regard to the Constitution promulagated in
1936 which, however, had been tainted by the crimes or the errors –
according to which version one believed – of the Stalinist 'personality
cult'. Thus the left adopted the implicit renunciation of confronta-
tional tactics, of class against class and power-bloc against
power-bloc, of the theoretical necessity of 'violent revolution' and
of armed struggle (we should not forget that in 1960 in Italy the PCI
was still a structure endowed with insurrectional inclinations and
tendencies left over from the anti-fascist and liberation struggle)
and instead stressed the objective conditions for developing the
productive forces. And all this took place at the centre of the
Western echoes of the great split in 1961 between Chinese
communism and Soviet communism and then the Cultural Revolution.

During this period Chinese communism (beyond or within the
often tragically misunderstood reality of China) seemed very
attractive to generations of young European communists. War was
declared on economic determinism and opportunism which forgot
the class struggle, the 'principal determinism and opportunism
which forgot the class struggle', the 'principal contradiction' thus
disarming 'the masses'. 'Revisionism' was a direct criticism of
Stalin, and the watchword of peaceful coexistence was coined at the
expense of the Third World countries, the flashpoints, Fanon's
'zone des tempêtes'. Indeed, Fanonism and Maoism shared much
in common in the last years of the 1960s. As for the anti-
authoritarian and anti-hierarchical dimension, it aimed to emphasize the contradiction between 'controlled labour' (as represented
by manual labour) and reproductive labour (as performed by guard
dogs, petty bosses etc.). This theme, taken up particularly during
student struggles, came up against that of the scientific and
technical revolution which could only envisage the problem in
terms of the means at the universities' disposal, and not in terms of
the universities' function as an 'ideological state apparatus'.

From the point of view of the critique of political reason, beyond
the alibi which for some was the Cultural Revolution in China, and
for others was Vietnam or Cuba, it is more interesting to note how
these tendencies represented the search for an ideology which could
break with the Marxism of the Third International (one that
Trotskyism or anarchism could no longer provide) without
abandoning the revolutionary ethic in the process. But Italian

operaismo, distrustful of ideological splits, brought about theoretical ruptures which certainly coincided on many points with that critique of 'revisionism' formulated most effectively by Althusser. This rupture entailed a return to the scientific Marx of *Capital*, to the revolutionary character of the epistemological break from 1965 onwards, giving priority to the class struggle from 1969 and refusing to abandon the concept of the 'dictatorship of the proletariat' from 1974.

The initial reflective themes of the *Quaderni Rossi*, which were some of the most fertile and revolutionary themes in the Marxist tradition, respond precisely to several of these fundamental criticisms. First there is the theme of the workers' debate and of concrete analysis to offset the more and more glaring insufficiencies of a traditional working-class movement which was frozen in institutional debates from which the proletariat and the workers were completely absent, both as the protagonists and as stakes to be fought over. Then there is the theme of the function of intellectuals in the class struggle. In this the role formulated by *operaismo* is very close to that brought into focus by the Polish Workers' Defence Committee, KOR [*Komitet Obrony Robotnikow* – renamed in 1977 the Social Self-Defence Committee] and the 'experts' within Solidarity in 1980. But above all else the dominant theme remained the return to the Marx who had enthusiastically analysed the birth of large-scale industry in Manchester. And this was precisely because the dominant object of fascination for all the political groups of the extra-parliamentary left was the largest factory in the world – the one hundred thousand Fiat workers at Mirafiori.

More significant than the lure of the factory gates was the appearance of maps of this factory-city on the bedroom walls of the militants, replacing posters of Che Guevara or Mao. The imagery of Epinal gave way to the diagram and with it there arose a concrete problem: how could one re-establish the circulation of information and gain an overview of the chain of movements composed of discrete activities in hundreds of attic rooms? How should one interpret the hundreds of daily incidents, the absence of conflict, or the workers' strike which happened the day after the official union strike? How could one explain the unforeseeable explosions when the 'least conscientious' workers, those 'unaware of tradition', the more 'peasant-like' workers suddenly stopped work and went to ransack union headquarters? The questions raised by Tronti – what are the laws of the working class? – or by Romano Alquati – what is the invisible party of the Mirafiori workers? – are not rhetorical. From them the cardinal rule of the correct investigation into workers' conditions emerges: it must be *active* investigation – 'hot investigation' – distinguished from the passive and detached investigations – 'cold investigation' – conducted by professional sociologists. It reveals much more effectively the real structure of production and the power relationships; in short, it reveals class composition.

Here we can grasp the discrepancy of the term 'class composition' in relation to its application to social class or professional category: it is a question of an essential quality linked to dynamics and a field of force. Only the intensity of conflict can make apparent the collective labour power of the working class. The working class is a political category, not a sociological term. Only 'hot investigation' is capable of being used by the workers for their benefit without ending up, like the majority of 'neutral' studies paid for by companies, in the work-study department as a means to increase work productivity, thereby appropriating the workers' free time and handing it over to the supervisors. Only 'hot investigation' immediately poses problems of organization in non-ideological terms.

From 1965–6 the militants who had gone through the experience of the *Quaderni Rossi* believed themselves capable of evaluating the impact of the forms of struggle which, until then, had been cast out into the dark depths of anarcho-syndicalism by Stalinist and Stakhanovist communism: absenteeism, sabotage, wild-cat strikes, 'turnover' and deliberate passivity regarding institutional obligations; in short, all those forms that Hirschmann, in *Exit, Voice and Loyalty*, was to call 'exit solutions'.

The editions of *Classe operaia* which appeared between 1964 and 1967 on wild-cat strikes in Europe, on absenteeism, and on the work-force in the Ford factories constitute a model of lucidity unparalleled during the sixties.[25] Moreover, the texts of *operaismo* rapidly became the object of sustained attention among employers who recognized that they could learn more about the functioning of their own factories from reading these heretical publications than from their own studies. Certainly the attention paid to the factory and its real operations on the shop floor was more systematic than in France or Germany. In Italy it is more an 'intellectual' than an ethical issue, but the same subjective enthusiasm and the same attempt by revolutionary militants to go beyond their sociological horizons can be discerned. However, *operaismo* does not limit itself to a simple, detailed phenomenological analysis of the daily anthropology of the modern worker; and if it had, it would not have been any different from the 'productionism' which recurs in the working-class movement. The latter moreover is over-anxious to accuse *operaismo* of the fault of 'workerism', as it is called in English and French; that is to say of a purely trade-union oriented viewpoint, and not a political one.

In its understanding of how the large modern factory works, *operaismo* made two essential discoveries: (1) the essentially social character of capital's power, what it was to call the 'plan of capital'; (2) the determining role of the working-class struggle in the dynamism and the ruptures which lie at the heart of capitalist relations of production. Let us begin with the first point which characterizes the work of all of those who contributed to the *Quaderni Rossi* following Panzieri, Rieser, Lanzardo, Alquati and Tronti. The second point is one which was taken up by the only adherents to *operaismo* who would find themselves in the journal *Classe operaia* between 1964 and 1967, in agreement over the principle of direct and autonomous intervention in the factories, without passing through the mediation of a syndicalist left, as had been the case with the *Quaderni Rossi*.[26]

1   An understanding of the ideas of Taylor, of Fordism with its 'modern times', the Fiat-Mirafiori factory-city, and the Keynesian state, ensures above all that the essential trait which characterizes high capitalism will not be missed: the essentially social character of exploitation. The classical or ideal-typical form of domination by capital is embodied by the town against the factory, the spheres of circulation and reproduction in society as a whole against the dominant position of the collective worker in the sphere of production. Workers' power is thus captured and domesticated. The theoretical correlative to this is that orthodox Marxism has remained at the stage of 'competitive capitalism' wherein the composition of the sum of individual capitalists' interests turned out to be contradictory. In this case only socialism would be in a position to represent the general interest both of society and of harmonious and well-integrated accumulation. *Operaismo* effects a

radical rupture with this literature which by different degrees denounces the irrationalism of capitalist production and presents the working-class movement and socialism as sole guarantors of the meaning and value of work and of 'progress'. Capitalism has carried out transformations at its very core which the working-class movement and Marx to a large extent (except in the *Grundrisse*) saw as the *raison d'être* of the *socialist transition*.[27]

This vision of capitalism which proceeds from the Marxian category of *Gesellschaftskapital* (social capital) reduces the inter-capitalist contradictions to a subordinate role (we would not even say 'secondary', to avoid confusion with Maoism). The power of capital is exercised above all as a power of society as a whole, as the power of the planning of large-scale equilibria and of science. It is therefore useless to demand planned socialism in the face of anarchic capitalism, when the latter responds to the workers' struggle by a transformation in the socialization of its own mechanisms and takes on the form of the Keynesian planned economy. Five texts mark this theoretical acquisition which is highly consequential for 'socialism in transition': *Surplus-value and planning: note on the reading of Capital* by Ranièro Panzieri, *Social Capital* and *La fabbrica e la societa* by Mario Tronti, and Negri's *Keynes and Capitalist Theories of the State Post-1929* and *Marx on Cycle and Crisis*. All these texts appeared between 1962 and 1968. In them, this form of Marxism is clearly differentiated from all the orthodox reaffirmations, be they ossified and liturgical, or even more subtle (like the true historical leftism of Pannekoek, Mattick, Korsch and Lukács or the 'return to scientific rigour' of Althusserian Marxism). This is the *first post-socialist Marxism*, nearly twenty years before the radical questioning of 'real socialism' by the Soviet Union itself.

This rejection of the Soviet model was a trait specific to the cultural 'élites' of the PCI from the 60s onwards. But it did not take as its goal the iconoclastic and theoretical form of demonstrating the uselessness of socialism. This trait, which was hardly stressed at all by the adherents of *operaismo* themselves in the political arena and which was concealed even more effectively as they re-addressed Leninist themes both on an organizational level, and on the level of armed insurrection, explains their isolation in relation to all the large left formations in Europe. This is all the more understandable since this exaltation of the positive side of capitalist development, of

its ultimate superiority over the historical accident which constituted 'real socialism' is linked to the Bernsteinian tradition: 'The
movement (the struggle) is everything, the goal, socialism, any
other mode of production is nothing.' The same thing happens with
ideology, where the preference is for capitalist cynicism rather than
for the humanist 'moralism' of the working-class movement. This,
in short, is a 'theoretical anti-humanism' raised to the level of a
system.

The theme becomes gradually more blurred in autonomous
Marxism with the appearance of the full-scale crisis which began in
1975. 'Reformist' situations wherein the workers' struggle accelerates institutional reforms, disturbing their rhythm and the repressive function, to transform capital for 'working class use', are much
more rare. After 1968–9 one rather had the impression that
working-class struggle completely blocked any positive transformations. This theme remains a methodological and rhetorical argument (the rejection of catastrophe theory) but Negri rejects it as any
kind of positive thesis in the present work.[28] On the other hand,
experience demonstrates that priority should be given to global and
social mechanisms of exploitation instead of the 'obsessive detail of
life on the factory floor': in the 1960s it was believed that it was
necessary to take the city in order to win the factories;[29] the realm
of confrontation during the crisis of the seventies moved to the
realm of monetary circulation;[30] the mass worker who was already a
circulating worker has been succeeded as the central figure in the
extraction of relative surplus-value by the *socialized worker*;[31] and it
is now believed that domestic labour produces surplus-value.[32]

In the same way *operaismo's* analysis of Taylorism differs
fundamentally from the radical current of Marglin in the United
States and André Gorz in France. Both Marglin and Gorz accept
the effect of the expulsion of workers' control on the production
contained by the scientific division of labour (the side of class
decomposition) but they remain in the grip of a micro-economic or
micro-social perspective of the work process. Taylorism, Paolo
Carpignano explains, contains the conviction that society as a whole
functions and should function like a factory. It is because of the
existence of this socialization of all relations of production that the
division of labour is made possible. In other words, contrary to the
unilaterally catastrophic visions of the Taylorian division as
rendering useless the individual's labour power (as absolute

surplus-value) the decisive operation for relative surplus-value as realized by the *Organisation Scientifique du Travail* [the scientific organization for work in the Fordist factory] consists in making use of such abstract, interchangable labour, its fluidity, and its unlimited reserves in society.

Where a radical micro-economic analysis sees the assembly-line worker only as a member of the labour force who is less qualified than the professional worker, as s/he is stripped of all control over the labour process, *operaismo* (one is tempted simply to say Marxism) above all sees the quality of this mass, abstract labour power taken collectively, the vector of a valorization process which is far superior in its mobility and its indifference to the process of specific work. It is clear that, according to this analysis, both the 'overtaking' of Taylorism, and the enrichment of labour, far from representing a rupture with the spirit of the 'social engineer' represent a new translation of his ideas into a situation where the abstract labour available in society has become more complex. That is, the situation where the factory worker goes to school to get some qualifications and he can no longer be ordered about in the same way as before even though his indifference to the particular content of his work has reached another level.

This movement to extend the analysis to the sphere of society as a whole implies in particular a drastic revision of what is considered to be productive and unproductive labour, of the role of the sphere of reproduction and of the orthodox dogma according to which the sphere of circulation is neutral in relation to surplus-value, i.e. it adds no further value. This problem has been tackled several times by contemporary Marxist schools: theories of the articulation of modes of production[33] in the Althusserian mould of the domestic mode of production[34] have attempted to answer this question in a more static way. But if these attempts are all united in confronting Marxism with the most recent developments in capitalism, in its 'socialized' dimension[35] when it is not 'socialist', a totally different situation obtains when the second major discovery of *operaismo* is considered: the determining and almost exclusive role of working-class struggles in the genesis and development of the capitalist mode of production. This point continues to draw a clear demarcation line between those Marxisms which while acknowledging the important place of the class struggle (frequently first-place in their declarations of intent),[36] continue to analyse social formations 'at the heart of capitalism'; and *operaismo* which sees 'the whole of capital in the working class'[37] or in 'class composition'.

2   Let us now turn to *operaismo's* second major discovery: the central role of working-class struggle in the dynamics of capitalist production. If the metaphor had not already been done to death, we would be tempted here to talk about a Copernican inversion of Marxism, using the analogy of a Galilean revolution, in which Copernicus would be Marx, and Ptolemy would paradoxically represent Marxist dialectical materialism. What dialectical materialism teaches us, in fact, is that class relations are dependent upon relations of production that are caught up in a development of the forces of production in which the economic aspect is the determinant, certainly in the final analysis but also overall. Class relations are engraved on this implacable necessity. We know the rest: feudalism is embodied in the water-mill, the bourgeosie in the steam engine and the soviet in electricity. And the 'socialist' mode of production will follow the capitalist mode of production when the development of productive forces (science, technology, the accumulation of capital) bursts through the chrysalis of obsolete superstructures, particularly juridical and political ones.

It can scarcely be doubted today that this poor-quality Marxism, 'these children's fables' as Mario Tronti christened them in *Operai e Capitale*, was the most formidable extinguisher of political rationality in the guise of a kind of 'structural follow-my-leader', and should have been the best way of maintaining the *status quo* in the developed countries (by means of imperialism) or for the development of the stages in the 'construction of socialism', which was the 'accumulation of capital' in disguise. In the sixties, it took a strong preference for minority provocations to sustain this kind of Marxism. In fact, twenty years later, it is still this principal inversion which constitutes the profound unity of *operaismo's* ideas in the eyes of its various opponents, and which creates all the problems involved in penetrating its methodology, even more than certain of its component ideas which almost passed into theoretical morality. We could mention for example the concept of the mass worker as opposed to that of the skilled worker, which has been picked up as a fragment of the theoretical edifice and which is completely alien, even opposed to its spirit.

But what does *operaismo* assert as its main thesis? It claims to comprehend one of the most complex formations that have ever existed, 'integrated global capitalism'[38] from an axis around which *operaismo* organizes itself in its choice of strategy to mirror capitalism's most impenetrable recesses and makes it comprehensible even in its irrationality. Where the contemporary academic historian, prudent and sceptical, enjoys emphasizing the plurality of causes, the crucial moment where chance 'encounters two independent series' (as Cournot says) plays an essential role. Where Gramscian Marxism historicizes the contradiction, where Althusserian Marxism 'overdetermines it by the effectiveness of an absent structure', *operaismo* returns to an almost unbelievably simple level of explanation. Asor Rosa stressed this when summarizing Mario Tronti's *Operai e Capitale* which was of great theoretical importance for one generation: 'His fundamental discovery can be summed up in a formula which makes the working class the dynamic motor of capital and which makes capital a function of the working class. . . a formula which in itself gives an idea of the magnitude of the inversion of perspectives which such a position implies politically.'

The only way of making sense of the world of capitalist production, profoundly and exhaustively in such a way as to reach its ontological cortex, is to examine the history of what we shall call its 'working-class articulation'. This means seeing the whole of capital in the working class and not the other way around. In this programme, which is the exact opposite of the economism of the working-class movement, some will undoubtedly recognize, to their horror, a phrase bearing some relation to Gdanovist theses: an 'exaggerated emphasis on political activity'. Of course when Tronti explains that there is but one class situation and two points of view – that of capital and that of the workers – it is easy to slip this thesis in alongside that of the two sciences – bourgeois science and proletarian science – and the whole stream of outrageous ineptitudes which followed during the Stalinist communism of the 1950s, and of which Lyssenkoism was one of the purest products. And doubtless by the same token that Althusser ventured into the French Communist Party under cover of scientific Marxism and Spinoza,[39] the adherents of *operaismo* proceeded to use formulae that would not have shocked the old Stalinist communists. One could even say that part of the strange character of *operaismo* in the years 1964 to 1971 lies in this paradoxical way of saying in the very language of the Communist Party things which are so contrary to its whole theoretical foundation as to imitate its internal rupture.

However, one cannot help thinking that this philological *tour de force* has been paid for dearly on the political level, notably when the 'Leninist' vocabulary – by aesthetic or voluntarist prejudice a prisoner of the specifically Italian context – grafted itself on to a European practice which had very little in common with the composition of the Bolshevik class, particularly over two issues, that of organization and that of the role of armed struggle in insurrection.[40] In reality none of these ambiguities is crucial to the central core of *operaismo's* line of argument. This argument reveals in the first place the priority of class relations *vis-à-vis* the relations of production; and in the second place the asymmetry of socialization and power between the two classes which is constituted in the cash/labour exchange nexus to the benefit of the working class.

The first point proceeds from the constitution of capitalist relations,[41] from the separation [*Trennung*] from the instruments of labour which can most often be gained by the pure coercive power of the primitive accumulation of labour. Bringing together the worker selling his/her labour power and the conditions of labour (tools, salary) into a contradictory unity constitutes class relations. But classes do not exist before the unity of this relation, they are born of this union. Classes are thus proleptic.

The second and most crucial point is that in the genesis of the capitalist mode of production there is no simultaneous birth of the working class and the capitalist class. The worker selling his labour power, then the proletariat, then the working class in its different modes for bargaining with large-scale industry, from the Fordist factory to the cybernetic factory, all these forms always have a more advanced degree of socialization over their opposing class. What is the superiority of the capitalist mode of production over any other social relation? It is that the form of wage exchange leaves the use-value undetermined. On the micro-economic level waged workers do not know the use-value of their labour power, nor its productivity, both of which will be determined only retrospectively by the mechanization which faces them. This is what happens when young workers holding professional qualifications in tailoring are set to assemble electronic transistors.

But we can see that in a long-lasting relationship, by trial and error, even with an imbalance of information on the side of the workers (asymmetrical information), an equilibrium will re-establish itself, with the worker foreseeing the use of his/her labour power, and weighing it up to modify its exchange-value. On the other hand, on the macro-economic level, another operation is produced which is the real crux of surplus-labour and relative surplus-value. Opposing money (a condition of labour) as a condition of capital, and possessing the ability to refuse to valorize it, labour accelerates the socialization of the relationship, and its struggles (on condition of course that they do not cut off the relationship completely)[42] accelerate the real subsumption of labour.

But what does the working class bring to the social relations of production? It brings its tendency to conflict and it is from the capacity of capital to organize itself to control this tendency that relative surplus-value is born (in for example the struggle for a normal day's work). This is the meaning which we must give to Tronti's obscure formula: the particularity of commodity labour power is its use-value, and its use-value is to constitute itself as the working class. In other words, without working-class struggle, capitalism would remain a system for tapping absolute surplus-value or income, a system which offers as dismal a prospect as slavery. Without the continual pressure which capitalism under-goes internally, there would be no mechanism, no invention, no progressive incorporation of science into the labour conditions, and the accumulation of capital would come to resemble even more closely the accumulation of castles and jewels, rather than the accumulation of machines and equipment. Accumulation, 'the famous law and its prophets', is thus not an economic mechanism endowed with some kind of autonomy (relative or absolute): accumulation represents the only consistent way of controlling the antagonism in which the whole mystery of surplus-value resides. The modalities which are particular to accumulation (rhythm, sectors, periods, etc.) are the manifestation of capitalism's reaction to class composition, that is the decomposition of the technical and political power of class composition.

However, the road is full of pitfalls in this transformation of socialization beyond the relations of production as a response to the rigidification of class relations. The capitalist class did not spring fully formed from the head of Marx or Taylor: it forms itself, after a delay, on the model of the working class. Employers' associations grow within the co-ordinates which allow them to oppose a unified reaction from workers' leagues, or from the mass behaviour of workers (regulation of inter-capitalist competition, the banning of dismissals for example). And this dissymmetry, the false homology of class relations, can clear the way for the 'miraculous' events which become revolutions.[43]

Like every explicitly monistic principle, the *operaismo* theory takes drastic action which is as sharp as Ockham's razor. But it is futile to point to its reductionist character independently of its results, and of what it enables us to understand. If the system of deductive hypothesis which the *operaismo* theory develops facilities the explanation of phenomena and situations, it should be preferred to the orthodox hypothesis which makes class movements dependent (with more or less relative autonomy) on capital accumulation which in turn is understood as an objective law. Moreover, this hypothesis does not tell us very much about the discontinuities and the changes brought about by the 'regime of accumulation',[44]

Without dwelling any longer on the significance of *operaismo's* epistemological rupture and on its research programme, we can cite as an example of the productive character of this analysis the internationalization of capital and imperialism. We already know the Leninist correction of the definition of an imperialist power: it is not the country which exports the most commodities, but the country which exports the most capital.[45] If we remain faithful to *operaismo's* methodology, in short to the Marxist method, in interpreting the export of capital not as a thing but as a social relation, we should say that the dominant imperialism is the one which exports class struggle the most, i.e. its way of controlling its own working class. A re-reading of Vernon's 'productive cycle'[46] as the Schumpeterian dynamism of the entrepreneur shows this to be possible. This is also shown in the vicissitudes of the international monetary system from the gold standard to the standard after the suspension of convertibility in 1971. And in all probability it becomes possible to impute the unifying growth of capital on a global scale to a reaction against a homogenization of class composition which is much more unified in its individual behaviour than one would like to acknowledge.

The inversion of perspective practised by *operaismo* and the autonomist form of Marxism contains a reaffirmation of the directly political character of what Marxist orthodoxy had rejected since *Capital* in the economic aspects and the 'objective' laws of accumulation, as, for example, the famous tendential fall in the rate of profit, or pauperization. And it is true that the apparent return to the dominant paradigm contains a re-evaluation of the role of the worker's subjectivity in the broad sense and not only in the institutional working-class movement. The reconstruction of the transformations which took place in class composition[47] begins the history described in Lukács's *History and Class Consciousness*, a history which was quickly brought to an end. The conceptual mechanism which is thus proposed is less ideological and more technical than the extremely Hegelian and historicist teleology of the passage of class-in-itself into class-for-itself. Its 'subjective' dimension contrasts well with the viewpoint of E.P. Thompson in *The Making of the English Working Class*.[48] Thompson, through amassing subjective facts, shows above all the progressive 'domestication' of the 'proletariat', as do the analyses of those who following Foucault write of the 'disciplining of the wage-earning class', that is of 'the decomposition of class'.[49] By contrast the analyses of the *operaismo* of the sixties extract from an accumulation of almost purely objective facts the image of a working class which is exploited but 'not submissive', and which in any case poses a threat.

Thus we can see how *operaismo* and its different theoretical manifestations differentiate themselves from the major contemporary currents of critical or Marxist thought. While sharing much in common with the critique of 'revisionism' and of the programme of the return to the Marx of *Capital*, and of Althusserianism, *operaismo* completely rejects the economic and political articulation that remains structuralist, the link between Marx and Hegel and the role of ideology.[50] The theme of the *refusal to work* which *operaismo* emphasizes as a fundamental dimension of the class struggle, and the rejection of the utopia of 'liberated labour' separates *operaismo* from the critique of the division of labour propounded by American radicals such as Marglin, or by Gorz. The argument that at the heart of the capitalist system there exists another way of working corresponds either to utopia or to the ideological packaging of the new social productivity of waged labour. As for *operaismo's* links with the Frankfurt School, they were clearly hostile at the beginning. If they have developed since the sixties it is particularly because the problems of the constitution of revolutionary subjectivity and the analysis of the processes of legitimation have taken on more and more importance for 'autonomists'. On a theoretical level *operaismo* affirms the internal and structural limits of capitalism's capacity for integration. For *operaismo* in fact, the working class must certainly be *within* capital, but above all *against it*, otherwise capital could no longer function. Therefore the unilateral domination of capitalist control can never obtain. Subversion and revolution constitute a permanent possibility which lies at the very heart of the system, and not on its cultural margins, as Marcuse argues, nor with those excluded from wage-labour by the effects of crisis.

Can we say that *operaismo's* paradigm presents a flawless unity and that it has not come up against any serious limitations? Of course not: and we shall now discuss several of the milestones which have marked the principal lines of fracture. They merge to a large extent with the political and theoretical progress of the author of the present work, to which Negri himself makes frequent allusion in the text.

II

If the first form of *operaismo* offered a means of understanding the functioning of capitalism between 1945 and 1975 from a new perspective, and in particular the role of wage struggles, there were several traditional and prohibitive questions, which were still insoluble from a revolutionary point of view, while other questions were raised specifically by the epistemological inversion of the old Marxism. The first questions concerned the revolutionary party and the relationship with the historical working-class movement. The second set called into question more radically the usefulness of political activity itself, and the usefulness of the very idea of revolution from the moment when achieved or achievable socialism was no longer constitutive of the tactical nor the strategic path towards communism.

Operaismo had discovered a sort of *objective subjectivity* which was the decisive operator behind the activities of capitalist accumulation. The usefulness of this type of schema has been to spare militants the exhausting succession of emotions from enthusiasm, through to depression at the time of the decline of volatile social movements, since strategically the worker's subjectivity is always in action. The flip-side of this optimism, contrasting almost feature for feature with the sombre prognostications on the definitive integration of blue-collar workers, is a continual questioning of the usefulness of a subjective subjectivity, *in progress*. What in effect would knowledge of the laws of movement of workers' spontaneity add, if not a sterile redundancy? And if the workers wanted *some* power in capitalism and over capitalism, though certainly not *absolute* power, this would lead one to wonder if this 'as yet unseen use' of the economic mechanisms of capital, as Tronti put it, looked anything like a revolution at all, in the style of 1964, 1789, 1917, or whether it was just a wonderful Bernsteinian mental exercise.

The adherents of *operaismo* had judiciously driven out the question of 'class consciousness' in order carefully to avoid the aporia of the Leninist stereotype of consciousness imposed from the outside. But as can clearly be seen, it returned covertly in a more sophisticated form: that of the passage from class decomposition to class recomposition. When crisis and stagnation hit Italy in 1971, well before the internationalization of the crisis, it was interpreted as a capitalist counter-attack against the levels of power that the proletariat had attained during the 'hot autumn' of 1969. All in all, the current that emerged from *operaismo* explained that the organization had the capacity to anticipate this crisis that had been deliberately hoped for by capital and could prevent it from happening as a political operation of class decomposition. The schematic structure remains unchanged whether it be seen from the point of view of its content by the adherents of *operaismo* in the PCI as a use of all the margins of autonomy of the political carried either by the institutional parties, or by the state administration, or from the point of view of the autonomists in *operaismo*, as a recourse to all forms of social contradiction contained in the restructuring of production.

Knowledge of the situation, the capacity to predict it, like old-style class consciousness, allowed a sabotaging of the capitalist operation, a jamming of its gears, its rhythm, without being driven back into the position of a utopian denial of the transformation in the technical composition of the working class. If the organizational idea contained in this schema is intellectually seductive, it is like proofs of the existence of God, in that it is wrong in presupposing that which it must prove. For the adherents of *operaismo* in the PCI, all this would be perfect if the historical party of the working class were really to be able to fulfil such a role.

In short the question of the specific role of subjective subjectivity remains open. And here *operaismo's* refusal of an ideology, its sovereign disdain of 'consciousness', its refusal to believe that any future project outside capitalism could have a positive content and not be just about refusal, dissolve into weakness. To exist *within and against* can constitute an interesting perspective in a period of full growth, when businesses' profit margins are comfortable and when workers' use of social democracy constitutes a luxury that capital can afford. In the seventies the game became harder. Full employment disappeared for the foreseeable future. The question became one of consolidating the spaces for the liberation of work, of letting them exist outside the wage nexus. It should be no surprise that the two strands of *operaismo* found in 'autonomy' a way of naming this slackening of the capitalist grip: 'autonomy of the political' in the first form of *operaismo*, 'workers' autonomy' for those who had totally renounced the 'workers' use' of the PCI.

The thesis of 'autonomy of the political' reactivates a traditional theme: that of entryism into the historical Party of the working-class. Added to this was a more noble justification of the historical compromise (the union of the national government with the Christian Democrats). Since the war the Christian Democrats had been the party that was synonymous with the state. Alliance with the Christian Democrats would thus allow the PCI to take control in the state and to reach the highest degree of utilization by the workers of large-scale capital. This would create a situation in which the workers' movement would be within and against the state and would not fulfil the petrified programme of the workers' state trapped in 'real socialism'. The PCI side of *operaismo* which occupied the prestigious but essentially cultural functions of the apparatus (the relationship with intellectuals, problems of culture and the youth organizations) justified this path by a political autonomy which often took the form of the strict opposite of the theses of *Operai e Capitale*: in both early and late capitalism that of the existence of two transitional phases where the category of the 'political' proved to be capable of overdetermining (if not completely, then in any case effectively) the revolutionary mechanism of class relations in the 'economic'.[51] In that period, this political capacity of 'decomposing' the working class was illustrated in the constitution of 'two societies', that of the excluded extremists and that of a working class trapped in an impotent syndicalist corporatism.[52] The solution adopted by this strand of *operaismo* in response to the difficulties raised by the class situation and by the analytical paradigm consisted in adding new elements which were intended to enrich the analysis.[53] In so doing, the cutting edge of Ockham's razor, of the first paradigm, loses its sharpness: the explicatory power becomes more uncertain and *operaismo's* system of the second kind, full of axioms, falls back into classical internal contradictions.

Retrospectively, in the political sphere, this *operaismo* never had any luck with its political choices. In 1967 it chose 'mass entryism' into the PCI, while elsewhere in Europe the great rupture between the communist parties and the student youth organizations dating from 1968 burnt itself out. In Italy itself, with the 'hot autumn' of 1969, the serious beginnings of organizations appeared which were outside the unions in the factories and outside parliament in political life. Ten years later, the theme of the 'autonomy of the political' appears very out of touch in relation to the conjuncture of the extreme radicalization of the class struggle, except as a final justification of the retreat carried out by the groups claiming to represent the avant-garde army of the working class, in relation to the 'movement'. This involuntary effect of the thesis of the 'autonomy of the political' is not the only one. The historical compromise of which it was the noble and uncynical justification was roughly treated by the social movement of the *emarginati* in Bologna,[54] the showcase of PCI-style socialism, and then this disaffection spread rapidly through the rest of Italy.

The separation of new revolutionary movement and workers' movement had become established in Italy too. The cultural and political hegemony of the PCI was severely affected. The colossus of Eurocommunism began a process of decline to which it reacted with brutality. It had to abandon the historical compromise and return to an oppositional role which was slowly being whittled away and marginalized with the rise of the Italian Socialist Party. The fate of the PCI's *operaismo* is not without similarities to the fate of Althusserianism in France. Both had the same considerable influence, in the second half of the sixties, on the most active revolutionary currents, both had the same unresolved ambiguity regarding the Party, the same difficulties in their political interventions, and experienced the same failure to modify their function in curbing the accelerated laxity in theory and the ever-increasing sectarian rigidity in practice. Finally, both underwent the same withdrawal into the political philosophy of the universities.

But how did the other side of *operaismo*, that which had chosen to break with the official working-class movement, respond to the challenge that it had itself constructed: to organize spontaneously, to think and to act so that the working class might assert itself *outside of* capital *for* communism? Up until the beginning of the eighties, theoretical debate and political confrontation in militant action were inextricably linked. The radicalization of the confrontation in Italy at the same time as the institutional and international freezing of the situation, and the eruption of 'leftism' led to very strong inflexions of the old themes of *operaismo* and to the appearance of preoccupations which were less and less Italian, that is to say borrowed from the European class situation and from the revolutionary European movement.

This ongoing mutation was accelerated in the intellectual sphere by the 1979 wave of repression which led to the arrest and detention and then to the underhand banishment of almost all of the main members of the leading groups in the constellation of 'organized workers' autonomy'. On the political level the continuity of experience which had begun in 1959 with the foundation of the journal *Quaderni Rossi* was broken. It was a complete catastrophe in revolutionary subjectivity. The 'Italian anomaly', which had been characterized until then by this continuity of struggles and of militancy was gradually reabsorbed and realigned to the current situation of the other European countries.

We can characterize the evolution of the paradigm of the first *operaismo* in the following way: the two basic elements of the paradigm are maintained. Far from being subjected to corrections by juxtaposition with other elements which weaken the paradigm, the elements are purified and developed to their logical conclusion. Working-class and proletarian antagonism remain the sole key to interpreting this evolution. The 'relative autonomy' of civil society, of the state, in short of the 'political' is challenged.[55] The method of class composition is maintained and developed either on the community or the cultural level (taking into account the ideologies of liberation),[56] or on the level of technical composition and of its inscription in a given territory.[57] The second great discovery of

operaismo, social capital, is purified of its contamination by the era
of the Keynesian planned economy, and retains above all the
Marxian significance of the movement to real subsumption made by
labour under capital.[58]

The characterization of this essential trait of modern capitalism
comes about through the method of 'determinate abstraction'
which is analysed by Marx at the beginning of the *Grundrisse*:[59] the
anatomy of the man explains that of the ape and not the other way
around. High capitalism allows only the understanding of its
genesis and its antecendents. Autonomists in *operaismo* are not
alone in making this reference to Marx pure and simple. But their
originality lies in having found the true Marxist correlative of the
Weberian ideal-typical method which Negri exposed as being the
method of tendency:[60] the tendency is postulated as realized. The
present totality is real subsumption and the levels of antagonism
contained within it. We are no longer in the break between
capitalist factuality which is full of contradictions and the virtuality
of a tendency which only political struggle could liberate. The
tendency works as a principal force of capital relations since it alone
directly controls the class composition as a force which has reached
this degree of socialization.[61] And the important corrective which
this mechanism produces is the socialized worker who appeared as a
theme in *operaismo* in 1976. This formulation replaces that of the
mass worker. Once the socialized worker, the essential figure of
capitalism, has completely realized the movement to real subsumption, the socialized waged labourer had absorbed what was still
called the working class.

On this level therefore, we can see a continuation of the
important factors presented at the beginning of *operaismo*. On the
levels of organization and content of the revolutionary transformation, on the other hand, a profound recasting has been produced,
which is sometimes masked by the permanence of the vocabulary of
operaismo. Thus working to this different rhythm, all the figures
centred around the group *Potere Operaio* in the years 1969–71
abandoned all reference to Leninism.[62] This process of organizational upheaval dated from 1972, from the moment the organization
no longer constituted a point of reference for the large factories of
the North and became once more a fringe group like the others.
With the movement of 1977 the last residues of the old culture of
the Third International among young people was removed.

Deleuze, Guattari, Foucault, Lyotard, Baudrillard were translated into Italian. A new culture was born, a culture which was international, eclectic and radical in its refusal to delegate to the old parties' sphere of institutional politics as well as to anything that might resemble an extra-parliamentary party.[63] A third element to have played a major accelerating role in this dissolution of Leninism, was armed struggle. And this emerged not as a theoretical question, but as a concrete problem which increased from 1973 onwards, reaching a dimension which had previously been unheard of in Western Europe, except among some nationalist minorities.[64]

Workers' autonomy found itself more and more trapped in a vice. On one side there was a militant Leninism, that of the Red Brigades, whose initial strength among the workers[65] masked a rigid communist orthodoxy,[66] and ultimately its profound similarity (minus the Italian anomaly) to all the small groups emerging from May 1968 which descended into terrorism in Europe. On the other side there was a diffuse violence, rooted in the movement of the 'metropolitan indians' of 1977, which was anti-authoritarian and anti-Leninist, and which state repression tipped over into terrorist groups, the most famous of which is *Prima Linea*. The attempt to define an organizational outlet of mass violence which was not terrorist in form ended in a failure whose outcome was the operation of 7 April which presented Workers' Autonomy as the organizational kernel, or the legal face of terrorism. Among the constant themes of the critique of armed action, two are important: first, the critique of the delegation of the exercise of revolutionary violence to any clandestine structure outside the poltical structures of social movements; second, the rejection of a military theory of the impact of illegal actions, as a 'propagandist' and 'symbolic' theory which is supposed to break through the media wall, but which does not really control the situation.[67]

But the sum total of radical corrections affecting the question of revolutionary organization by 'autonomy', can be summed up in the question of the 'constitution of the new revolutionary subjectivity'. The impasse suffered by the workers' movements in the sixties, by the student movement in 1968, by the movement of 1977, and finally by terrorism always leads us back to the same question: how could these struggles of resistance reproduce themselves in such a way as to construct a new subject independent of material constraint, but which was also cultural, symbolic and imaginary? Here lies the real key to the rebirth of the organization and to the change in content of the social radical transformation. This theme became dominant in the Italian movement which was confronted more dramatically than other movements elsewhere in Europe with the perverse constitution of the terrorist subjectivity, the shadow cast by state power, and then with the decomposition of the revolutionary figure simulated and propagated in the media imagination by the phenomenon of the *pentiti*, those who publicly disavowed their adherence to the movement.[68]

The willingness to take seriously once again the subjective side of the principal actor in the class struggle implies being interested in his/her representations, in the cultural and ethical manifestations of his/her concrete existence. Thus ideologies of liberation are integrated into the analysis of class composition to the extent that they reinforce the autonomy of the collective subject and constitute it as a subject which is virtually independent of capitalist relations. Revolutionary culture, that of the exploited, is no longer from this point of view the acculturation of bourgeois culture, or a poor reflection of the latter. Revolutionary culture safeguards the space for the values which belong to the exploited class. It allows it to engage in struggle, but above all to reproduce itself as a subject.[69]

This is what Negri, since 1976, has formulated in the expression *autovalorization*. Like the Spinozian *conatus*, autovalorization increases the power of the struggle and widens the separation of work from capital. It is the concept which allows the reunification of various kinds of behaviour under one category: the refusal to work, the refusal of orders, the reappropriation of time and use-values. This concept does not go as far as the underground economy which cannot be read as a manifestation of autovalorization on which the market has been obliged to model itself to continue to exploit relative surplus value.

And if we consider Negri's contributions at the level of philosophy from his *Descartes politico o della ragionevole ideologia*[70] to his work devoted to Leopardi,[71] via his magisterial work on Spinoza[72] or from his notes on the philosophy of right in *La Forma Stato*[73] to his recent *Fabbriche del soggetto*[74] via *La Macchina Tempo*[75] we can see the progress of the same radical idea: the ontological foundation of the revolutionary subject, a reconstruction of reason as a liberation project which is linked to the

Enlightenment of the Revolution. It is tempting here to plunge into the body of the argument. However, let us be content with looking at a few examples which show at what point the first form of *operaismo* was both superseded and preserved. Negri's work on Descartes shows the process of keeping in check the Renaissance subject, and revolutionary reason during the first re-ordering of Absolutism which also saw the appearance of the bourgeois class and the manufacturing state. Ten years later Negri's work on Spinoza brings to light the anti-figure of Descartes and Hegel: the character immediately given to the politics of the multitude (the composition of the collective subject) as opposed to the social contract, to the dialectical mediation between the individual and the state.[76]

His work on Leopardi, like his interpretation of Kant, is strongly characterized by his reading of Heidegger which is a complete reinterpretation, taking up again the question of the progress of spirit in the face of the catastrophe which brought the French Revolution to a close.[77] The true romanticism of Leopardi and Hölderlin marks the refusal of the dialectic – the Hegelian solution – in favour of a poetic ethics, while the programme of a schema of reason beginning with the events leading up to the revolution that took place, brings out the analytical dialectic of the battle between master and servant, with its false symmetries.

It could be said that at this stage the loop of Italian *operaismo* has been reached and is converging with the large questions forged in the embers and tears of 'European leftism': can a non-artificial solution of the crisis of legitimacy of democratic representation be found? How can the revolutionary transformation be legitimized and inscribed into the material constitution? What horizon of positive rationality and what new collective actor of politics can be reconstructed if the return to the old socialist humanism is definitively excluded and if post modernism is an inventory of fixtures and not a programme?

This book offers the English-speaking world a condensed account of the progress of Antonio Negri and the theoretical and political movement with which he has been so closely associated. The elements we have provided here will enable the reader to assess the continuities, with relation to his works previous to 1976 – that is, up to the appearance of the concept of the socialized worker as well

as his increasing distance from early workerism.[78] Thus the concept of
the *subject* relating to the students of the 1976 Parisian movement (a
movement which Negri followed with passionate interest) is not the
actor of which Alain Touraine writes, but a *mechanism* and an *acting
tendency*. As for the socialized worker, the worker under capitalism
in the era of real subsumption, s/he represents an essentially
intellectual labour force. An invention out of necessity, s/he
produces intellectual cooperation and communication.

One of the innovations contained in this essay concerns the
positive determination that Negri assigns to the antagonism of the
socialized worker in its most elevated form: that of the *ecological
system*.[79] If Negri accepts that the concept of the nuclear state
expresses the radical rupture of the latter with democratic
rationality (see Part 2, chapter 4), he does not hold with this
characteristic which remains part of the Frankfurt School's
programme of underlining the modern manifestations of capitalist
domination. What interests Negri is that the subject of the
antagonism in capitalism of real subsumption and of nuclear death
is also undergoing transformation. The social subject of the struggle
is a new type of worker whose enterprise is society as a whole and this
society, in the face of the absolute threat of the nuclear bomb, has
become an ecological system. Ecology is therefore the system in
which the socialized worker works. But the ecological system is not
a first nature from which human activity would be excluded or
would not be admitted except as a minor disturbance. Ecology also
corresponds to the highest degree of social conflict of the socialized
worker when s/he 'acts upon the totality of the conditions of
production and reproduction of the social' (p. 87). Ecology is
therefore second nature.

Something new really has happened in Western Marxism. The
first and second forms of *operaismo* have served their time as a
specific theory. Let us hope that their effects on the other great
currents of critical thought will fulful the promise of these
precedents. This will again confirm William Morris's words in *A
Dream of John Ball*: '. . . Men fight and lose the battle, and the
thing that they fought for comes about in spite of their defeat, and
when it comes turns out not to be what they meant, and other men
have to fight for what they meant under another name. . . '[80] And
we can hope that the catastrophe of 7 April 1979 and Negri's exile
will not be a conclusion but merely a deferment.

Notes

Yann Moulier teaches economics at the Institute of Political Science and the Ecole Normale Superieure, Paris.

The author and translator would like to acknowledge the assistance of Michael Hardt in the preparation of this Introduction.

1   The adherents of *operaismo* were accused of fabricating false unpublished works by Marx. For example a particularly caustic extract by the founding father of Marxism on wage-labour which was published on the front page of the weekly magazine *Potere Operaio* was said to be pure invention. It was in fact a real text: the *Critique of National Economy of 1845*. Finding texts by Marx to back up one's interpretation is not convincing in itself, but the complete transfer of the texts by Marx cited by the adherents of *operaismo* compared to common texts of different historical currents of Marxism is itself very significant. There was also a joke about Enzo Grillo's translation of the *Grundrisse*, which said that the translation was better than the original! This shows there was a current which was violently hostile to the socialism of the nascent working-class movement on a theoretical and strategic level; it was not just a simple tactic for an uncertain takeover of control. See also Marx's *Critique of the Gotha Programme*.

2   In providing important sources of *operaismo*, in particular in Negri's work, Rosdolsky's *The Making of Marx's Capital*, trans. P. Burgess (Pluto, London, 1977) plays an important role.

3   Marx, *Manuscrits de 1857–58* (Editions Sociales, Paris, 1980).

4   Marx, *Grundrisse: Foundations of the Critique of Political Economy* (Penguin/New Left Review, Harmondsworth, 1973).

5   Negri, *Marx Beyond Marx: Lessons on the Grundrisse* (Bergin and Garvey, New York, 1984).

6   This point is stressed by Harry Cleaver in his Preface to *Marx Beyond Marx*.

7   If we are to return to the use of the Hegelian dialectic as a tool, then the Althusserian critique on the formal level of 'inversion' or of 'the extraction of the mystical shell from the rational kernel' is completely justified.

8   Both *ouvriérisme* and 'workerism' correspond rather to the Italian word *fabbrichismo*, that is they bear a pejorative connotation.

9   On the legend created around Gramsci, created by Togliatti, and on the particular acculturation of Gramsci in Italy and France, see Gallimard's edition of Gramsci's *Ecrits Politiques* (Political Writings) and his *Carnets* (Prison Notebooks), selected and edited by Robert Paris.

10   Lucio Colletti, *From Rousseau to Lenin* (Monthly Review Press, New York, 1972).

11   Perry Anderson, *Considerations on Western Marxism* (New Left Books, London, 1976).

12   See my postscript to the Portuguese translation of Mario Tronti's *Operarios e Capitale* (Affrontamento, Lisbon, 1976).

13   Only the following extracts from the book have been translated: 'The struggle against labour' (chapter 14 of the first theses), in *Radical America*, 6, no.1 (May–June 1972) pp. 22–5; 'Workers and Capital' (the postscript to the second edition of 1971) in *Telos*, no. 14 (Winter 1972), pp. 25–62; 'Social capital' (original title 'Le plan du capital') in *Telos*, no. 17 (Fall 1973) pp. 98–121; 'The strategy of refusal' (chapter 12 of the central essay of the first theses) in *Semiotext(e)* vol. III, no. 3 (New York, 1980), pp. 28–34; 'Lenin in England' in *Working Class Autonomy and the Crisis*, (Red Notes and CSE Books, London, 1979).

14   Among other classic texts which have already been translated apart from those of Mario Tronti, there are: Raniero Panzieri, 'Surplus-value and planning: note on the reading of *Capital*' in *The Labour Process and class struggles* (CSE pamphlet no. 1, London, 1976) pp. 4–25. Maria Rosa Dallo Costa and Selma James, *The Power of Women and the Subversion of the Community* (Falling Wall Press, Bristol, 1972). Sergio Bologna, 'Class composition and the theory of the Party at the origin of the workers' councils' movement' in *Telos* no. 13 (1972), pp. 68–91. Ferruccio Gambino, 'Workers' struggles and the development of Ford in Britain' in *Bulletin of the Conference of Socialist Economists*, March 1976, pp. 1–18. Sergio Bologna, 'The Tribe of Moles' in *Semiotext(e)* vol. III, no 3 (1980), pp. 36–61. Gisela Bock, 'Italian Analysis of Class Struggle and the State' in *Kapitalistate* no 1, Berkeley, 1973. Potere Operaio, 'Italy 1973: workers' struggles and the capitalist crisis' in *Radical America*, 7, no. 2 (March–April 1973), pp. 15–32. Sandro Pescarolo, 'From Gramsci to Workerism' in Raphael Samuel (ed), *People's History and Socialist Theory* (RKP, London, 1981), pp. 273–8. None of Romano's works has been translated. There are however two reviews which have been largely influenced by

operaismo and 'autonomous marxism' and all their collaborators, M. Montano, Peter Bell, G. Caffenztis, C. Marazzi, B. Ramirez, P. Carpignano, H. Cleaver: they are *Zero Work* no. 1 (December 1976) and no. 2 (December 1977), and *Midnight Notes Collective* (Jamaica Plain, Massachusetts). We can also recommend Henry Cleaver's *Reading Capital Politically*, (University of Texas, Austin, 1979), which contains an excellent reconstruction of the global conjuncture of non-academic Marxism; see also the *Texas Archives of Autonomist Marxism* (University of Texas, Austin, 1977 and 1978) which are an attempt to catalogue systematically the contributions to this current of thought and to the wider mainstream.

15 'Domination and Sabotage' (first published in *Red Notes*) in *Semiotext(e) Italy: Autonomia, Post-Political Politics*, vol. III no. 3 (New York, 1980) pp. 62–71.

16 See n. 5.

17 'Is there a Marxist Doctrine of the State? A reply by Antonio Negri' in Norberto Bobbio, *Which Socialism?* (Polity Press, Cambridge, 1987), pp. 121–38. There is also the whole volume *Working Class Autonomy and the Crisis* (Red Notes and CSE Books, London, 1979) which contains several articles.

18 See the Preface by Jim Fleming, pp. xiff and the Preface by Maurizio Viana, pp. xxxviiff.

19 H. Cleaver, 'Karl Marx: Economist or Revolutionary' in S.W. Helburn and D.F. Bramhall (eds), *Marx, Schumpeter and Keynes: a centenary celebration dissent* (M. E. Sharpe, Armonk, 1986), pp. 121–45.

20 This was evident particularly in Germany with the publications of K.H. Roth's *Die andere Arbeiterbewegung* (TriKont Verlag, Munich, 1977), or with the publication in the United States of B. Ramirez's *When Workers Fight* (Greenwood Press, 1978).

21 On 7 April 1979, Toni Negri, who had already been dubbed the *cattivo maestro* ['malign genius'] behind the events of 1977 for which he had been prosecuted and then released, was arrested on a charge of armed insurrection against the state and direct complicity in the kidnapping and murder of Aldo Moro. Around sixty people comprising all of Negri's department in the University of Padua were also arrested. Their trials ended for the most part in acquittals or were dismissed for lack of evidence. The second accusation against Negri was dropped after two years. The first, which was supported solely on the assertions of a 'witness for the crown', C. Fioroni, who was himself found guilty of the kidnap and murder of

his friend, resulted in a thirty-year sentence for Negri, which was reduced on appeal to twelve. However, the continual stream of accusations forced Negri, who was freed from prison on his election as Radical Party candidate to the Italian parliament in 1983, but who faced the prospect of returning to gaol indefinitely, into exile from Italy.

22   Negri, *L'Anomalia selvaggia: Saggio su potere e potenza in Baruch Spinoza* (Feltrinelli, Milan, 1981. English translation forthcoming, University of Minnesota Press).

23   For a contextualization of the 'Italian anomaly' see my essay 'L'Opéraisme italien: organisation/représentation/idéologie ou la composition de classe revisitée', in A. Corten and M.B. Tahon (eds) *L'Italie: le philosophe et le gendarme* (Actes du Colloque de Montréal, VLB, Quebec, 1986), pp. 37–60.

24   See for example Rolf Bierman, *Tupamaros, Berlin Ouest* or Alain Geismar *L'engrenage terroriste*, not to mention the interminable stream of works by those in Italy who renounced terrorism to varying degrees.

25   Only a few isolated texts by C.L.R. James, Martin Glaberman and D. Mothé, which appeared particularly in *Socialisme ou Barbarie*, are anything near comparable.

26   Cf. my postscript to the Portuguese edition of *Ouvriers et Capital*.

27   Cf. for example Negri, *Fabbriche del soggetto* (xxi Secolo, no. 1, Sept.–Oct. 1987), *Massa-Livorzno* p. 162.

28   See for example Negri's discussion, in chapter 2 of the present work, of the experience of the American New Deal, which he interprets as the epitome of the twentieth century: impossible capitalism or impossible reformism; also his discussion of the concept of the nuclear state which Negri interprets as a translation of a return to pure coercion (chapter 4).

29   The slogan of the student and workers collectives of *Lotta Continua* in 1969 'Prendiamoci la città', appears in the same extension of Tronti's essay which appears in *Classe Operaia*, 'La fabbrica e la società'.

30   Cf. the contribution of Christian Marazzi on this theme in *Zero Work* and in *Magazzino* and also that of Sergio Bologna in the review *Primo Maggio* on 'Marx the analyst in the Herald Tribune on the financial crisis of 1857'.

31   On this theme in Negri's works see his *Proletari e Stato*

(Feltrinelli, Milan, 1976) which used the expression for the first time, as well as the important issue of the review *Aut Aut* which was devoted to a research programme at Padua University (in particular see the contribution of Romano Alquati). See also Negri's *Dall'operaio massa all'operaio sociale* (Multhipla, Milan, 1978).

32   See the work of Maria Rosa Dalla Costa and Selma James, the former having taught at Padua, who defended this theme as well as that of 'wages for housework' which aroused much discussion in the feminist movement after the publication of their book (see note 14).

33   Cf. P.P. Rey *Les alliances de la classe* (Maspero, 1974) for a critique of the structuralism implicit in this position. Cf. also H Cleaver, *The Origins of the Green revolution* (Stanford University, unpublished Ph.D. dissertation, 1975).

34   Cf. Meillassoux, *Femmes et Capitaux* (Maspero, 1976).

35   Even if it ultimately refused it, the reactionary liberal theory of Friedman and Hayek takes this mutation of capitalism into account – this is what the French 'regulation school' calls the transition from competitive capitalism to monopoly capitalism.

36   See Althusser's last texts from *Lenin and Philosophy* (1971) to *Eléments d'autocritique* (1973) to 'Soutenance d'Amiens' (in *Positions*, 1976), as well as the sensational declarations of Terni on the anniversary of the Paris Commune (cf. M. A. Macciocchi, *Deux mille ans de bonheur*, Paris 1983, pp. 531–4), and several works which were unpublished after 1980, all translate the pathetic return to this principle to the actuality of communism, however without themselves being part of the body of the analysis.

37   Cf. the declaration of Tronti's programme in *Operai e Capitale*.

38   This formula appears in a joint work by Negri and Félix Guattari, *Les nouvelles alliances* (Paris, 1986).

39   Althusser in the preface to an interview given to F. Navarro in June 1986 (unpublished).

40   On the very particular form of *operaismo's* Leninism, see Negri's little-known work *La fabbrica della strategia: 33 lezione su Lenin;* (ARBA, Padua, 1976). We will recall that the adherents of *operaismo* maintain the ideas of the possible revolutionary rupture of the capitalist system, but reverse the role which was devolved to the Party in the process. The Party loses any strategic function absorbed in the spontaneity of class composition so that ultimately

it represents no more than a tactical function of the *socialization* of working-class antagonism. In the light of experience it appears that Tronti's elegant formulation of the problem in 1966, then Negri's in 1976, highlight the problem rather than solve it. On the return of some adherents of *operaismo* to the PCI, then the dissolution of all the organized structures of 'autonomia' cf. in particular the critiques by Sergio Bologna in *Primo Maggio* from 1976–7, or Negri's own self-critique: *Fabbriche del Soggetto* (1987); *La Macchina Tempo: rompicapi, liberazione, costituzione* (Feltrinelli, Milan, 1982), pp. 221–4.

41   The analysis led by the adherents of *operaismo*, particularly in Tronti's central essay in *Operai e capitale*, 'Marx, forza-lavoro, classe operaia', is a detailed commentary on the chapter on money in the *Grundrisse*.

42   Instances are possible when the proletarian struggle of labour power manages to block capitalist penetration. The separation (*Trennung*) does not happen 'spontaneously': from the capitalist point of view of course, brute strength is needed, or the imposition of forced labour, of a monetary inducement to 'liberate' the workforce.

43   Cf. the two articles we have already quoted where we have tried to develop all the implications of the schema of class composition, by crossing the figures of waged labour with the dynamics of conflict (composition, decomposition, recomposition).

44   This is the major reproach that one can make against the more traditional formulations of French 'regulation theory' (the more adaptable formulae being pluralist in their explanation, but they encounter the same difficulties).

45   See Lenin's polemic *Imperialism as the highest stage of capitalism* against Hobson's *The Export of Capital* (Constable, London, 1914).

46   Cf. the collective work under the direction of Luciano Ferrari Bravo, J. O'Connor, M. Nicolaus, E. Mandel, C. Neussüs, R. Vernon, S. Hymer, N. Poulantzas, F. Gambino, *Imperialismo e classe operaia multinazionale* (Feltrinelli, Milan, 1975).

47   We must remember that the notion of 'class composition' is a concept which aims to replace the too static, academic and in general reactionary concept of 'social classes'. Class composition comprises simultaneously the technical composition both of capital and of waged labour, which refers to the state of development of the

productive forces, to the degree of social cooperation and division of labour. But this level of analysis is not separable from the political composition which is its *ultima ratio*. We can find in it all that characterizes the collective subjectivity of needs, desires, the imaginary and their objective translation into the forms of political, cultural and community organisation. For works on class composition, less on its definition than on its operational character in the analysis of concrete situation, cf. Romano Alquati, *Sulla Fiate altri scritti* (Feltrinelli, Milan, 1975) and *Sindacato e Partito* (Stanpatori, Turin, 1974). For an historical application cf. Sergio Bologna, in *Telos*, no. 13 (1972), or on the Movement of 1977 in Italy cf. Bologna, in *Semiotext(e)*, vol. III (1980).

48   E.P. Thompson, *The Making of the English Working Class* (Victor Gollancz, London, 1963).

49   For a similar analysis in the legal sphere cf. F. Edelman *La légalisation de la classe ouvrière* (Christian Bourgois, Paris, 1978).

50   The lines of convergence with Althusserianism become more pronounced after 1974. For a 'restrained' conception of Marxist analysis in particular, and the basic character of the antagonism in relation to the two classes cf. E. Balibar, *Cinq études du matérialisme historique* (Maspero, Paris, 1975). Two even more clear-cut points are the rejection of Hegelian dialectics and the interest in Spinoza: cf. P. Macherey, *Hegel ou Spinoza* (PUF, Paris, 1979); L. Althusser, *Positions* (1976); and the rejection of 'socialism and the transition', L. Althusser in interview with Navarro (1986).

51   M. Tronti, *Sull'autonomia del politico* (Feltrinelli, Milan, 1977).

52   A. Asor Rosa, *Le due società* (Einaudi, Turin, 1977). Cf. also Napolitano, Tronti, Accornero, Cacciari (eds) *Operaismo e centralità operaia* (Editori Riuniti, Rome, 1978).

53   M. Tronti, *Il tempo della politica* (Editore Riuniti, Rome, 1980) pp. 71ff.

54   The unfortunate word used by Berlinguer, when he called the *emarginati* [marginalized people] of Bologna *untorelli* [= literally 'plague-carriers' this word carries overtones from its use by Allessandro Manzoni in *I promessi sposi* to describe those children who were falsely accused of wilfully spreading the plague in seventeenth-century Italy] recalls the behaviour of the Communist union leader, Georges Marchais, who in May 1968 called Dany Cohn-Bendit 'the German Jew'. Between 1977 and 1986, lawyers,

magistrates and academics linked directly with the PCI distinguished themselves in the persecution of 'workers' autonomy', which was initially presented as the real strategic command behind the Red Brigades. Nearly ten years later one can see how grotesque these accusations were. And still to come was the detailed history of the trials of 7 April as an operation of the state and a Stalinist exercise led directly by the PCI.

55   Cf. 'Sur quelques tendances de la théorie communiste de l'Etat les plus récentes: a critical review' in *Sur l'Etat, Contradictions* (Brussels, 1976) pp. 375–427. Cf. also Negri, *Proletari e Stato* (1976).

56   Cf. the work of the journal *Primo Maggio* or F. Gambino 'W.E.B. Dubois and the Proletariat in Black Reconstruction' in Dirk Hoerder (ed.) *American Labor and Immigration History, 1877–1920: Recent European Research* (Illinois University Press, 1985).

57   Cf. *Quaderni del Territorio*, nos 1 to 5 (Celuc Libri, Milan, 1976).

58   Cf. Negri, *Fabbriche del soggetto*, (1987) pp. 75–80.

59   Cf. Negri, *Marx Beyond Marx*, Lesson Three.

60   Cf. Negri, 'Crisis of the Planner-State', in *Revolution Retrieved*, (Red Notes, London, 1988).

61   Cf. Negri, *Proletari e Stato* (1976).

62   The abandonment of Leninism as an organizational reference on the theoretical level follows step by step the process of the dissolution of *Potere Operaio*. This was punctuated by S. Bologna leaving the organization in 1972, Negri leaving in 1973 and finally the dissolution of the rest of the group centred around F. Piperno. From 1974 on, the debate continued by means of journals and reviews like *Primo Maggio, Quaderni del Territorio, Metropoli, Rosso, Magazzino, Attraverso.*

63   The appearance of the first free radio stations in Italy and the role played by Radio Alice in Bologna in 1977 profoundly modified the terms of debate about organization and brought down one of the main arguments in favour of centralization.

64   At the height of anti-terrorist repression, the Italian Ministry of the Interior considered the 'armed party' to contain at least 100,000 members – partisan but significant dramatization of the scale of the problem.

65   Unlike other European groups of the same kind, the Red

Brigades commanded a real audience among workers' collectives.

66 This criticism which Negri frequently takes up, was also emphasized in a famous editorial by Rossana Rossandra in *Il Manifesto*, in which she describes a 'family album' to stress the profound kinship between the Red Brigades and the insurrectional culture of the PCI's Stalinist period.

67 The simulation of civil war which constituted the operation of 7 April 1979 and more generally the close links between media communication and terrorists' appeals led the second wave of *operaismo* to give more attention to the problem of ideology as something which could be 'set-up' and not as a 'reflection'. Cf. *Attraverso* and the numerous works on the trials of 7 April.

68 The common ground between the major Italian trials and the Stalinist trials of the 1930s is their attempt to rewrite and to falsify memory and history (by erasing dates, practising a kind of inverse teleology) in the police files, coupled with a need to deconstruct the *subjectivity* which had formed. For such an operation one cannot proceed without the active, subjective consent of the subjects under attack.

69 A very good example of the historical reconstruction of the social subject of liberation is George Rawick's *From sundown to sun-up, the formation of the Black community* (Greenwood: Westpoint, 1972).

70 Negri, *Descartes politico o della ragionevole ideologia* (Feltrinelli, Milan, 1970).

71 Negri, *Lenta Ginestra: Saggio sull'ontologia di Giacomo Leopardi* (SugarCo Edizioni, Milan, 1987).

72 Negri, *L'anomalia selvaggia* (Feltrinelli, Milan, 1981).

73 Negri, *La Forma-stato per la critica dell'economia politica della Costituzione* (Feltrinelli, Milan, 1977).

74 Negri, *Fabbriche del soggetto* (1987).

75 Negri, *La Macchina Tempo* (1982).

76 Cf. Gilles Deleuze's Preface to the French edition of *L'anomalia selvaggio: L'anomalie sauvage* (PUF, Paris, 1982) pp. 9–12.

77 Cf. Negri, *Fabbriche del soggetto* (1987) pp. 20–1, 63–7, 75–80. We know that the interpretation of Heidegger and Kant (*Kant et le problème de la métaphysique*, Gallimard, 1958) consists in maintaining that the author of the *Critique of Pure Reason*, having foreseen the possibility of founding pure reason and practical

reason on transcendental imagination, renounces this and re-
establishes the primacy of the analytic and the concept, and thus
relegates transcendental aesthetics of the ontological terrain of
factitious experience to the formal conditions of cognition. Negri's
interpretation is distinguished in that it dares to accept Heidegger's
interpretation, but transforms its significance by inserting revolution and the immediate experience of liberation in the place of space
and time.

78   Cf. p. 88 where Negri rejects the 'rotten dialectic of
workerism' as well as the definition of the twentieth century as the
century of impossible reformism and capitalism.

79   Cf. chapter 3, *From the factory to the ecological machine*.

80   William Morris, 'A Dream of John Ball', in *Three Works by
William Morris* (Lawrence and Wishart, London, 1977).

PART 1

1

Paris 1986, 26 November – 10 December

There were fifteen days of struggle against the proposals to reform the universities and secondary school teaching and the struggle took place both in the secondary schools and in the universities. After exactly fifteen days the proposals were withdrawn: this was a result of several gigantic student demonstrations and violent clashes with the police – as a result of which one student was killed – which promised a veritable social upheaval against the government. This is the first datum – macroscopic, but in and of itself incidental, superficial and insufficient. What risks being hidden by this initial perception and which, on the contrary in this book I wish to emphasize, is that here we have witnessed *the emergence of a new social subject*: an intellectual subject which is nonetheless proletarian, polychrome, a collective plot of the need for equality; a subject that rejects the political and immediately gives rise to an ethical determination for existence and struggle.

Let us be clear about this: it is an *intellectual* subject but also a *productive* one. This means that the productive side of work is now apparent principally on the intellectual level. The intellectual power of this subject is inextricably and emotionally linked to the principal characteristics (exclusion, selection, hierarchy) of the labour market: as a result of this, even though in its essence it is intellectual, the subject is proletarianized from the very beginning. That is to look at it from the negative point of view. What is positive, let us repeat, is the fact that intellectual work has become eminently productive. As a consequence, the new subject is *central in society*: in 1968, students sought the factory as a point of identification; today the workers look to the students as the only possible and continuous detonator of social action, and within the social market of productive labour, they identify with the students and with their intellectual productivity. It is an *ethical subject*: but in what sense? Since it becomes political while rejecting the political – that is, the whole machine and the individual cogs of a state which is dominated by parties – it reappropriates political methods, using them in the service of truth. Finally, it is a *rebellious subject* (that is, now; tomorrow, it may, perhaps, become revolutionary) which attempts to appropriate social communication, and by doing that, to challenge radically the workings of contemporary society: in contemporary society communication is, simultaneously, the connective element and the point from which to exercise control, in that it counterposes the equality of community to that of money, utopia to cynicism and productive cooperation to capitalist control.

If we bear in mind these initial elements we can immediately appreciate the particular originality of the scene of struggle before us, as well as its great clarity. As often happens in France, owing to characteristics of that country which were already apparent to Marx, a month of political struggle has revealed, in a completely developed and pure form, that which in Germany only the continuing influence of ideology and the metaphysical efforts of the historical consciousness have been able to disclose and then only imperfectly (and which in Italy only the daily ebb and flow of the revolution sometimes hints at, though in an attractive way): that is, the concept of a new class-composition and a new political subject. During these Parisian struggles, in contrast, the intensity of the experience was already abstract and the mechanism of needs reached maturity in a very short period. A week, or ten days, were enough for an enormous and joyous mass to establish the concept. The same space of time was sufficient to allow recognition of the tragic dimension of the political, to reveal the violence of the state, and as a consequence, to identify the entirety of the forces that had an interest in accentuating the authoritarian characteristics of the regime, or, on the other hand, of those forces that sought the unity of the protest. This eminently political operation was accomplished by virtue of the *proletarian hinge of the movement*, which was constituted by the students of the technical schools and by the 'beur' people: here is one of the immediate forms of the reappearance of the political. In its proletarian form it consists in the capacity to discriminate between the front of unity and of opposition and to bring to awareness, through these relationships, the reality of the new social composition of the class.

Thus a new movement exploded and grew, leading to an exceptional outpouring of analysis and political criticism – this after almost twenty years, at any rate *after a decade*, of absolute silence, of cowardly and atrocious conversions, of widespread repentance, and after both the Left and Right had given each other a helping hand by indistinguishably exercising the craft of mystification and of repression. In Germany, the resistance to all this and the growth of new movements was the result of social division; in Italy the resistance had become invisible and had permeated every stratum of society: now all this has been put back into play on this new political horizon. Those fifteen Parisian days have reinvigorated a debate that had seemed dead and buried: namely, the critique of the present starting from the identification of a new subjective force. All this has been possible because, in opposition to the disgraceful distortion of history that has been carried out by the official workers' movement, *an ontological awareness* has demonstrated its residual and deep, yet powerful permanence, and has re-emerged both in people and in the collective movements. From the disaster of ideology a 'gay science' of the present has emerged. In this case, the relationship between the movement and history constitutes neither a tautology nor a vicious circle; on the contrary, the way in which it manifests itself is completely new. Even though we are unable to make complete sense of it, we can say that it is productive; and we are raising the hood behind which the movement had hidden its new power [*potenza*].*

Let us, then, examine this new movement closely, not by constructing a narrative, but by posing at once the essential

---

* In English is difficult to highlight the difference between two terms which are expressed separately in other languages : *potentia – potestas*; *puissance – pouvoir*; *potenza – potere*; *Vermögen – Macht*, etc. This difference, which I consider to be particularly important, is rooted in a philosophical tradition inherited from Spinoza (see my *L'anomalia selvaggia* (Feltrinelli, Milan, 1981)). This distinction marks the poles of the political dialectic: on the one hand *potentia* which is constitutive social activity, and on the other *potestas* which is the totalizing and fixed dimension of social making.

questions. Is it really a subject that is at issue? If one sees it as a form of consciousness which is accompanied by a material determination, then certainly, yes. It is a consciousness of needs, interests and potentiality. If, however, one claims that this relationship between consciousness and its material presuppositions is something definitive, concluded – a species of new individual, arisen from where one doesn't know, endowed with what creativity one knows even less – then one is talking nonsense, just like the idealists and Stalinists do. In fact *the new subject is a mechanism*: as a result of material conditions, its consciousness tends towards subjectivity, towards a constructive articulation of real needs. And we can immediately add that the activity which determines this articulation is intellectual. The new subject is an intellectual subject. It constitutes an eminently intellectual labour force. The work it carries out is *abstract*. As such, it is work which is carried out by multitudes of people, but which, at the same time, is singularized. To the extent that it has a vast number of determinate, specific potentialities, it is work which tends to appear simply as activity. When the Parisian students gathered in the squares, their only common element – their only medium of self-identification – was their intellectual style, their ability to express themselves with eloquence and irony in challenging authority – above all, in the form of paradox. In this way, the students revealed the essential nature of the work that is embodied in the current class-composition: its highly abstract character (which is a necessary condition of its singularization); its highly intellectual character (which is a necessary condition for its 'soft' application); and its basic equality as the only and exclusive foundation of a plural and convergent order, and of a complex articulation and division of the social labour. Whoever denies these characteristics of contemporary work, *whoever denies the mechanism the possibility of becoming a subject, is an enemy*. Consciousness constructs subjectivity by going beyond the material conditions of its expansion. As intellectual operators (as ever changing functions of intellectual labour and of its material conditions), and as the protagonists of a general and inarrestable movement towards the hegemony of intellectual labour, the students are, through their movement, the manifestation of a new formation of subjectivity. Just as the Spinozan power [*potentia*], by means of the multitude of determinations of the real, forms new subjective protagonists, so today a very rich, and increasingly intellectual mechanism is constructing and manifesting a *radically new organization of social labour*. Others will object that this is not a revolutionary condition, and that, on the contrary, capital will be able to gain control of these events. . . Now, if what is meant by this is that such is the capitalist programme, then these events are banal. But when this criticism is heard from the workers' side (for example, through the traditional denunciations of spontaneity in favour of a consciousness that is created from external experiences) however doggedly it might be repeated, it is nothing other than a case of simple vulgarity. Later we shall return to this problem and the formidable, and potentially catastrophic, difficulties that it creates for capital. For the moment we simply add: the faces of the intellectual proletariat are beautiful, open and sincere; they are an ontological power made visible. To say the word 'subject' is to say that this power cannot be expropriated under any circumstances. The activity of these youths, these intellectuals that are taking shape along with a new society, is beautiful: for at the same time as, and for the same reason that, they are being formed as a subject, they are giving material force to utopian criteria of liberty and of equality. These youths are more beautiful, then, than many other people, and more so (unfortunately) than their worker-fathers who are always corporatist and often resigned. This proletarian intellectuality, on the other hand, is different: irony, paradox, and a critical spirit constitute the fabric of utopia; and hope nourishes it.

In this way the new intellectual subject is established as a principle element of the definition of the proletariat and is shown to be the supporting structure of the critique and revolt of the entire proletariat. If in 1968 the students sought legitimation of their struggle in the workers' organizations and in the factories, *today it is the workers that look to the students*. Recently, here in France, the students requested the participation of the trade unions in their programme of agitation. The trade unions arrived, perplexed; but when their leadership tried to prevaricate, the rank-and-file forced them to remain united. From the objective point of view, the fact is that by virtue of its power, intellectual work reveals the mechanism of *interaction for all social labour*. From the subjective point of view, it produces a specific social constitution – that of cooperation, or rather, that of *intellectual cooperation*, i.e. *communication* – a basis without which society is no longer conceivable. Elsewhere I have described this process as both characteristic of, and the basis for, *the epoch of the socialized worker.** My friends and I have been studying this hypothesis for more than ten years. But why should we continue to call it a hypothesis? We now know everything about the socialized worker – how it moves, how it works, how it reproduces itself, how it organizes itself. The events in France that we are dealing with and that provide such strong confirmation of the truth of our hypothesis and prognostication, now show us how the socialized worker 'dances'. It is as well never to forget the socialized worker's intolerable fickleness (that is, intolerable for whoever has aims which are exploitative or instrumental in nature). Our 'hypothesis' is no longer a hypothesis as such. In 1968 the students went to the factories; today legitimacy and leadership are found among the students. They are aphorisms of the new nature of productive labour, traces of the new processes of an intellectual formation of the proletariat. Therefore, those who ignite the social movements, exercise countervailing power, and reappropriate and recompose (for the entire society) that which capital and the state have expropriated are those who produce value through intellectual labour: namely, students and others. Their power expresses itself through tenderness. *The theme of equality* (that phantasm which is, objectively, the community of communication, and, subjectively, the generosity of the subjects and the tenderness of their collective relationships) provides the movement with its power (and if necessary, its violence) against all corporations – even those of the workers who, precisely with regard to the theme of equality, are often caught off balance. The movement acts not only against corporations but also against the state because the state is the guarantor of the reproduction of inequality. In this way, a movement which has been strongly characterized by specific objectives and determinate demands can become a general and political movement for proletarian struggle against inequality, corporations and the state. And it can prepare itself to become a revolutionary movement by applying the method of equality to itself (to its own organization) and by using equality as a

---

* This is a translation of *operaio sociale*, literally 'social worker'. However, the use of the latter term is obviously inappropriate, therefore, we have chosen to use 'socialized worker'. On this and other problems regarding the definition of terms, see my *Revolution Retrieved: Selected Writings* (Red Notes and Blue Heron, London, forthcoming).

fundamental yardstick by which to judge all proposals. Let us take communism for example: this paradoxical password has become the motor behind every organizational proposal and it constitutes a demonstration of the centrality of the socialized worker. Let us again consider equality: to begin again does not mean to go back; on the contrary, it means to reaffirm the materiality of intellectual labour, the centrality of the subjects that it produces, and its mobility and power.

At this point, we should say something about the *racial question*, because this has raised, indeed imposed, the issue of equality in the French movement of '86 in a concrete, immediate and insistent way. This is a very large topic so I will, therefore, limit myself to a brief comment. In France, the question of civil rights and their uniform application has encountered and crossed the racial contours of the society. The young Arabs of French nationality (of whom there are at least a million) are directly confronted by inequality; that is, they are doubly discriminated against because they are subject both to economic exploitation and racial exclusion. This situation is dramatized by the climate of violence – which is sometimes also a climate of terror and always one of ghettoization and repression – that is found in the coloured districts and in the proletarian *banlieux*. Now, during the recent struggles, this *multi-racial labour force* not only mobilized around issues relating to equality, but translated these into an immediate and aggressive form. As a consequence, this great mass of Arab youth that attends the schools, lives in the districts and agitates politically in French society, has appeared as an unconscious, but nonetheless effective carrier of the fundamental interest of those class fractions that are made up of the foreign workers in France: an interest in an integration that is the appropriation of wealth and power. Moreover, this mass of Arab youth has already been introduced, from both the academic and productive points of view, to the highest levels of the capitalist organization of work, and is thus a highly abstract, intellectual, mobile and highly modern labour force. It is in terms of these characteristics that the mass of Arab youth is subjected to the ancient laws of racism; and it is for this reason that it becomes so important to study the racial question. (It is no accident that the reactionary forces of French society have here identified an equal and opposite lever of mobilization.) The racial question demonstrates the power of the historical development towards equality, that is, the dynamic of the communist subject as a central and irreducible element; it also allows us to trace this historical development in terms of how it affects those (horrible) concrete class-divisions brought about by racism. Racism is a class point of view, but through racism, the violence of the class point of view is multiplied a thousand times. This is, therefore, an explosive point: it is not true that Frantz Fanon and Malcolm X are shadows of the past; they are still with us – as scientists of the future. Certainly, outside France or the other countries where the racial question is quantitatively central, there is a tendency to minimize the significance of what we are saying here, objecting that racism (and thus the dialectic that is described here) is only rarely a moment of irresolvable contradiction and that elsewhere in Europe, where the labour-market is more regulated, the different races are in such minorities that they are easily assimilated, or else are subject to a regime of mobility that destroys all possibility of political aggregation. This objection might stand (in which case we would have to tone down our expectation of a new revolutionary explosion of racism quite substantially) if it were not for the fact that *behind the framework of the racist society* it is possible to perceive *that of the dual society* – one of the most recent and most ferocious products of the capitalist mode of domination. The dual society constitutes the end point towards which the racist society tends; it is an extension of the racist model. In each of the countries of advanced capitalism – whether a multi-racial labour-market is present or not – a South Africa is taking root. In this way we can appreciate the significance of the issue of equality which was raised during the recent struggles by the multi-racial subject – a subject that contrasts the fact that it is an intellectual, socialized and proletarian subject with the depth of racial discrimination in natural and cultural terms. Racial discrimination constitutes a scandal, one which appears even more profound when it is borne in mind that the design of a higher communist organization of society is not only a product of the will but something which is fortified by the ontological reality of the racially excluded. These movements, these emergencies and these mechanisms, are irreversible. Here, then, is another lesson of the recent struggles.

All this would seem to be sufficient to demonstrate that in France since the events of those weeks (independently of how the struggles are likely to develop), *a new revolutionary subject* has emerged. We have used the word 'emerged', but this is not quite correct because the subject was born already fully developed, and what it illustrates is not a beginning but an end result, an actual condition: this is because it is an *insurgent* subject. It is a subject which has risen against a power structure that has been reformed and firmly consolidated over the last two decades. It has arisen within and against those old and new ideologies of inequality and negative value: neo-liberalism and postmodernism. In saying that the subject has emerged already fully developed, we mean that it is fully developed ethically. Hardly had this characteristic (which is an ecological determination) of the movement been recognized, than it was subject to a 'moral reductionism'. It is therefore necessary to explain at once the precise significance of the term 'ethical' and to counterpose this to moral reductionism. There is no sense in which the ethical multitude can be reduced to a mere sum total of moral individualities, of innocent and beautiful souls. What we have been dealing with is not individual morality, but collective ethics. Things could not be otherwise because everything concerning the origin of this generation is collective in nature. This generation has taken the collectivity as its starting point in order to turn it into something ethical. The utopia of this generation is, and could not but be, a utopia of equality and community. To capitalistic socialization (as it is expressed by individual market initiative and subordination to the yardstick of money), this proletarian generation has counterposed communist socialization: that is, *an ethic of the community* (which reveals how profound social cooperation is), and the truth that collective production is reflected in communication. This is a disturbing dimension to those who have observed it: it is no accident that once it had been understood by the political representatives of capital, these struggles (which in and of themselves seem child's play) were followed, paradoxically, by a certain panic and a sharp fall in the value of the franc on the international exchange markets. This was only to be expected: money is both the means to, and the symbol of, capitalistic socialization, so if the latter is overtaken by a crisis, the value of the currency collapses. In this way even the blockheads in charge of the French government's economic policy were forced to recognize the real significance of the '86 movement. Apart from this one, we shall leave all other paradoxes aside: the ethical character of the movement is too profoundly inherent in the realty of European and

French society to be explicable – or even illustrated – in terms of paradoxes. The permanence and insistence of the postmodern and late capitalist crisis of values has been brushed aside by the ontological power of a collective morality based on equality. This ethic is immoral as long as morality is individualized; it is an ethic which reflects the collective constitution of equal individuals. Several not unintelligent, reactionary ideologists, whose aim is to contain the damage to the established order at any price, have claimed that these youngsters are more liberal than neo-liberalism (which continues to be an ideology of the state) can allow. This is not true; rather, these youngsters have taken the declaration of the rights of man of '89 seriously; theirs is a revolutionary liberty, a liberty that embodies freedom and human solidarity. The mayonnaise can be stirred as much as you like, but if you don't do it in the right way, it won't thicken. To the generations that knew freedom without equality, the present generation has counterposed fraternity, community and the collective reappropriation of control over communication and productive cooperation. In the liberal societies fraternity (as far as it went) meant 'insurance', and in the socialist societies, 'sacrifice': for the present generation *fraternity means 'subject'*.

We have thus arrived at what is most essential about our analysis of the 1986 events in Paris; that is, we have grasped the problem of the *actuality of communism*, because it is this which in the end stands out. Certain jokers having theoretical pretensions have said that the movement has *an ethic without a utopia*, and they have said that it is for this reason that the movement is so wise (where, by 'wisdom' they mean moderation, good behaviour and a lack of excesses). These jokers have approximated the truth, not in their definition of wisdom, but in their recognition that this movement is without utopia. What was still utopian in 1968 is today something natural, second nature and fixed in consciousness. Certainly, in the absence of the movement of '68, without the Foucaultian tangle of genealogies and powers, in short, without parents, the movement of '86 would not have come into existence. Such parentage is not ideological, however, for what the movement illustrates is the unfurled consciousness of the socialized worker. In 1968, given the enormity of the transformation and the genuine changes that were being felt, the weakness of the subject suggested that the political was the necessary and hoped-for site for the establishment of new values and the consequent stabilization of the movement. Today, the extraordinary maturity of the collective consciousness induces alienation from the political which is seen as useless tinsel, and often as a disgusting excrescence. The direct and collective democracy of this movement reacts to the official institutional set-up (together with its liturgies and symbols) with derision. The collective clarity of this consciousness is based on the technologies which it knows and possesses. It has the luminosity of the 'media'. It is pure visibility. It is probable – as some other joker will say – that only the study of angels can describe these regions of being. But these angels of ours have been down to hell, and since they are acquainted with all its misery, and are full of its arrogance, they have once more raised their eyes to heaven. A new and original revolutionary tradition (which has been influenced by, but not reduced to, the tradition of the workers' movement) has established itself in the last twenty years. Revolutionary conceptual sequences have been established: community, understanding, communism are paths which can be followed in all directions. The actuality of communism, then, is the actuality of community. Thereby, the desire for community is formed in a mature, visible and immediate way during the process of reappropriating the means of communication. Communication is the means by which the community appearing as truth begins to be constituted. Community is inconceivable if communication is not founded on truth. The current generations are attempting to understand their *communicative 'second nature'* rigorously and forcefully: to be opposed to the political is to be opposed to the absence of transparency, the exhaustion of mediation and the growth of elements of irresponsibility and secrecy in political life. To be opposed to, or rather, *alienated from the political* is a sign of insurrection. To be born again: this watchword was supremely important in the mystical beliefs of classical antiquity and was revived by the Christian change. There is no reason why it cannot be made use of – with good taste and allusive efficiency and without mystical satisfactions – during the course of the communist revolution. For we have reached the point which Marx said we were capable of reaching: i.e. the point at which the material basis of private appropriation and the law of profit itself are too weak to resist the growth of the collective individual.

The socialized worker has come to develop the *critique of*

exploitation by means of the *critique of communication*. Production is, in fact, social, and it has become so to an increasing extent. Productive cooperation is diffused throughout society; it permeates productive networks which in their turn are entirely social in nature. Precisely because it is social, production finds its exclusive centre in communication, in the processes of information and in the spheres of communicative structure. Under the domination of capital, however, the mode in which communication functions and takes shape is simultaneously a mode of expropriation. Therefore, to aim at gaining control over communication (i.e. to desire its reappropriation) is to influence in a direct way the social relations of production and exploitation. It is on the new organization of communication that the determinations of exploitation are based. One can thereby understand why socialized work (both that of the factory and socialized work in the true sense) tends to be concentrated on intellectual labour: by virtue of the cohesiveness provided by the communication which is involved in social cooperation, socialized work tends to establish new processes of hegemony. In this way the fight against exploitation conquers and adapts itself to the new conditions of exploitation. It needs to be emphasized that this change of sign in the sequences of the social channels of communication (which used to run from society to the factory and which today run from the factory to the society) does not remove the suffering and cruelty involved in exploitation. Neither does it annul its past. Manual labour tends to become intellectual labour in order that it may rid itself of the wounds inflicted by the brutality of exploitation, and in order that it may thereby continue the struggle to destroy not only the single manifestations of exploitation, but exploitation itself. A large element of *pietas* was felt in the major street-demonstrations that took place in those weeks: the students felt filial compassion for the pain and effort suffered by their mothers and fathers – whether the latter are immigrant workers, mass workers, coloured workers, man – or woman-servants. There was a sense of anger as well as *pietas*. The modification of the class composition does not negate, but rather enhances liberation from the most backward stages of exploitation: because of its higher productivity, intellectual labour has a larger capacity to solve the problems of exploitation.

Once more, then, the specific subjectivity involved in socialized work and communicative intelligence gives rise to the *power of subversion*. This subversion is a subversion of all existing structures, or rather, of all those that are aimed at exploitation, either in the first or second instance, directly or indirectly. Subversion is the destruction of the violence that is inherent in exploitation and which runs through society, indistinctly, massively and terribly: subversion is *countervailing power*. The more the labour force, or the working subject, becomes intellectual and social, the more the violence inherent in exploitation acquires an intellectual and social character. Violence is spread out in a generalized way; it occupies the whole of society and permeates all of its pores. Violence is no longer merely ideological; rather, it is functional and innate. How can it be uprooted and destroyed? It is a violence which we feel bearing down on us; often we are its prisoners and our thoughts and nightmares are implicated in it. In this light countervailing power might be thought to be equivalent to countervailing violence. It would, however, be mad to draw such a conclusion, and when violence was recently expressed through terrorism, it did indeed have a feel of madness about it. But what does subversion imply then? Subversion is a force which is powerful and clear; it is the positive aspect of destruction. The subversive character of the demonstrations that took place at the end of 1986 was not a consequence of the influence of a few guerrillas over the mass processions. In this respect police blackmail, impressive for its vulgarity, was completely exposed and useless. Rather, the subversive character lay in the non-negotiable and irrenounceable declaration of a certain number of truths, such as: equality, freedom, opposition to selection, opposition to death, the promotion of life, the future, plans for knowledge and society – and a number of other small things of a similar degree of ethical importance. Subversion is the radical nature of the truth. It is an applied form of this radicalism. *Subversion is the calm and implacable countervailing power of the masses.* This latter characteristic needs emphasizing: the obvious truths, in particular the norm against killing, are expressions of a very high level of determination. This determination is as great as that which has always been traditional in social-revolutionary movements, at least at their beginning. This traditional determination has not been negated, but rather integrated into the recent struggles. It has also been transformed in some way, because while persisting throughout the development of the struggle and the project, it has been expressed in very radical (though always transparent) ways, by a violence which, because it is creative, destroys without killing.

The movement has discovered its true tendency in a very short space of time: it has discovered this tendency by revealing its communist nature and forcefully counterposing it to the political level and to the institutional dimension. Between these extremes which immediately constituted the terms of the problem, a specific dynamic has developed which for the first time can be clearly identified. The project of *reappropriating communication* and establishing community thus lies between ontology and power. Here, then, we find the thousand watchwords that organize and give shape to the passage from ontology to the attack on the ruling powers: No to instrumentalization, No to the politics of the pot-boilers, No to the falsifications, No to the mockery etc. etc., Yes to truth. The truth is a means to an end. The action can be extended, between ontology and *the struggle for power and against the ruling powers*, and thus become ethical, only if it is based on truth. Truth destroys the owners' political domain. In this respect, *the critique of the political* reveals the ethical importance of the determination of truth. It is this declaration, its repetition over a long time-period and its continual verification, which determine how long the realization of the project will take. The subject will realize the project by claiming the truth. Ideology will fade away and be lost; it will give way to truth. In these terms, it will soon be recognized – as it was for a moment during the struggle when a comrade was killed – that the enemy not only represents 'non-truth', but that the enemy is also, and above all, an adversary subject. The enemy's machines too will be identified, fought and destroyed. Within the perspective of class struggle, war is certainly not ruled out; it is just that at the moment we are the more powerful contender.

These are the lessons of a formidable movement, or rather, they are the indications which the movement offers to whoever wishes to heed them. Then again, there are those who do not wish to do so. Antagonism has been rediscovered and the asphyxiating crust beneath which we lay has been broken.

2

The end of the century

The twentieth century is drawing to a close. In the West the need to define it is certainly less intensely felt than was the anxiety to experience it of those living at its outset. At first sight, Western humanity is emerging from the twentieth century in a sorry state. However, let us attempt to characterize this blessed century and understand what it has been. This is no easy task: it was already a point of contention for our grandparents since they were unable to agree on when the century began: 'Fifteen years before, or fifteen years after 1900', said Friedrich Meinecke, for example; 'With the great slump of the 1880s or with the 1914 war', argued Schumpeter. Schumpeter also asked, however, whether there was still any point in posing this problem when, surveying the political and social scene, it was necessary to acknowledge that, round about the time of the first world war, the concrete determining factors of the economic cycle and of centuries had gone mad. *What period of time, then, does the expression 'the twentieth century' represent?* What has happened to those beliefs in indefinite modernization and progress and the aim of a well-regulated capitalism which were so dominant at the century's outset? Isn't the century which is now coming to an end rather the century of crisis and malaise? From an alternative point of view – and it is an observation that concerns a large part of humanity – the twentieth century can be said to have begun with the revolution of 1917. From this point of view this revolution is what constitutes the specificity of the century, gives it its originality and raises it to the status of a great historical period. After all, the shadow of 'Red October' was subsequently cast over other parts of the world: initially over Europe and central Asia, and then over China and Latin America. But though irreversible, does this fact really constitute the specificity of the twentieth century? Or was 1917 not, rather, the last of the revolutions of the nineteenth century, its extraordinary world-wide success being nothing more than a trick of capitalist logic and a means to the establishment of a world market disguised as emancipation? Then there are those who sarcastically conclude: 'So you want a characterization of the twentieth century. Why look for it in terms of capitalism or socialism? These are merely nineteenth-century ideologies. The specificity of the twentieth century is to be found in the collective madness in which each and every one of the century's protagonists has been a participant. This collective madness is represented by such events as the war of 1914 and then fascism and nazism; the 1940 war and the mass exterminations that characterized it – first Auschwitz and then Hiroshima and the Gulag; uncontrolled decolonization and neo-colonialism; today the Iran-Iraq war, Three Mile Island, Chernobyl. . .' – and so on and so forth: 'Come into this chamber of horrors and see the horrific specificity of this abominable century!' And so we could continue, discovering ever newer defining characteristics and ever more original scars. But to what purpose? For, corresponding to the relative validity of each *particular* appraisal, there is the extreme fragility of every proposed *general* characterization, that is, a kind of incomprehension. Why?

Because *the twentieth century really is incomprehensible*. We could therefore say, perhaps, that it doesn't exist, that it is merely a numerical abbreviation, an empty series, or a nominal expression. To a certain extent it is a repetition of the ideologies, hopes and mystifications for which the nineteenth century is well known. However, the repetition of these elements has taken place at a faster pace and pushed them to their limit, in a word, made them extreme. Hence, such repetition represents a '*temporal exasperation*' *that has launched us into the twenty-first century without having first let us emerge from the nineteenth*. Therefore, it is not possible to establish the essence and originality of our own characterization by focusing attention on a specific content, for the twentieth century really is incomprehensible. But this void – in which temporal innovations have unfolded and cataclysms intervened (the power of semantic innovation of the latter being recognizable only *post factum*) – nevertheless amounts to something. Not by chance, the greatest minds of the twentieth century – from Weber to Sartre, Joyce to Eliot, Benjamin to Brecht, and Wittgenstein to Heidegger – found their common identity in some positive or negative idea of *cataclysm* or *innovation*, that is, in a passing of time which, by depriving reality of every metaphysical resonance, endowed it with meaning only 'after the event', at the moment of the revelation of the actual, or the discovery of the real. 'Only when I have answered a question, can I know what it was aimed at.' This is an appropriate adage for the twentieth century. The twentieth century has no content, but has, rather, the form of a cataclysm and the sense of an innovation. It constitutes a puzzle which contemporaries, other than by simply living the dizziness of the uncontrollable acceleration of every moment of transformation (or better, of every moment of the life cycle), have been unable to solve. When we examine the matter more closely, the incomprehensibility and the paradox which the twentieth century represents becomes even more apparent – both in an intensive and an extensive sense. In the *intensive* sense, it would seem that the specificity of the twentieth century can be grasped: only while crises explode and the most passionate and tragic questions of our epoch must be asked; or only where cataclysmic transitions from the past (which, though ontologically precarious, nevertheless asserts itself) to the future (which is inserted into the present but which cannot yet be grasped conceptually) can be perceived. The historical consciousness is torn by this dilemma. In the *extensive* sense, the paradox is made even more apparent by a whole sequence of cataclysmic transitions. Through a multiple of these transitions, the direction of a substantial change which is taking place is established. That is, we can establish the nature of the change from a world dominated by capitalist power and relations of production (which can be described in terms of the law of value) to an integrated, indifferent world devoid of value: to a totalization which is a mysterious, metaphysical privation. Yet paradoxically, in the shadow of this veritable apocalypse – which threatened the multiple changes and spread and overhung temporal *décalages* – conceptual distortions, or perversions of finality, while seeming to magnify to excess the historical difficulties of the transformation to the point of confusing every theoretical profile, were not enough to cancel out the reality of the innovation or its power (which is a formal power).

There is in the history of the twentieth century, however, a moment (which we shall proceed to outline) when the apocalypse (and the innovation that resolved it) *took on a concrete form*. That is, it appeared and was acted out in a determinate historical conjuncture. By addressing ourselves to the particular events which took place in this conjuncture, we can identify that historical period which, by hypothesis, alludes to, or rather, establishes, the general characteristics of the century as a whole. The period in question represents a radical transformation and, that is, the conquest of a new reality which exists beyond capitalist crisis and pushes forward the threshold of being. Through such an analysis we will at last, perhaps, arrive at the beginnings of a definite characterization of the century. The period is the one that extends *from the Great Crash of 1929 to the enacting of the policies of capitalist reformism*. These policies represent a gigantic effort, a noble gesture on the part of capital which, having recognized the limits of the market and the latter's capacity to throw everything into disorder, resolved upon a project of control and promotion, of authority and progressive democracy. The policies represent, in addition, an operation that powerfully embodies the spirit of the century; this, precisely because the operation was a *mise en forme* of old elements, and therefore a paradoxical innovation. It was a new formation that emerged explosively from old elements. Capitalist reformism, born in the United States and realized as the project of the first Roosevelt government, is probably what constitutes the 'concept' of the twentieth century. To put it another way, this concept is experienced as the peculiarity, or the specificity, of the century and it expresses the solution to the problem which is peculiar to the century. As a consequence, the concept has proceeded to spread, in time and space, all over the globe. We find ourselves confronted with enormous *décalages*, in terms of both time and political culture. It is in the midst of such discrepancies that capitalist reformism is enacted. There is, therefore, no continuity: in this case *natura facit saltus*. In the United States, the Rooseveltian experience in fact lasted for three or four years at most. It started in 1933, and by 1937 was already over. Then there was the war, and afterwards, the upheavals involved in the post-war reconstruction-period and the new partitioning of the globe. A new phase of capitalist reformism, this time involving the entire Western world, was to come about only at the end of the fifties and during the *sixties*. On what grounds, then, can we say that this decade represents the essence of the twentieth century? The reason is as follows. During the sixties we witnessed a capitalism that was highly innovative and democratic in the sense that profit margins were sufficiently wide so as to allow a continuous redistribution of incomes in favour of the working strata and the socialized proletariat in general. There was, therefore, an enormous pressure: towards the legitimation of capitalism in terms of development, and the motivation of individual and collective consciousnesses in terms of consumption; and in favour of basing social transformation on abundance. Now this overall project manifested itself in many different events which were dispersed throughout the century and which were different in form. If capitalist reformism represents the nub of the twentieth century, it also represents the radical guiding-thread that runs though it: it found its impulse in the United States in response to the Great Crash, and the Europeans reinvented it in the post-war period following the much more tragic response to the self-same problems of crisis represented by National Socialism. A form of capitalist reformism modified by domestic traditions and a fundamental authoritarianism was developed in Japan; and finally, in the seventies and eighties, similar indications of the tendency have made themselves felt in those developing countries which, in the meantime, have escaped destruction through repression of the periphery – the latter as a consequence of monetarism at the centre. Then again, at various times even *the socialist countries* have been contaminated by capitalist reformism, so that concomitantly, we have seen the productive pulse of these regimes submit to the incentive to consume and, in this respect, rediscover new entrepreneurial motivations and an associated participation.

Having said this, it is necessary, however, to pause and reiterate the aspect of incomprehensibility and fragility displayed by the specificity of the century, since it is also in the fast, neurotic motion we have talked about that the tragedy of the century consists. By this I mean that the reformist and capitalist specificity of the twentieth century, appearing like lightning – like a dazzling flash as strong as it was immediate and sudden – by the same token displayed an *extreme ambiguity*. On the one hand, it repeated capitalistic reliance on economic expansion and the belief in the liberating force of capital (a conviction that had been crucial in organizing the bourgeoisie as a class ever since the eighteenth century). On the other hand, however, it was at once apparent that this conviction rested on a void, on a *recognition of the existence of an irresolvable crisis*. The activities of capital and its own reformism display the characteristics of something that has been irremediably destroyed – that is, both the suspicion that capitalism represents a form of the relations of production that has already been superseded, and the fear of no longer managing to contain labour processes and processes of valorization within a virtuous circle. It is above all in the way that reformism concerns the very working class which capitalism itself has brought to a high level of maturity and strength, that the sense of ambiguity and the feeling of fragility – to the point of precariousness – make themselves felt. This, then, is the specificity of the twentieth century: a flash of lightning, an ambiguous thunderbolt that was able to produce a bourgeoisie which, in the middle of the century, displayed that dull dignity which is typical of restorers of a lost age. This should not be thought of as having been a reactionary attitude, but on the contrary (to the extent that capitalist restoration was by that time felt to be impossible) a utopian one, and thereby much more justifiable. It is immediately worth adding (or rather, re-emphasizing) that the characteristics of capitalist reformism have nothing to do with the policies of restoring the 'free market', or with the business of deregulation – in other words, with the attempts to redistribute income in favour of the already wealthy and to dismantle the welfare state (that are typical of Reaganism, for example). These positions are unambiguous and without illusion or malaise – or hope.

Twentieth-century reformism, as it emerges from economic crisis (and which the entirety of political regimes and economic systems have incorporated), can be likened to Julian the Apostate who is mistakenly thought of as a traitor and who claimed and sought an irremediably lost birthright. But just as Julian's restoration of paganism was both abstract and vacuous, so too is reformism. Reality is not determined by such dreams; instead, it rejects them. When these dreams appear, they only retain any substance in actuality for a very brief period of time. Julian was like an apparition – an apparition both bright and permanently uncertain – because, confronted with the uncertainty of the existent, he designed a perfect model – which reality refused to accept. But that is not all: in effect, Julian the restorer – that is to say, the reformist, or our idealized Roosevelt – pushed the confrontation with reality so far forward that not only did his aims become unrealistic, but all capitalist projects which followed came to be felt as such. Since discrepancies between the project and the reality are no longer possible, *capitalism itself is impossible.* If capitalism can exist only as reformism, then, when reformism is shown to be impossible, so is capitalism, and nothing remains but impotent desire and empty nostalgia. Nostalgia for paganism died along with Julian the Apostate. The twentieth century represents the explosion of a reformist project on the part of capital. It was to have given form to the whole of the twentieth century; but the century slipped from its grasp. Everything coming before this experiment should be thought of as still belonging to the nineteenth century; what comes after is something extraordinarily new: the twenty-first century, perhaps? We shall see. For the moment it is enough to say that, located *in the thirties and sixties*, capital's *reformist phase* was an experience which was simultaneously enthusing and *ephemeral*. Thus, returning to our collective biography, it is only right to acknowledge that we ourselves had found cause for optimism in that fragility, for example through the idea of pushing reformism forward, of shattering its limits, and of marrying capitalist reformism with socialism etc. But now what is to be said? What is to be done? The reformist giant had feet of clay. It was an illusion. We had believed it possible to build our transformative power from within the processes of capitalist transformation – and in this respect our destructive intentions were themselves adapted to reformist aims. Anti-fascism, the determination of consumption by the unsatisfied pressure of needs, exploitation of the wages-question: what else was all this if not a waltz with the authors of reformism? Keynes and Roosevelt were the flags we carried within the workers' movement, not to speak of Kennedy. Without confusing the cards on the table, yet incapable of discriminating correctly – i.e. of precisely identifying those material, constitutional and structural determining factors that render the limits of capitalism insuperable, or better, intraversable, or impassable – we were engaged in a class struggle to the rhythm of the Beatles. To go beyond this is to choose to construct something different.

It is precisely at its limits – i.e. in its twentieth-century-reformist guise – that capitalism is revealed, in a flash, as being impossible.

We are at last approaching a definition: the twentieth century is impossible capitalism. 'What has reformism been?' Answer: 'A handful of decades, distributed here and there on the face of our planet, and including Europe, America, Japan, *chez nous* and "down under"'. *The twentieth century is impossible reformism* – that is, the impossibility of the only form of possible capitalism. Reformism has been the only possible response to the October Revolution and to the nineteenth century which was responsible for the results of this ideology. But since reformism is impossible, there has, in fact, been no response to the October Revolution. The twentieth century has existed only insofar as it has produced an impossible dream. Therefore, caught by this impossibility and suffocated by it, it itself is impossible. The twentieth century exists as much as reformism exists: it is merely a thunderbolt, a brief flash of lightning (though a very bright one), or a brief period of light during the night.

Consequently, and only for this reason, the night as a whole has been somewhat less dark. The twentieth century is rooted in the nineteenth. Socialism has spanned both centuries, as have various forms of authoritarianism, such as bonapartism, colonialism and racism for example. Imperialism has continued to be *fundamentum regni*. Traditional forms of legitimation were prolonged from the nineteenth century until the explosion of capitalist reformism: only then did 'the rule of law' make room for 'consensus'; only then were the authorities obliged to strive to demonstrate a democratic dimension – in *theory* at least. In *practice* such democracy was no less constricting, tragic and heavy than the authoritarian tradition, the latter having become like a machine – that is, a sort of 'fixed capital' of the state. What we have, then, is a dark, threatening foundation that is prolonged for half the century, then the reformist explosion, and then, in a very short space of time – its defeat. The light of the twentieth century consists solely in this explosion and defeat – that is, in the very brief period of time that connects the two. In turn, this period of time corresponds to the experience of reaching the outer bounds of capitalism and to the exhaustion of any idealized conception of the latter. In addition, therefore, the period also corresponds to the paradoxical determination of capitalism's impossibility. This revelation can be likened to fireworks: during the course of the century it appears multiply, briefly, and in a uniform way. The apocalypse can be glimpsed lurking behind the plurality of appearances of reformism. The ideologies and aims of the nineteenth century have cast their light over the first half of our own century and beyond. In repeating itself here and there, this inheritance has assumed a new – reformist and transformative – guise. This was the only way of overcoming the economic crisis and the accumulation of contradictions, and of bringing about a renewal which tended towards the real. When this moment is described, it is as if we were approaching one of those *historical conjunctures in which humanity reformulates its own destiny*: such as, for example, the period round about the year 1000; the thirteenth and fourteenth centuries in Italy and the sixteenth and seventeenth in Northern Europe – or else the period at the end of the eighteenth century that constitutes the dialectical storm of the Enlightenment. I use the expression *as if*, because in fact, though echoes of these historical conjunctures obviously make themselves strongly felt, nevertheless, there is no comparison, even of a *formal* kind – nor any analogy in terms of *content* – to be made between the latter and the moment I am describing: in the twentieth century the great reform did not consist in a reconstruction of the real. The enormous urgency, determination and manic character of reformist policies (which were intended to be 'the crisis to end all crises') leave us, as it were, exposed on a frontier where the concentration of social pressures and illusions results not in a reconstruction but rather in a radical rupture and a leap forward – the consequences of which we are entirely ignorant (save that a 'forward leap' might *in fact* turn out to be a leap into emptiness). This period is presented to us in the form of catastrophe: it attempted to be reformist, but ended in despair. With that, the twentieth century – if it can ever really be said to have existed – comes to an end. It is precisely the catastrophe of meaning which gives continuity to the century. The latter is like an accumulation of rubble exposed on waste ground – that is, an accumulation of experiences on the basis of which we confront the, perhaps novel, unknown.

Now that we are at the end of the century, we must begin to concern ourselves with the adventure that we are about to embark on in 'unknown territories'; in other words, we must begin to concern ourselves with our ethical propulsion beyond the limitations of our previous theories and experiences. *The very brief reformist period has modified, in a substantial and decisive way, all political and social determining factors*. It has been *the* apogé *of a change of direction*: at the beginning of the reformist period the worker was the only subject, but his/her principal preoccupation was increased wages and from the moment s/he obtained them s/he lost his/her privileged status as the unique 'contracting party' of social and economic change. At the same time, the capitalists wanted greater mobility of the labour force, but once they'd got it, they found themselves confronted by the latter's indistinguishability, i.e. by its pure, socialized form. In this way, a new, unknown and unpredictable subject emerged – or at least seemed to emerge. As a consequence, those capitalists that wanted greater fluidity in the circulation of commodities found themselves challenged by social movements which, precisely in the area of commodity-circulation (and thanks to the choices made by the capitalists), wanted, and were able, to impose their own needs and values. So, in order to maintain expansion, the support of the state was sought – but the public deficit soon became unsustainable, and therefore incompatible with the reproduction of hierarchical social arrangements. Subsequently, therefore, another path was tried, namely the ravaging of nature in order to reduce labour costs and so obtain wealth at a lower price; but here too – indeed, above all here – the reaction that was provoked was very lively, strong and determined. The social classes seemed unrecognizable, but nevertheless, the struggles persisted; and so a search began for countries where 'peripheral Fordism' might be implemented. It quickly became evident that the countries concerned which, through loans and the decentralization of technology, were developing rapidly, were the same countries which, by reneging on debt repayments, constituted a direct threat to the entire structure of the international monetary system. In short, every reformist search for equilibrium and every innovative strategy, resulted in conflicts and antagonisms which were new, and also, perhaps, irretrievable and irresolvable. The end of the century represents an accumulation of these changes of direction and of the overflowing of experience in the direction of the unknown. Why did all this come about?

It might be objected that the situation described above is nothing other than the normal state of affairs associated with economic development, but such a view is mistaken. It is not even true that we are about to witness a simple rearrangement of the normal, or even exceptional, difficulties that always (and in an unpredictable way) inhere in economic development and that are its episodic products. On the contrary, in the situation described above, the arrangements themselves are modified: the significant structures within which actions acquire their meaning, are transformed. The concepts of 'production', 'reproduction', 'circulation', 'crisis', 'innovation' and 'subject' acquire a radically new meaning; this for the simple reason that the experiences of exploitation, struggle and organization (and, on the other side, of imperialism, repression and the state) are themselves radically new. What is it that has brought about such a decisive change in the framework of our thought and our production? To talk of a change of paradigm is correct, but insufficient, because the paradigm that we are here borrowing from scientific epistemology has become an ontologically pregnant concept. Movement, passage, actual transformation: *in the chapters that follow* we will analyse these various concepts in detail together with the different social processes we have mentioned and their past and present character. For now, we wish to continue analysing the nature of the transformation, its profoundness, and the rupture that it implies.

Elsewhere, in analyses which were undertaken almost a decade ago (and which were therefore the product of earlier phases of struggle), we identified the dynamics by which substantial changes in the character of the mature capitalist societies were taking place. At that time, our attention was above all attracted by certain phenomena which, at the high point of capitalist reformism, illustrated the connection between the expansion (and the change of nature) of the welfare state on the one hand, and the rejection of work (or the present form of the class struggle) on the other: in fleeing the factory, the worker sought socialized forms of production, and as a consequence, *the welfare state was transformed from an instrument designed to support the capitalist firm, into an instrument of socialized productivity. From the welfare state to the state as producer; from the mass worker to the socialized worker.* Having traced out and described these processes in the past, today it remains for us simply to confirm, expand and make our description more precise. We shall return to these themes in the following chapters, where it will become clear how correct our approach was even ten years ago. Furthermore, we analysed the above-mentioned evolution in the forms of control of the labour-process, within the conceptual framework of a *transition from 'formal subsumption' to 'real subsumption'*: Marx, as is clear at various points in his work, foresaw this transition and described it as the achievement of the subjection by the capitalist mode of production, of the whole of society. I believe that this theoretical framework will withstand scrutiny. It might then be asked: 'So why so much political excitement about (and literary dramatization in the description of) a period that was thought to be already well understood?' The answer – as is obvious – is that there is something which, while pertaining to the inner nature of the transformation, at the same time hails it as the radical innovation that it is, and which had not been sufficiently explained. Here we wish, above all, to emphasize this hidden something.

There is also a paradoxical aspect to the way in which we 'situate' ourselves with regard to the century since we tend to think in terms of a sort of negative dialectic – that is, in terms of a conceptual continuity (even though it is mystified, i.e. negative but real) between capitalist development on the one hand, and innovation on the other. In this way, we are unable to present an effective challenge to the manœuvre which this century has carried out, and which consists in the exaltation of continuity in all its forms – that is, in its self-exaltation. The twentieth century has been the century of psychoanalysis, hermeneutics and historicism; of illustrated history and science fiction. All these are a thousand individual and collective ways of narrating to ourselves, in linear fashion, the past, present and future; and it is like this on the political and social terrain as well: the great changes of the thirties and sixties have been experienced as no more than the epiphenomena of a continuous (even if eventful) historical journey. But change has not been recognized and, therefore, not commented upon, and when it has been perceived, it has been described as a *deus ex machina*, a suspension, a parenthesis, or as something exceptional. We can, perhaps, explain all this if we bear in mind another of the elements that are characteristic of, and fundamental to, a characterization of the twentieth century, namely communication, or in other words, the triumph of a network of connections and information between people, which is profoundly new and totalitarian. By concentrating our analysis on innovations in communications, it can be seen that the latter have been effective, from an early date, in determining in a negative way our collective perceptions of secular change. That is, the new forms of communication maintained defunct images of the relationships of capitalist domination – beyond their effective duration – and this served to make the transformation which this domination was undergoing seem like something strange, exceptional and alien. As far as we are concerned, then, to overthrow the dominant image of the century (and this may also require some self-criticism) is to demonstrate how the latter contains completely different continuities, and how, beyond the description of surface phenomena and every possibility of their cancellation, there is an ontological horizon where change is constructed and in which change is inscribed. We must give proof of this level – which is not so much profound as hidden – of being. It is a reality that no repentance, no violence, no apostasy and no communicative inertia will manage, in the long run, to conceal.

The twenty-first century – that is, that open temporal series starting from the crisis of reformism, and thus from the discovery of the insuperable limits of capitalist becoming – spreads out before us. This is the hidden moment. *The twenty-first century is already inhabited by new realities, subjects or machines; by new projects or concrete utopias.* It is inhabited by a new race of people that capitalist knowledge and control can no longer subdue. The twentieth century, with the experience of reformism and its crisis, has shattered all continuity. Beyond those limits, a new individual is advancing. This individual is a bundle of knowledge, power and love, the likes of which have never been seen before. Science, the artificiality of knowledge, ethical deterritorialization and communism, constitute the elements of an irreducible ontological determination – that is, a decisively new, highly original, *ontological break*. The new individual is atheist because s/he can be god and his/her imagination has the violence of one who knows how to reconquer the universe, annul death, and propagate and defend nature and life.

The quality and the intensity of the perception of this transformation are at stake. There is no doubt that in the twentieth century, the real subsumption by capital of the whole of society followed the latter's formal subsumption. However, it will never be possible to explain the intervening transformation simply in terms of capital's ability to reduce every social relationship to the unidimensionality of control. The change could be interpreted in this way only from a purely objective point of view, that is from the point of view of capital. We must, rather, consider as being fundamental the *acceleration of all social relationships*, the precipitation of the crisis, and the encouragement that capitalist reformism has given to the recognition of the limits of the system. These limits have been interpreted, or better, represented, by a catastrophe of rationality. It is useless to try to deny this. It is useless to limit oneself to the simple definition of the limits. The genetic mechanism is something else; it is the free irruption of the future into the present. We must proceed by tracing the hidden contours of development, and above all, by unravelling the meaning of those cataclysmic innovations which cursorily reveal what is hidden, namely the turgid, clandestine life of a well-endowed future subject.

We ourselves shall proceed in this way: from the mass worker to the socialized worker; from the hegemony of factory production to that of socialized production. We shall proceed by using a series of correlations and conceptual frameworks in which the form of the labour processes and of the circulation of commodities (together with the diffusion of the determinations of control) are all altered. We shall proceed within a horizon on which peace and war, and politics and terror, change roles and at that point constitute a new framework for the state-form.* In addition, however, we must consider the ontological transformation of the subject. The latter represents a leap of nature that is analogous only to what we discern between death and life, between inactivity and movement. Machiavelli has taught us once and for all that this metaphysical determination derives from the political. But he was unable to imagine that the ontological drama which politics represents would, through capitalism and its crisis, involve collective essences, and that it would develop potentialities and ever more organized desires. Once more *The Prince* is comparable with communism, though in a way radically different from the ways in which we have seen the comparison made on other occasions, because here politics is at the service of ontology.

The century's close represents an immersion in the future. The twentieth century has added nothing to our knowledge; it has merely pushed our passions to their limits. But at the same time it has been – often in terms of the derisory quantity of time for living that it has lent to the imagination – a creative century: it has left us with the experience of revolution, and it has created new ontological determinations. It is in terms of these latter that we shall judge ourselves.

---

* This is a translation of *forma-Stato*. It refers to the entire complex of determinations which pertain to the state when it is considered as a structure, both formed by and formative of the relations of domination which are developed between the different classes. This form is modified in relation to both the changes in the modes of production and the variations in the relationships of hegemony. For a detailed analysis of this concept see my *La forma-Stato* (Feltrinelli, Milan, 1977).

3

From the mass worker to the socialized worker – and beyond

When, round about 1968, we began to think that the epoch of the mass worker had come to an end, our enemies smiled maliciously and our comrades began to get worried: since we had been using the concept of the mass worker only since the beginning of the sixties, they felt that too short a period of time had elapsed for us to be justified in simply abandoning it. But it was not our fault if we were unable to keep abreast of historical developments! For in a large part of Europe, *the mass worker had been conceptualized and had become a reality just when its period of existence was in fact about to end*. In organizing the 'rank and file committees' and disseminating the plans for a 'trade union council', in effect what we were doing was rediscovering certain of Gramsci's perceptions and bringing to light something which, after Gramsci, everybody had tried to make us forget about. In the 1960s, acknowledgement of the concept of the mass worker was above all a means of restoring our memory in view of Stalinist ignorance and the events associated with Mussolini, and above all in view of American imperialism's victory against the workers' soviets in the 1930s. Such was the superiority of that little piece of reality when compared with the prevailing mystifications, that when we launched it onto the 'political market' we won our battle immediately – and we are still amazed by it. In this way we deceived ourselves: we ourselves believed (even though for a very short period) that we could 'anticipate' (as we put it) capitalist development. In reality, we came last – and that by a wide margin. The capitalist revolution which produced the mass worker and assigned the task of producing value to mass production, had its apogée in the crisis of 1929. This crisis had, however, been developing since the end of the first world war. After the crisis, by means of state intervention, Roosevelt's policies brought about mass consumption (whereas mass production had been underway possibly since the beginning of the century, and certainly since the war period). The mass worker is a strange animal born between town and country, and between the two coasts of the Atlantic. At first, the mass worker produced everything and consumed nothing – this was a state of *Metropolis* – until his/her massive productive capacity brought about a crisis in the circulation of commodities and in the reproduction of capital. Confronted with the extraordinary growth of the mass labour force at the end of the 1950s and the beginning of the 1960s, in proclaiming the birth of the mass worker, what we were *in effect* doing was paying tribute to the passing of his/her historical period. Indeed the latter had perhaps already passed by. Illustrated in this instance by that 'rejection of work' which a broadening of struggle and action would have made a reality, the mass worker already constituted, then, an important element of class-consciousness.

By contrast, *our perception of the historical and political constitution of the socialized worker was a genuine anticipation*, an anticipation both cognitive and political. We were confronted with a number of incontrovertible facts: for example, in the ferocious conflict that took place over the destruction (by the bosses) and the defense (by the workers) of the institutions of the mass worker, paradoxically, neither side was victorious. The trick was this: on the one hand, even though it required an enormous effort, the employers succeeded in asserting their authority. That is, they managed to restore order to production, to increase the mobility of the labour force and to impose redundancies. On the other hand, after having fought – and indeed, brought the forms of conflict to a very high level – the workers were no longer particularly concerned about the redundancies or about increased mobility (and the trade unions were left to fight alone). On the contrary, on the basis of their reconquered freedom, the labour force set new productive initiatives in motion. Moreover, the bosses' victory was a Pyrrhic victory since they were not able to reimpose order in the old factories or to restore *Metropolis*; rather, they were obliged to restructure and automate production processes and agree to a new contract which gave workers much more favourable conditions and which was much better adapted to the 'rejection of work'. As far as the workers were concerned, the new compromise had nothing to do with the traditional contractual preoccupations (i.e. wages and conditions) of the mass worker: the directions, perspectives and horizons in, within and on which productive cooperation was beginning to develop were all new. These facts required an explanation. The concept of the socialized worker allowed us to relate the new social dimensions of productive cooperation and revolutionary organization to new and effective working models. It is by starting from this point that we ask how *an adequate theory of value* can be reconstructed. In other words, we are no longer interested simply in knowing whether, and if so, to what extent, our anticipation was valid, for it was; we know that we had genuine knowledge. The hypothetical anticipation has reached its real synthesis. It is, therefore, necessary to pose the problem of the law of value (that is, of surplus value and exploitation) in terms of the entirety of its implied effects. We must ask ourselves how it works and how it can be reformulated in terms of the social activity of production.

It is necessary to point out some phenomenological elements. Firstly, work has become diffused throughout the entire society. This is because it is carried on both within and outside the factory. The channels of recomposition may involve the factory or else contribute to social syntheses within long-term production-strategies. The scale of production has become vaster and the integration of the various labour processes more complex than ever before. How can one calculate the value, surplus-value, wages and profits that are produced and distributed within this new productive structure? It is necessary to experiment. Any argument proposing formulae (whether complex or simple) with which to define the processes of value-composition and wealth – distribution will undoubtedly be problematic. There will be a lot of hard thinking to do in this regard. Yet *in practice*, this confusing system actually works. It represents a massive operation which coordinates and integrates a range of activities at the level of economic sectors and national markets; and which, on the international level, facilitates coordination and integration over the entire surface of the earth. Every subject of this productive complex is caught up in overpowering cooperative networks. This, then, is the context within which the socialized worker begins to take shape. What more need be said? The professional worker was the first great representative of wage-labour within the system of large-scale industry. There, tools in hand, precisely because of his/her perfectionism, study and dedication to work s/he was capable of producing masterpieces however oppressed s/he was. As for the mass worker (the second great representative), s/he was animated by an awareness of the productive cooperation which was involved in large areas of mass production. Because of the revolutionary impulse which mass production gave him/her, his/her development was exciting; but at the same time, in that hell that was the Taylorized factory of organized subjugation, his/her development was also terrifying. By contrast, the *socialized worker is now recombining conception and execution within a universal horizon.*

On the one hand, what needs to be emphasized is spatial universality. This is manifested by the social and international diffusion of work, and by the contemporaneity, and the homologation, of various types of activity going on under different forms of association and which show increasingly varied levels of productivity. These things represent a network of various, highly differentiated, yet confluent mechanisms: a Foucaultian spatial universe. On the other hand, however, this assemblage of contrivances is organized temporally. Value – which was variously distributed and then socially consolidated by the historical process of capitalist accumulation – has now become reactualized. The social immersion of production is a recuperation of temporal lags; it is the production of continuity across gaps in realization; it is a merging of epochs, forms and different labour processes. In short, it is neither more nor less than *a new, original accumulation.* The whole of society is placed at the disposal of profit (as if under Colbert) and the infinite temporal variations that compose society are arranged, set and made malleable in a unitary process. The latter is a new primitive accumulation, which gathers and unhinges inveterate positions (and rents) and which mixes, in new and indefinite labour, all that is potentially productive.

The agents of this enormously powerful engine are the new proletarian subjectivities, the subjective workers, or the socialized workers. They coordinate different work-cycles; they construct social watersheds within which the most diverse productive potentialities are gathered and developed; they overthrow old work-practices; they disorganize and throw off the habits and rules of corporatism. In this way they allow *value to flow freely* between the various strata of a society which has become inflexible. The sabotage of command and of contracts embodying ossified compromises, opens new flow-channels for value. Only the arrogance and insane bad faith of the old leaderships of the workers' movement, attached as they were to the most sinister corporatism, could have left a monopoly on the interpretation of this new process of the liberation of the labour force to the mystification of the neo-liberals, of the imperialists and even of the fascists! Just as our ancestors were in favour of free trade in grain (i.e. in favour of the class struggle *tout court!*), we are *in favour of deregulation in order to facilitate the class struggle of the socialized worker*. In this way a new human potential can be developed, one which has the capacity to break the sclerotic systems within which late capitalism has imprisoned us, and create the conditions necessary for a new mode of production. These conditions consist in new ways of thinking and new forms of collective action. It must be emphasized that it is here that sabotage finds its creative and innovative function. In societies such as the ones we live in, oppressed as they are from top to bottom and bound to asphyxiating customs, destruction is as important as innovation (and not only from the political, but also from the productive point of view). *Sabotage is innovation.*

Thus we are at this point able to begin to describe the subjective make-up of the socialized worker. It is by virtue of the very high degree of cooperation that this person is productive; and it is through the power of cooperation that contemporary capitalist organization has been set in motion again: i.e. by pursuing the process of the social liberation of the producer. That which the socialized worker places before industry in general is like a process of incubation. In other words, it is like a stimulus to the change of paradigm of industrial organization, to that obscure but substantial change which the twentieth century has witnessed, not only in general terms, but also from the point of view of particular sectors and individual undertakings. Thus the socialized worker produces value 'naturally'. S/he produces a given amount of value which the entire capitalist organization then subdivides into those well-known quantities called necessary labour and surplus labour; wages and profits; value and surplus value. The internal connections between these conceptual pairs are admittedly complex. It would, however, be very foolish to think that it is impossible to understand them and that they should therefore be abandoned. The only practical outcome of such attitudes has always been that use of these concepts (together with the continuous and consequential evaluation of their possibly limited utility) is left to the capitalists. Paradoxically, the latter are the only recognizably convinced historical materialists that exist these days. If we too are willing to recognize the practical validity of these concepts (apart, that is, from the partiality of their application and the possible theoretical obscurities involved in their traditional formulation) we will gain undoubted advantages from them. That aside, let us return to the *socialized worker*. S/he is a producer, but not only a producer of value and surplus value; s/he is also *the producer of the social cooperation necessary for work*. This function, which formerly pertained to the capitalist (and in more general terms, to the varied and manifold types of control exercised over the labour force during the centuries of capitalism's consolidation and development) now pertains to the worker. The principal and most apparent characteristic of the productive labour of the socialized worker consists in the fact that s/he is the originator of social cooperation. We can acknowledge, then, that the operation of the market has been undermined. Within the market proletarian subjectivities come to the fore and, powerfully and effectively, prevent capitalism from asserting the exclusivity of its own point of view. Incompetent theoreticians are amazed at these phenomena and with their incredible *short-sightedness* they actually believe that such phenomena constitute evidence of proletarian embourgeoisement. In fact, let us repeat, the process consists in the exact opposite: it represents the reappropriation by workers of control over the cooperative process. Consequently, it is natural that description of these new phenomena in terms of traditional categories should become increasingly problematic. Nevertheless *we continue to be Marxists* and will remain so with the socialized worker until we are convinced by a new theory (and a new theory is already necessary) having at its core the pervasiveness of exploitation and the class struggle. This theory must take account of the radical phenomenology of the transformation in progress which we have said is a genuinely new, original accumulation.

The socialized worker is, then, the originator of the social cooperation necessary for work. S/he does not want to have bosses because s/he cannot have bosses. If these imposed themselves, his/her own role would no longer have any purpose and his/her nature and identity would not be what they are. The socialized worker has a collective identity because workers' consciousness is always collective – and this is even more the case from the moment in which the workers recognize themselves to be the exclusive organizers of the collective labour. As we have said, this function has been reappropriated. Such reappropriation stems from the fact that the collectivity realizes that it has been expropriated, and thus delegates to the members of the same collectivity the task of recomposing the power of organization as it concerns the productive purposes of the collectivity. From this point of view, everything finally becomes clear and irreversible. The socialized worker is decisive in the development of the class struggle. S/he represents the ultimate overthrowing of the subjectivity of this process and its ultimate attribution – from the exploiter to the exploited. The socialized worker represents the final resolution of the dialectic between liberation and emancipation at the liberation end of the continuum. From now on, *emancipation will be a by-product of liberation*. At this juncture – i.e. when the socialized worker becomes the controller and direct organizer of labouring cooperation – the rejection of the capitalist's role as the controller of work becomes critical enough to become transformed into material exclusion, endowed with the violence of the capitalist's physical contrivance. *In this way, every historical and progressive justification of capitalism loses its validity*. The socialized worker is a kind of actualization of communism, its developed condition. The boss, by contrast, is no longer even a necessary condition for capitalism.

Clearly, the subjective aspects of this process should be described more fully. In fact we will do this in the following chapters, above all when, from the phenomenological description of the genesis and affirmation of the socialized worker, we proceed to examine the questions surrounding the latter's political organization, namely its character and how it can be distinguished from the organizational forms of the mass worker, not to mention those of the professional worker. For the moment it is sufficient to add a single observation, namely that the development of subjectivity remains such even if this development is completely contained, almost confused, within the objective conditions – whether material (and by that we mean the organization of work, elements of content etc.) or formal (that is, the forces that activate these complexes). Thus, because of this entirety of the subjective pulse even when it is crushed by structural conditions, revolutionary theory and the utopian appeal are not only possible but present and increasingly effective. It seems paradoxical (though in reality it isn't) when, for example, we say that while the logic of capital has ended up in asphyxiating structures, the workers' dimension has become ethical. This amounts to saying that the latter has extricated itself from the structural logic of capital and that, at the moment of this extrication, it has shown that it has overtaken capitalist development. Therefore, capital combats an ethic, a working-class ethic, an ethic of rejection and a manifold ethic of subjectivities that want to destroy capital. Therefore, when we return to the question of working-class subjectivity, we shall be involved in discussions about ethics. At that point we shall discover what incredible metaphysical paths have already been tried out, and how the ethic of the social producer, of the socially insubordinated worker, by now anticipates the same violent determinacy of the revolution.

Let us return to the structural dimension in which the subjective figure of the socialized worker is formed and situated. This genesis is given between the two phases of development of the capitalist mode of production, which, *following Marx*, we shall call the phases of 'formal subsumption' and 'real subsumption'. Below I cite some Marxist texts that may assist the reader in focusing attention on these topics (see Appendix, pp. 219–24). In reading these texts the thing that needs to be emphasized above all is the way in which the movement from capital's subjection of society to the active prefiguration of society by capital involves, within it, the constitution of an increasingly high and intense degree of productive cooperation. Given that this is objectively the case, we believe that experience demonstrates that – even though with marked asymmetries of historical development and ontological consolidation – this process leads to a genuinely new subjective determination. By this I mean that here the *collective combination becomes a collective worker*. At this point, in order to exist, individual labour needs to be inserted into the framework of social labour. The collectivity is a necessary condition for work and for the very subjective realization of singularity. Furthermore, the high degree of interdependence of these processes means that the collective worker represents not simply a function, however subjugated, but a qualitative evolutionary entirety, a change of nature. The structural dimension in which the socialized worker is formed is something exceptionally productive. (We describe it as the movement from formal to real subsumption, though this framework serves almost exclusively to clarify, through difference, the novelty of the concept. In short, given the nature of the process and its ontological depth, the Marxian classification has the analogical utility of an orthogonal projection.) In Marx, as the process of subsumption progresses, we are only given the objective outline of the socialized worker, i.e. its historical possibility; but the subjective worker does not yet actually exist. We know, however, as Marx himself added, that this objective process is already, in itself, a revolution. It is a process of destruction by capitalism considered as an industrial culture and practice, based on the penury of the subjects, on the theft of their labour time, on the reproduction of the exploited masses and on the non-labour of a few etc. But when, by contrast, production and the capacity to sustain and develop it are taken over by the collective social subjects (who constitute the new proletariat), and when the subjection of society to capital shatters the restrictions imposed by the latter (in its role as holder of the means of control and expropriator of communication), then the revolution has begun its completion. Capital is directly exposed to the antagonistic action of the social subjects. The guiding principle of the great transformation has been established and the very intense nature of the transformation has adapted itself to innovative contents, i.e. to new productive dimensions. *The collective has been established as a subject.*

'With that production based on exchange, value breaks down, and the direct, material production process is stripped of the form of penury and antithesis.' Does this mean, then, that the class struggle has come to an end? Or does the very analysis which allows us to identify the new material determinations of the collective subject – that is, the socialized worker – not perhaps oblige us to situate the latter outside and beyond the class struggle? The quotation from Marx at the beginning of this paragraph (as well as the others we have cited during the current phase of our research) undoubtedly betrays a profound ambiguity. In making the above statement Marx is actually exceeding the limits of his analysis and in operating on an ethical level (in a utopian sense) he implicitly asserts that there is a linear relationship between the processes of subsumption and liberation. Such continuity is a mystification. This doesn't alter the fact that the idea of continuity lies at the heart of the ideology and politics of socialist emancipation, and that Marx, given the specific conditions of his research, could not but adhere to it. But as far as we are concerned, the current situation is profoundly different: *we have gone beyond Marx, and the socialized worker has become a reality*. In Marx's outline of the successive phases of subsumption, the idea of the socialized worker is merely hinted at and described as a possibility; we, on the other hand, experience the actuality of the concept. This is what gives Marx's utopian appeal its great significance, because it is up to us to go beyond the confusion of emancipation and liberation and to turn the latter into an effective theoretico-political practice. This, however, makes it difficult to retain the terminology and conceptual definitions used by Marx: for example, one might ask why a worker should still be described as a 'worker' rather than an 'operator' or a 'social actor' – or by any other term which, provided it does not repeat the errors of workerism, might be more or less suitable. For the moment, however, this is not the problem. Rather, given that the socialized worker is the collective agent of productive cooperation, the problem is that of explaining whether, and if so how, antagonism can constitute the basis of the actual and powerful movement of liberation – i.e. of that movement, the condition for the possibility of which, is real subsumption. In other words, the problem is whether, and if so, how, antagonism can exist, starting from the ontological realization of the socialized worker in real subsumption.

The socialized worker has an antagonistic character. If the term 'worker' must be retained in our analysis this is not because the term takes us back to the heights (or depths) of workerism, but because it captures the most reliable and solid paradigm of an antagonism which has never ceased to exist. This antagonism is not simply directed at the capitalist: such opposition is permanent; and the more that property-rights and managerial prerogatives are reduced to, or resemble, old aristocratic privileges, the stronger, more aggressive, arrogant and joyful is the opposition. Such aristocratic privileges are dead, however, and it remains only to bury them. The antagonism is, therefore, something much more profound and radical. It concerns the quality of social production, the alternatives that make themselves felt within it and the values that can be discerned on the horizons of the world of real subsumption. What this amounts to is that only the presence of the workers saves the subsumed world from an indifference of the senses and an indifference of values that are typical of this world. How and why does this come about?

We can begin to answer this question by recalling that the principal defining characteristic of the socialized worker is *his/her capacity to reappropriate control of the labour process*. However, control over industrial labour is not some sort of whip which is blindly used to beat slave-workers. Neither is it simply a technique, or an applied science which organizes and gives shape to disparate elements of the labour force. Rather, control over industrial labour (which, under real subsumption means control over the entire society) is a complex structure combining: science and democratic participation; the determinants of the goals of production and the conditions of the labour process; and the ability to utilize latent social forces and suitable measures of policy, assistance and training. Now, to assert that this complexity generates indifference, and in any event eliminates the antagonism, simply means to obscure an essential fact, namely that production, and thus present-day society, subsist by virtue of the socialized worker's independence and by virtue of his/her singular and separate power to constitute existence. From this point of view, the existent antagonism, far from having disappeared, is the only active key to the existence of the subsumed society. In order to reappropriate control, the socialized worker challenges every manifestation of this antagonism and tackles the complexity of the structural determinations of the social process. Moreover, this antagonistic means of reappropriation – which is by now the key to production, or the only condition of existence of the society – even goes as far as to challenge that specific articulation of science and power which characterizes the subsumed societies. To appreciate this, one only has to bear in mind the extent to which the socialized worker's relationship with science is organic; such a relationship is inherent in the very definition of the concept of the socialized worker. The rejection of labour, typical of the mass worker, is the rejection of a labour which is overdetermined by abstract control, and such rejection often takes place when control is scientific. In this case, the rejection of labour by the mass worker can (and has) become a rejection of science or, as far as it went (and with a certain cynicism, pompously disguised as utopianism), a demand that science be put to alternative uses. Today, all this has to a large extent been surpassed. The decisiveness of the socialized worker touches the heart of the problem, namely *the control of science*. Science is a body of knowledge which is utilized according to the determinations of power. It is necessary to break this connection between knowledge and power and to establish alternative controls. Science is one of the sites of antagonism (probably the principal one), because it constitutes the terrain on which the extent of workers' reappropriation of the productive process will in the end be revealed. And there is, alongside science, interwoven with, when not subordinated to it, the system of the social dimensions of production and reproduction, of politics and ethics. Antagonism runs through these systems in the same way; it destroys both their form and their content in order to construct (in conformity with the act of destruction) other values. These values are both antagonistic and adequate to the concept of the socialized worker.

The socialized worker is, then, universal in both spatial and temporal terms. At the same time, however, *it is necessary to identify contents* adequate to this universality. Thus, we must insist once more on the intensity of the form of this process and on the socialized worker's singularity. That is, we must return: to the extraordinary historical acceleration that has been brought about by the socialized worker's appearance; to the acceleration of the ontological processes concerning such appearance (above all, the irreversibility of the genesis, of the process, and of the constitution of the socialized worker); and to the pressure towards the reappropriation of control over productive cooperation, which leads to the irresistible constitution of a new subject. At this point we should mention a paradox relating precisely to the constitutive process of the socialized worker. The paradox is that when the workers reappropriate power and take possession of the means of knowledge, power and knowledge are not centralized as they are in all political regimes which precede the communist revolution; but rather, power and knowledge are socialized and devolved, and all centralization and monopolies on control are creatively destroyed. The one and the multiple exist simultaneously, but from the ontological point of view, the one is at the service of the multiple. The 'time' of the boss (who in his inner essence continually turned in on himself, on a zero-sum calculation) was a control time, a state of negative acceleration and of the annihilation of all concrete values for the sake of reducing them to pure money, to the absolute zero of phases of circulation. All this, in the perspective of the socialized worker, corresponds to: a time which is diffuse, articulate and manifold; a body of knowledge which tends to a maximum of diversity because it is localized and territorialized (without thereby becoming parochial or corporatist, however). What this amounts to is that the socialized worker identifies the nature of the antagonism in the universality of his/her own social being and in the indefinite microphysics of his/her powers. He/she counterposes such antagonism to capitalistic centralization of power, to the exhaustion of the capitalist's will to power, and to the nullifying stamp of the capitalist's dialectic. Thus the antagonism is not presented as a logically rigid determination but as an ontologically variable, dynamic and constitutive dimension. The new is not something unitary, but something manifold. The paradigm is not solitary, but polyvalent. The productive nucleus of the antagonism consists in multiplicity. The paradox which we have emphasized is not only thereby resolved, but constitutes the specific form of existence of the socialized worker.

In moving from the mass worker to the socialized worker and *beyond*, 'beyond' consists in a stabilization of the antagonism at the highest level. There the socialized worker acts upon the totality of the conditions of production and reproduction of the social. *We shall call this totality 'ecology', or the 'ecological system'.* The totality is not simply naturalistic but also ethical, political and productive. It is a second nature which capital has constructed and which the socialized worker must re-humanize. Ecology does not exist, then, without a definition of social, productive subjects; ecology does not exist apart from within a specific dialectic with production. We will come back to this later, however: for the moment it is sufficient to have introduced the concept of ecology. For now, we do not want so much to describe the link which exists between Red and Green politics, as much as to emphasize Red politics – together with the material and productive make-up of the antagonistic and subjective protagonists which we are defining. Yet, from this point of view, it is necessary to stress that as long as there exist organizations capable of innovation within classes and in society, the enormous gap which separates the mass worker from the socialized worker can be bridged. Certainly, it will not be possible to entrust this task to the *rotten dialectic of workerism* (and of dialectical materialism): that connection which saw proletarian struggles continuously induce restructuration of the forms of capitalist control – and which was confronted by a new subjective outline of class (and all that indefinitively) – has been definitively broken. A useful dialectic would be one that facilitates recognition of the full, entire socialization of the process of the destruction of wage-labour and of all mediations – whether capitalistic or socialistic – of development. Can such a dialectic be attributed to the real movement, i.e. to the workers' movement in its immediacy and spontaneity? Probably not; whether positive or negative, the dialectic is always a weapon of the adversary, a form of the illusion that the antagonism is destructible. We can therefore induce that though latent and clandestine (and with diverse movements and unexpected explosions), these means of reconjunction of the various strata of classes (and of the diverse historical explosions of the composition) can be realized. That is, if not guaranteed, they can at least be indicated by the depth and the power of the material modifications that are taking place on the body and on the brain of the working class – that is, of the children of the mass worker. These are experiences which many of us have had – whether as the children, or simply as neighbours, of the mass worker; and our change does not obstruct our loyalty to a destiny, the vendetta carried out because of the exploitation suffered by our parents, or the joy of a reconquered liberty and the material liberation which is close at hand. On the contrary, because of this, our memory has never consisted in nostalgia, but in hope, in organization and in overcoming.

4

From the factory to the ecological machine

While production is carried on through social networks and is closely connected with the processes of commodity-circulation, and while productive labour (which, though diffuse, is above all *socially integrative*) is to be found everywhere, *by means of the social, production and reproduction constitute a completely uniform, undifferentiated network*. A limit beyond which productive moments are innovative experiences and creative moments in the reproductive whole of life, is perfectly visible. From this point of view, work has even less to do with the factory. The latter is no longer recognized or considered to be the specific site of the consolidation of labouring activity and its transformation into value. Work abandons the factory in order to find, precisely in the social, a place adequate to the functions of concentrating productive activity and transforming it into value. The prerequisites of these processes are present in, and diffused throughout, society. The prerequisites include such infrastructures as communications networks, semi-manufactured information systems. . . and so on. Industrial labour finds that a large number of the prerequisites of production are present and continually reproduced in society – just as the peasant found a large number of such prerequisites in agriculture. This accumulation of potentialities and their appearance in an unmediated form is both a product of capitalist development and one of its residues. That is to say, the accumulation of potentialities is something which capital has produced but has not been able to exploit. It is something which falls outside the framework of capitalist production and which only socially liberated labour can put to use. Society thus offers itself to work in the same way that, in the factory, a single machine, several machines and the entire system of machinery offered themselves to the labour force: namely, as a *system of preconditions*. The machines are preconditions in the sense that they represent accumulated labour, or concentrated labour-power, which only further labour-power can reactivate and in so doing, draw off further strands of value, know-how and wealth. The machines constitute a system because this world of technical conditions is an ordered universe and a sort of ideal schema to which new activity can and must be added in order to create new determinations of being. In advanced capitalism, society is an ontologically fixed technological system of enormous potentialities. It is inherently equipped to absorb vitalizing labour and as a consequence, to activate the system of reproduction. Thereby, once labour – i.e. the innovative activity of the labour force – is added to society, every determination of the social is invigorated.

In advanced capitalism *territory* becomes the framework of productive potential; that is, *it becomes the spatial ontology of the productive society*. Territory is not, therefore, just an impluvium which gathers all sources of creativity and all instances of aggregation of the labour force: it is also, – indeed above all – a water-bearing stratum which, just as in nature, gives rise to spontaneous springs. Work not only converges and is organized on the social terrain, but it here encounters one of its fundamental productive conditions. No one who is familiar with Marxism and with the materialist conception of the technological system will say that with the above description we have gone beyond Marxism (except to the extent that reality itself has superseded the limits of Marxist analysis). Rather, what we are observing is a real development and our one ability to anticipate it does not reside in the realm of the actual, but in the theoretico-practical tendency which is inherent in it. Neither, consequently, is it possible to accuse our Marxist description of having passed over into the realm of the magical. What *is* magical is technology's power (which is more mysterious the more sophisticated it is) to furnish accumulated value which has been sucked out of society. Technology holds onto this value secretly, discreetly and richly. Therefore, we are operating within a framework which is entirely, and in all respects, Marxian and we are interpreting the productive power of machinery (even more so if it is social), bringing it back to the concrete, determinate and demiurgical determination of human labour.

The same can be said of *economic cycles* or, in other words, of the *temporal dimension of the productive society*. Here, too, it is unnecessary to refer to obsolete theories – such as the one which sees the cycle as being an autogenous process, or the one which sees the form of the cycle as being determined by external shocks. Rather, it is necessary to refer to an horizon of cyclical microfunctions, i.e. to an horizon of small movements of self-valorization and accumulation in which the time-spans and temporal aspects of investment, consumption and planning become increasingly concentrated. Such a perspective provides at once an explanation for the impossibility of discovering regular patterns in the economic cycle in the current epoch, and the possibility of identifying a powerful, polyvalent and multidirectional determination of expectations and prognostications. The *concentration of time*, so characteristic of social labour, ties its measurement more closely to the living experience which people have of reality than to concepts and abstract types of average and measurement. The formation of economic cycles can be compared to the condensation of fluids or vapours: all of a sudden, before our eyes we discover, agglomerated and coagulated, that which was previously invisible. Whatever form it takes, by becoming concentrated, work gradually comes to occupy all space, filling all the voids. The process of occupying space is an atomistic process, or rather, a process of the construction of space starting from the void.

What is implicated in the *crisis of the concepts of average*, mediation and measurement, is above all the *theory of value*. The latter presented the production and existence of wealth not only as a flow but also as a drama, a naked antagonism and a circumstance of great historical significance. Therefore, we could not but appreciate (as we still do and to an even greater extent) the significance of the theory of value. But though we appreciate and are willing to reaffirm the theory on this level, we find it less useful as a theory of measurement, of current measurement, and – inevitably – of mediation. Value exists wherever social locations of working cooperation are to be found and wherever accumulated and hidden labour is extracted from the turgid depths of society. This value is not reducible to a common standard. Rather, it is excessive. It is a limit that we try to approximate. Its apprehension and quantification are impossible. As to the act of measurement, it is interminable. We can therefore do nothing other than continue attempting to trace all the spatial and temporal determinations of value as they are revealed by social labour. In doing this, we must abandon the illusory notion of measurement and the mystification of mediation. *Notwithstanding this, it is both possible and necessary to construct a theory of value.* By doing this, we would possess a systematic and fruitful framework within which to organize all the moments in which value is expressed. Our theory of value will have to be nothing less than *a cartography*. This will undoubtedly be a formidable undertaking. It will involve setting out 'maps' of value which approximate the detail of the movements of social labour and which outline, show and predict new objective possibilities of subjective coordination and cooperation. A law of value which responds to current needs must be one which allows us to navigate the flows of value and construct compasses which serve: to deepen the level of cooperation, to establish flow-channels and to grasp opportunities for original accumulation. If afterwards we wish to measure all this, there are a number of accounting techniques available which are highly complex, comprehensive and precise. But let us not confuse accountancy with a theory of value nor perpetuate the naturalistic illusion that it is possible to find a foundation: reality consists only of activity, construction and imagination. Realization of the theory of value was sought in economic plans and in planning. The only consequence of this, however, was the repression of freedom; and socialism, for so long hoped for, showed itself to be the end of hope. Indeed, socialism represented the planning of time without meaning; it was the measurement of nothing.

Let us, then, return to the description of the *system of social machines* within which the logic and reality of collective action are established. We have already seen that the factory is becoming less and less the specific site of the production and increase of value. Secondly, we have seen how work-processes have shifted from the factory to society thereby setting in motion a genuinely complex machine. In addition, when we analyse this complex machine from a synchronic and structural, rather than from a diachronic and historical, point of view, we become aware that we are operating within a completely new dimension, one which is irreducible to obsolete logical or linguistic determinations. We shall call this environment or this *Umwelt* a 'machine'; and we believe we are justified in doing so. When we add the adjective 'complex', however, we already find ourselves being driven back into the linguistic universe of mechanics and, thereby, we lose sight of the *qualitative*, vital and natural characteristics of the mechanism. It is essential to emphasize these characteristics. Undoubtedly, nothing could be more false than to pretend that the determinations of this machine are 'natural' in a literal sense; but it is also true that they are quasi-natural in the sense that this 'nature' is constructed and reconstructed by human beings. The wealth of this nature consists of accumulated labour and every one of its landscapes, creeks or depths has been effected by human labour. *What we have, then, is not nature, but 'second nature': not the factory but the environment, or the ecological Umwelt.* The latter is an ecological Umwelt-environment which is perceptible and definable also, and above all, in terms of its quasi-natural dimensions and qualities. It is definable in accordance with genetic cognitive processes and according to mechanisms and determinations which reveal the fundamental facticity of this universe. The social machine is a natural machine. It is an ecological mechanism. It is a complex dimension in the sense that many determinations contribute to shaping it. The social machine is a natural machine animated by human labour – even as a result of the ugliness and the destructive elements which this labour has imposed on nature. Once again, however, the abstract entirety of this machine and the rigidity of this ensemble of determinants must be destroyed. The antagonism of the choices in favour of life rather than death and in favour of collectivity and cooperation rather than profit must be counterposed to the indifference of social relationships.

But every alternative and every movement within and of the machine would not have been possible if the latter had not been reduced to a human dimension, one which presents itself as a destructive dimension and from that point on – from that desperate extreme – rediscovers meaning and gives human value to a world to be reconstructed. This world and this nature that we find before us and in which we are inserted and absorbed in suffering or in joy, is a hypothesis of humanity.

Therefore, I think it is vitally important to continue emphasizing the theme of value, especially the situation described by the new, allusive theory of value. This is because to demonstrate the extent of its impact and its implications for the concept of nature means to avoid lamenting the historical crime represented by the subsumption of nature within capital; or rather, it means to avoid being paralysed by the fear induced by this event. From a more positive point of view, to take up the theme of value again means that nature can realistically be related once more to the class struggle and the rules of antagonism. This is because, owing to the capitalist revolution, nature presents itself to us in a humanized form. It is because of nature's humanity that the ecological battle is possible and can be hoped for. What could nature ever teach us if this were not the case? Nature would present itself to us as a monster or an untouchable deity even in the midst of the filth of development and of the destruction brought about by advanced capitalism. Instead capital has restored nature to us. Capital has transformed nature into a machine. It is now up to us to take control of this machine, to change the directions which the bosses have set out in, to sanitize the concept and to restore to humanity a utilizable mechanism. We shall undertake the move to ecology in full awareness of the social definition of work. *For the socialized worker, society is constituted by ecology because ecology is the socialized worker's factory.*

The class struggle takes place within the ecological factory. That is, the class struggle takes place within the immediately given social dimension and within the new spatial and temporal determinations of production. We have already seen how difference and antagonism are established by the socialized worker. Diversity and antagonism represent a choice in favour of the values of life and the quality of reproduction, and a rejection of negative values, of the practices of death and the nullifying tendencies that are implicit in the capitalist machine. It must immediately be added that these alternative values (and the antagonism that nourishes them) are established within the new ecological dimensions of production. It is not that antagonism and difference do not emerge in connection with every singularity and urge that such singularity be attributed to one or the other fronts of antagonism. However, the complete significance of antagonism and difference will be grasped only when these choices, from the molecular level on which they emerge, reach the molar divisions; that is, when these choices are unfurled over the infinite relations that are typical of the ecological dimension of social production.*

These mechanisms of identity and difference, of unity and of the *molar generalization of the antagonisms* are central to our analysis. It is around these mechanisms that the entirety of the means of constituting the socio-ecological Umwelt display themselves. The machine of the constitution is here subjected to a maximum of tension, to an unshackling of directions, pulses and pushes, in order to make it function in one way or another, for exploitation or against it, on one side or the other. It is a pre-Socratic form of physics. Now the concept of exploitation reappears here as central. As is well known, the utility of this concept is generally denied: it is held to be unscientific and is said, rather, to be a moral concept. It is evident, then, that the concept must be mystified even now. But it is becoming less and less easy to do this. The denial of exploitation has become so difficult as to require a special science and a strategy. It is for this reason that in place of talk about exploitation, the bosses have recently imposed the *concept of exclusion* – something which is captured in images of the Bowery, of the Parisian metro during winter, of the *favelas*. Even the Pope is willing to regret exclusion from the labour-market, from the welfare state and from citizenship etc. For the boss, society has suddenly become a *dual* society – as, for the workers, it always has been. This has happened only to a certain extent, however. That is, society proceeded to become a dual society until the moment in which, following the unifying processes which the new dimension of social labour gave rise to, the two sides changed places: the workers realized that they were coming to occupy an increasingly hegemonic position in society (notwithstanding trade union efforts to organize the defence of minoritarian and corporatist interests) while the bosses realized that they had to establish positions of counterattack from which they might destroy proletarian and working-class hegemony. However, now that work has become

---

* 'Molecular' refers to the complex of relations which are developed either in a socializing or antagonistic (but in any case varied) manner, among the plurality of social subjects. 'Molar' refers to the reduction of this complex of multifarious relations to a relationship characterized by a dualistic opposition. I derive the use of these terms from Deleuze and Guattari's *Anti-Oedipus* and *A Thousand Plateaus* (University of Minnesota Press, Minneapolis, 1981 and 1987.) See also Guattari and Negri *Les nouveaux espaces de Liberté* (Bedon, Paris, 1985).

socialized, destruction of this hegemony involves destruction of the entire society and the nature which society has organized as its own environment. Consequently, the dualism invented by capital is as destructive and nihilistic as the dualism of the workers is (and will be to an ever increasing extent) constructive, gentle, spontaneous, generous and superabundant – both in practice and as far as utopia is concerned. Poverty is deliberately planned by the ruling powers in order to counter the tendency towards the unification of socialized work. If the unification of socialized work generates inflation – and this seems inevitable in view of the increased productivity brought about by the socialization of work – then the basic objective of the capitalists will be to stop inflation. This is an act of hypocrisy and violence which hides a precise aim: that of stifling the socialized worker's force, power and desire for unification, all of which lie at the root of inflation. As far as the bosses are concerned, if obstructing unification requires extensive poverty, that's fine: it will be a case of 'killing two birds with one stone' because a large number of poor people, besides effectively obstructing the unitary organization of the socialized worker, also gives rise to the vicious blackmail represented by the unconcealed manifestation of widespread misery – i.e. to the obfuscation of the imagination, the reawakening of atavic fears and the encouragement of monstrous piety. But why should we – products of the highest level of political and social constitution so-far attained by humanity – allow ourselves to be influenced by such blackmail? Turning to another matter, it is obvious why the bosses are currently struggling against all the more-or-less 'Keynesian' attempts to stimulate demand; and if such action contradicts the aims of profit-making imposed by the system, it is nevertheless completely consistent with the ideology of poverty and divisiveness which capital is promoting within the working class. Neo-liberalism and neo-malthusianism are twins. If there is inflation (or rather, what this means in terms of workers' power), then it is necessary to control the money supply. In this way, a powerful mechanism for the establishment of poverty is set in motion. In addition, in order that the social infrastructure too is utilized for the consolidation of poverty, it is necessary to reduce welfare (which represents a policy designed to prop up demand). Finally, highly sophisticated techniques for the repressive combination of monetary policy and other financial policies have been promoted. The aim of such techniques is a massive repression of the working class and the destruction of every means to the political expansion, translation and transformation of societal contradictions and struggles. The capacity for monetary control is aimed exclusively at the analysis and tight control of the relationship between public expenditure and wages, both individual and social. In this way, the series of privileged instruments for the construction of the dual society reaches its panoply. Capital is bringing to bear its *monetary destruction* on every point of the social unification of work. The dual society is a society which, being insensitive and gross, has been cut through by a powerful, sharp blade. *The ideal of modern-day capitalism is apartheid.* In constructing the dual society in opposition to proletarian unification of society, capital reimports into the metropolitan countries instruments hitherto used only by imperialism and colonialism. The Nazis, the Ku Klux Klan and Boer freemasonry have become the Father, Son and Holy Spirit of existing capitalist culture. The dual society is the most sophisticated and powerful product of the will to destroy the social unity of the producers. Thereby, capital has induced – as is only natural – fear and panic.

The fact is that the dual society, poverty and social exclusion are real. We also claim that they are mystificatory manœuvres carried out by the enemy. They are real mystifications which make us suffer. Our task, then, is to understand this reality better in order that we are, thereby, better equipped to fight it. First of all, then, let us consider the problem of how the relationship between the tendency towards the proletariat's social unification, and the political, economic and ideological obstacles placed in the way of such unification, has been articulated. Let us also examine the form in which it has sometimes been broken and the general way in which it must be challenged. Now it seems obvious that in capital's drive to gain control of the tendency towards unification, there is a contradiction between the centralized planning of this project and the aim of social (i.e. economic and institutional) deregulation. That is, there is a contradiction between the means and the proposed ends. By disregarding the surface appearances of this contradiction and penetrating to the level of class-relationships, it may be noted that, behind the contradiction and within the inertia and difficulties which the above combination of objectives generally involves, there exists *a rich combination of forms of resistance*, of partially antagonistic movements and of irreducibly alternative determinations. All this is fundamental: it means that deregulation is not only damaging to the interests of the proletariat, destroying the guarantees with which they were from time to time provided; but that deregulation also represents an opening of political spaces, i.e. a place where the new form of proletarian knowledge/power can show itself. I must, however, qualify these remarks since deregulation has not always had the characteristics we have emphasized. Rather, it has acquired them only by virtue of the post-reformist struggles characterizing recent decades; that is, it has acquired them within those processes – typical of the twentieth century – of disruption of the repressive dialectic between proletarian struggles and capitalistic restructuration. But this disruption is nothing other than the disruption of the economic cycle. Deregulation signals the cycle's disruption, and viewing such disruption as a tendency, deregulation also accelerates it. Therefore, deregulation allows the struggles, at least in certain phases, to bring about a new cycle which is by now incompatible with the continuity of the restructuration of control and with the repressive mechanisms of such control. Returning to the problem of the actuality and depth of the dual society, of poverty and of marginalization, we must conclude by pointing out that all these are governed by mechanisms of intervention (or rather, by the selective and teleological planning of non-intervention, or the dislocation of objectives and periods of restructuration). In other words, the dual society, poverty and marginalization are governed by mechanisms of deregulation which, while initially having a formidable impact, in the long run turn out to be problematic. Indeed, because of the accentuation of the proletarian challenge, the emergence of extra-systemic factors, or simply because of problems in the system's functioning, the mechanisms of deregulation may even bring about a situation which it is difficult to sustain globally, and thus to include (in a strategic form), within a framework of control.

During the course of capitalist development, there have always existed gaps – particularly in the sphere of circulation – which are independent of direct capitalist control. In these gaps, certain use-values have been defined, and sometimes, communities which are rooted in such values have come into existence. Marx himself talks in this regard of 'small circulation'. Now, we have often had occasion to describe the processes of self-valorization which existed in the gaps left by capitalist subsumption of society or which made themselves independent of the process of subsumption. But what is happening in the present (post-reformist) period is something fundamentally and profoundly different. This is because one is not dealing with elements which have been insufficiently incorporated into the overall framework of capitalism and insufficiently subjected to capitalist control; nor is one dealing with singular, ontologically separate elements. Those elements of proletarian self-valorization which appear in the gaps left by deregulation, in utilizing it or breaking it, have no resistance or residual character. They are moments, to put it in technical terms, of a structure which is linked to the real subsumption of society by capital, elements which have not yet been caught up in a process of subsumption, or else elements which are waiting on formal thresholds. Deregulation is a global policy: it brings about a leap forward in the entire political, economic and juridical system. The period of deregulation in fact began long before the comming to power of the Reagans and Thatchers of this world. It began in 1971 with the detachment of the dollar from the gold standard, and with successive measures (which, descending from that summit, were nevertheless cogent and uniform) of deregulation of the oil, raw materials and labour-markets. The theory of deregulation, then, represents a massive attempt to bring back the ideology of the market to the centre of the political stage. This can only come about, however, when work has become socialized and when the productive (and work) processes have already permeated the social totality and become so thickly sedimented that it is not clear exactly what degree of autonomy individual subjects can have. When it eliminates all differences between actors, the ideology of the market does not mystify such differences. (Socialist arguments attack this process of mystification.) Here *the ideology invents the market, pretending that it is a real fact.* Here, then, it is not a case of neo-liberal ideologies mystifying a reality which is in fact controlled scientifically: when neo-liberal theorists talk about the freedom which deregulation supposedly restores to private subjects, they falsify the scientific process, and that is very dangerous. In fact, particularly in the present decade, the countries that have been loudest in praising the virtues of leaving things to entrepreneurial initiative have been the very countries in which, at the same time, public debt and commercial and budget deficits have increased the most. The more such countries have preached financial restraint, the more they have lived on credit; the more fashionable they have made the free market in opposition to the state, the more they have had recourse to traditional methods of finance (such as military spending) and the more they have 'drugged' economic growth with exceptional measures of intervention etc. The fact is that after many (too many) years of asphyxiating theories of planning, after so much (too much) dismal socialism and after several totalitarian catastrophies, Hayekism has a nice feel about it. Why is this? Certainly not because the market can be reinvented and the private restored, but on the contrary, because through Hayekism, collective consistencies and collective subjects can express themselves at the level of complex options and in contexts of alternative possibilities etc. In short, given a situation of growing proletarian unification, in seeking to destroy antagonistic collective organizations, market rigidities and growing marginal difficulties, the price paid by capitalist deregulation for the construction of new differences *is extremely high*. Deregulation raises the level of struggle, recognizing it to be the global dimension of the subsumed society. It is here that new productive circuits and new tendencies tied to the emergence of collective subjects are formed. (Thanks to deregulation, these subjects are no longer corporatist but collective – and thus freer and more powerful.)

We are now in a position to summarize the basic themes of our enquiry. These can be expressed in terms of the phrase 'From the socialized worker to its universal expression in a situation of real subsumption'. A renewed nature – one which everywhere facilitates collective action (which has become progressively more intense and which is aimed at the constitution of a world full of life and experience) – stands before the socialized worker. The world and nature have become a fluid environment, a rich and dense communicative entirety in which (paradoxically) the subject has established itself in an increasingly universal way. On the other hand, a number of mechanisms for obstructing this force, or this tendency, have been set in motion. Yet inscribed in this same process, there exists *the potential for disruption and the invention of alternatives*. For example, there is the possibility to choose in favour of a higher quality of life and a constructive time for the imagination. There exists the enjoyment involved in the reproduction of life, and the ecological antagonism – which is at the same time the capacity to produce and reproduce existence. It is no coincidence, then – and we shall come back to this point in more detail – that in many ways and in many respects, the emergence of the socialized worker has been accompanied by, and bound up with, the emergence of the feminist movement. This is due to the fact that here and there, but above all in the feminist movement, the conception of production has been subordinated to that of reproduction, while the latter has itself been subordinated to the conception of nature. . .and so on, in circular fashion. However, this does not mean that everything has been reduced to indifference or to a recourse to obsolete values or that life as such – as the most significant expression of ontological innovation – does not continually reappear at the centre of this event, imposing itself as the paradigm of every deduction and every practical invention.

The reformist revolution of the thirties was sustained by political, trade-union and capitalistic alliances involving *big labour, big capital and big government*. If these have come to an end, and if the values which they expressed are now exhausted, today it is perhaps possible to begin to perceive new alliances and new values. New alliances and values have been constituted in the dynamic of the power/knowledge (or vice versa) of the socialized worker, of the feminist movement and of new groups of revolutionary intellectuals (especially those groups which, with regard to the issues of ecology, wages and the quality of life, have begun to make unsuppressible demands concerning liberty and wealth). On the other hand, today, new alliances are only possible if they are built on a revolutionary terrain: it is a fact that, at the stage we have now reached, reformism is impossible, and that every new form of social cooperation in work, directed at constitutive objectives, represents a catastrophic, revolutionary and ontologically innovative transformation. When transformative action installs itself in the ecological machine and in terms of the globality and extension that this presents, its weight, incidence and capacity to pose targets for action immediately become an irrecoverable projection towards the future – like a body which, released from the forces of gravity, floats freely wherever the winds of heaven take it.

5

The world economy of the socialized worker

So far we have seen in synchronic and analytic terms how the new subject has come to be formed and how the context in which it operates has gradually altered: the socialized worker lives in the ecological machine; there it locates its operating potential and through it, constructs and reconstructs the world. We now want to analyse how, in terms of living history, these synchronic moments (which, theoretically, are endowed with a strong transformative potential) can be grasped diachronically and constitutively. At first sight this theoretical passage should be possible – this for at least one fundamental reason: namely, that the process of the constitution of the new type of worker has developed in evident homology with the process of the formation and structuration of the world market. In fact, the stimulating economy no longer appears as a single 'world economy'. In this economy productive entities were developed and then – during the period of disastrous relationships between the centre and the periphery – propagated by the process of development. Today, all Stalinist or Rostowian models of development have exhausted their potential. There no longer exist 'stages' or a 'world economy'. Instead, there exists a world market in which, as a result of processes which are diffuse, continuous, homologous and contiguous, productive agents are being formed. These processes are not like a waterfall but like a series of interconnecting pools. This determination is fundamental as far as analysis of the socialized worker is concerned. *The world economy of the socialized worker is the unified world market.*

The world economy of the socialized worker came to prominence in the *decade between 1971 and 1982*. In chapter 2 we emphasized that it is essentially the thirties and the sixties which constitute the hallmark of the century. During these two decades, reformist acceleration created the structural conditions necessary for the emergence of the socialized worker while pushing capitalist development to the edge of catastrophe. From that moment on, the conflict between the new qualities of the socialized worker and the determinations of production, reproduction and the crisis became very acute. This conflict (or ontological break) became of prime significance as a result of the events of 1968. From this point onwards, a critical process constitutive of a new reality was set in motion, and as a result, in the seventies we witnessed a first exemplary manifestation of the conflict: in the decade between 1971 (with the *detachment of the dollar from gold* and the consequent deregulation of all international prices and disruption of monetary balances; the end of international Keynesianism of the Bretton Woods kind; the abnormal rise in the price of oil and its subsequent reverberations etc.) and 1982 (with the *Mexican debt crisis* and its demonstration of capitalist inability to control the effects of deregulation and the actions of the socialized worker in the world market) we were already in the *twenty-first century*. We were in the twenty-first century in ways which were still imprecise and prototypical (and perhaps because they *were* imprecise and prototypical, they were also particularly emblematic and powerful in identifying and highlighting the intervening break). As a result of all this, we found ourselves confronted by aspects of the crisis that were totally unlike what had previously been experienced. The construction of a policy of deregulation and the constitution of the socialized worker – both on a global level – went hand in hand. This gave rise to the development of antagonistic pressures on a new scale, and as we have seen, this new relationship no longer allows us to consider ourselves as living in the twentieth century: the regular economic cycles we once knew have disappeared and only economics professors still busy themselves with the vain attempt to identify them. The economic and political horizon is, rather, characterized to an increasingly significant extent by the simultaneous presence of partial cycles, incontrollable movements and sudden contractions on the one hand, and on the other, by the appearance of new autonomous cycles and the emergence of new dimensions of productive cooperation. During the decade we have referred to, the world economy or the world market became *the schizoid context for the completion of the socialized worker's historical constitution.*

In what follows we shall obviously come back to the seventies often. We have already hinted at a number of issues, and we shall take them up again. Having said that, let us try to understand what is essential about the enormous process which finally matured and reached crisis proportions in those years. Let us try to understand what were the potentialities, forms of planning and raw materials which capital used to further its aims of domination to such a large extent. Secondly, we shall see how the world market, or rather, the world economy of the socialized worker, has been restructured. Thirdly, we shall identify the locations and contexts of the crisis which, having reached maturity in the seventies, exploded in the eighties. For lack of space all this will have to be set out very briefly though we shall try to focus on the most essential aspects.

First of all it must be emphasized that the process of the constitution of the world market would not have been possible if *in the advanced capitalist countries* the conflict between exploiters and exploited had not already reached a high level during the years of triumphant reformism. How did all this come about? The answer is that it came about in exactly the way we described when talking about real subsumption: in this case, theory is merely an anagram of historical development. The socialization of exploitation was the result of the direct absorption by capital of all the conditions of production and reproduction. Capital consumed society, and thus became social. The same thing happened at the global level: capital consumed the entire world and thus became global. However, it must be emphasized that what became global was 'social capital', and that what is at issue is specifically the globalization of the exploitation of the socialized worker: we are not dealing with the generic aspects of exploitation (such as the relationship of the metropolitan countries to the countries of the periphery etc.). If the above analysis is correct, it is also correct to say that old-style imperialism is now as little possible as fascism in the mother-country is. But if 'old-style' imperialism (to which third-world conditions and protest stand as lasting monuments) is over, this does not imply that relationships of imperialistic exploitation no longer exist. On the contrary, the new type of exploitation is even more terrible and widespread (if such a thing is possible) than the old: a *new* participatory, liberal and 'democratic' type of *imperialism* is being consolidated. One can therefore say that to become global, social capital has had to pay an exceptionally high political price. This, then, is the point: an essential condition for the globalization of social capital, and thus for the exploitation of the socialized worker, is that *political forms of control* become the pre-eminent (if not exclusive) forms of control exercised by capital. Capital extends its political form of domination as much as possible. Only in its political form can domination be used to transform knowledge of the interdependencies of production (that is, of cooperation) existing on a world scale into a network of control (which may become a network of repression and which in any case is always a network of exploitation). *The international schema of control, therefore, is always and exlusively political in nature.* It comprises elements of centralization and expressions of local and peripheral identities and attachments. All these are caught up in a dialectic which from the point of view of exploitation is always unitary in nature. This dialectic is, and cannot but be, political, therefore. There are further points to be made in this connection. For example, as we have said, the law of value can clearly no longer be considered as anything more than a schema (though a necessary one) for the identification of relationships of exploitation; theoretically it is inadequate, useful (above all for the boss) only for the production of immediate, rough analyses. The difficulties which are experienced in using the law of value generally are enhanced by the world-wide scale of its application. The law of value highlights not only the extent, but also the intensity, of exploitation. It indicates the innumerable portions of value which the new original accumulation regenerates. However, given the process of the globalization of capital, it is impossible to describe the production of value by adopting a linear approach and by looking for points of reference that can be reduced to a system. As far as theories of imperialism are concerned, these are as unsuccessful as the theories of value. *Value has everywhere escaped capitalist control.* Or rather, it has overflowed and its presence is fully and widely felt: it circulates among the factories and in the metropolises, and even in the tropical areas hitherto untouched by industrialization. While there exist many different manifestations of value, at the same time, owing to the continuity, cross-over and superimposition of economic cycles, such manifestations cannot be differentiated from each other. Capital can only control the process of the globalization of capitalist relations of production, i.e. the establishment of a world market (which from another point of view is a global mercantile society, a world economy of an hitherto unknown, paradoxical kind), if such control is political in nature. The capitalist élite is a political élite, and as such it forges technological instruments which are adequate both for the extent and for the intensity of the control which is to be exercised. The political aspects of social production take on prime significance; the sectors which are usually defined as the leading ones are those in which the greatest capacity for control is produced; discipline and the organization of work relationships are exercised exclusively as political tools. Just as commodities were once conceived of as being produced by means of control, one can now talk in terms of *the production of control by means of control*. This is because the quantity – and even more so, the quality – of production, of the value produced, of the production of commodities in general, no longer has anything to do with control – either in the metropolitan societies or in the world-society as a whole. Unlike the epoch of the mass worker, with the forced cooperation of large numbers of labourers, control in the literal sense is no longer a necessary condition for production: today control is provided by book-keeping. The latter is an expression of the reproduction of power and the system over, above and beyond value. Production is now dominated by the socialized worker who rules over cooperation. Control by the employer is thus, in reality, empty, reflexive, cruel and sterile. *Automation and the computer revolution* constitute the heart of this epoch-making crisis of capitalist control. They are the symbols of the twenty-first century.

The transformation of the economic into the political requires adequate instruments. Automation and computerization are instruments designed to fulfil this purpose: they are concentrations of scientific knowledge employed according to the requirements of capitalist power; they are the symbols and the transmission belts of 'modernization'. Of the various functions permitted by automation and computers in the control of socialized and industrial work, we may note the following: the substitution of labour and thus streamlining of its turnover; checking of the precise times involved in every condition and phase of the production cycle and thus the subordination to it of all activities and needs of the socialized labour force; making immediately apparent the cost of a product with respect to every element that goes into its production thus allowing rational decisions concerning systematic inclusion or exclusion; and finally (as a result of the above panoply of conditions), success in establishing new hierarchies and a new legitimacy for socialized control. For the moment, we wish to emphasize these rather than other aspects (we will come back to other important aspects of the above issues later on) because by doing so we shall be able to clarify the means by which political control, armed with technology, is spread throughout the world economy. Wherever it exists (and it exists almost everywhere on the face of the planet), this technology is used to establish efficient forms of control both over and within the new forms of productive cooperation. Such forms of control are obviously powerful: above the great mass of social productive labour, they tend to constitute hierarchies and bases for the diffusion of control. To this end the processes of automation, and above all those of computerization, allow social actors to be homologized and classified with regard to the aim of control. We can now begin to appreciate the full significance of the notion of the production of control by means of control, which we introduced above. Political domination can be directly and efficiently linked to automated or computerized control structures. The computerized control structures are not only a reflection, but are the embodiment of command. The streamlining of production cycles (in particular of the more complex ones), and the construction of networks of information, knowledge and intervention, all represent a method of rationalization of the market which, when utilized in conjunction with the development of deregulation, becomes a favourite instrument for the efficient homologization of the social forces in accordance with schema which are functional for the legitimation and reproduction of the system.

The above combination of determinations structures the world market by establishing *an adequate international division of labour*. That is to put it in abstract terms. Concretely, processes of the unification of the world market have become so rapid that, rather than talking about an international division of labour or the specialization of given regions, it would be better to talk about *forms and hierarchies of production which are uniformly diffused*. By this I mean that capitalist control no longer requires a merely formal unification within each country of the sites and processes (that is, the temporal and spatial aspects) of production: these structures have already served their purpose. Rather, as in the case of control of social labour within each single country, so capitalist colonization of the world market is *integral, transversal and exterior*. This has several important consequences. For example, one can ask whether the concept of 'peripheral Fordism' actually means anything any more – even though, for a certain time the concept successfully captured the idea of a growth, in the periphery, of new labour-markets integrated with the central economies according to the classic criteria of large international economies of scale. Now, those countries which through the application of peripheral Fordism have crossed the threshold of advanced and autonomous growth, have become full participants in the world economy of the socialized worker. This integration has been at its most pronounced in the case of those countries in which corporative resistance (for example, by professional workers) to this enlargement of the market and to complete modernization has been weakest. In addition, integration has been at its most complete and compelling where preceding social-structural forms have been at their most subtle. In this way, precapitalist or artisan modes of production (which constitute by-now obsolete criteria of legitimacy and participation) now straightforwardly make up the new social structure of production. They provide new areas and situations to explore with a view to accumulation and the discovery of new productive possibilities; but above all they provide ideological support and legitimatory illusions. In this connection, *the Japanese industrial and political structure constitutes an exemplary case.* Here, technological success, rapid industrial innovation and the construction and conquest of leading markets, lie side by side with traditional forms of social control and with the consolidation of systems of collaboration (between the state, enterprises and families) in the provision and development of services. Such a combination has been possible because it has been politically controlled on the basis of an adequate level of technological development. This has lent great stability to the capitalist mode of production in that it has absorbed and obliterated differences between communities and work-processes. In the Japanese case, therefore, real subsumption appears to have preceded formal subsumption which it has adapted to its own requirements. However, acknowledgement of the importance of technological factors must not be allowed to obscure the fact that the whole complex is held together by the determining influence of the ruling powers. These are genuinely and exclusively of ancient heritage. They constitute a form of internal imperialism.

It may be that I have emphasized this tendency too much, so that – particularly when Japan is taken as an example – it appears as a linear function, and the structures which it produces seem, as a consequence, to be immune to contradictions of a more general kind. In fact it constitutes a set of conditions which, though extreme, are nonetheless real; and we can correct the above impression by undertaking a more precise analysis of historical reality. For this purpose we need to return to the period between 1971 and 1982. In this period, as we have said, capitalism's need to undermine the consolidation of the mass worker as the hegemonic agent of production, led – in the metropolitan countries – to the first experiences of violent deregulation, while production was increasingly shifted to the countries of the 'third world'. So-called 'peripheral Fordism' thus became increasingly widespread. (One should really speak of 'peripheral Taylorism' – which slowly became 'Fordism'. In other words, mass production utilizing exported technology slowly became production for a mass peripheral market.) From that point onwards, *the industrial map of the world was redrawn*. The countries of peripheral Fordism became full members of the world economy of the socialized worker. In this situation, the most important differences were not so much those within the world economic system which had taken shape, as those between it, and those countries falling outside the new boundaries of the system. In other words, just as there coexist within the metropolitan countries two levels of existence – one of integration, another of exclusion – so in the world economy there is the level of internal integration and a boundary of exclusion. Counterposed to the capitalist countries (including the ones that have recently joined this category) and to the world market as an organized structure, there is the world of the excluded – a world of hunger and desperation. In short, the 'third world' as such no longer exists, and after the accession of a large part of the latter to the 'first world', there followed *the discovery of 'another world'* which lives on the margins and is built on lower, more wretched conditions than those of the first world.

It is particularly interesting to trace the process of integration we have been describing, *from the perspective of the monetary develop-*

ments of the past two decades. Clearly, we cannot offer a complete analysis, but this is not our task. Even on the basis of a cursory analysis, however, we can show that enormous progress towards unification of the world market was made during the above period. This was due to a subterfuge whereby the large enterprises which financed development of the periphery brought together individual nations, continents and areas within a single plan of production, in this way bringing about the profound and lasting interpenetration of structures which – to an increasing extent – were rigorously homogeneous. This integration came about principally through the deployment of monetary instruments. Once integration had been achieved (i.e. once the structure had been established and its social significance recognized), monetary instruments became less useful and their effectiveness was questioned and challenged. The IMF was unsuccessful. The traditional means of managing international debt and the imposition of a rate of interest designed to establish the norm of aggregation (or exclusion) from the world market, were no longer adequate for their purpose. Every attempt to resurrect old systems of control – whether imperialistic systems of the traditional kind, hierarchical functions, well-known models of the international division of labour etc. – failed. The economies of the periphery refused to accept these measures for one basic reason, namely that they were no longer peripheral. They were already integrated into an economic structure having dimensions equal to those of the developed world (and of those economies that were genuinely undergoing development). Having recognized this situation, the countries of the periphery then began to refuse repayment of the loans they had taken out to fuel their economic development. In the face of this refusal the governments of the centre – and this is the novel feature – were unable to take repressive measures. Faced with the unpaid Mexican loans, the American government, from 1982 onwards, found itself in the same situation it had been in when faced with the refusal of the mid-West farmers to repay their loans. Integration is such that in both cases refusal had repercussions for other parts of the structure and this threatened to bring about its destruction. The world economy of the socialized worker thus began to reveal its true colours: the instruments which had been used to bring about integration in the first place were thrown into crisis by the very degree of advancement of such integration. In this way, the degree of integration served to indicate the limits of domination. Here too, then, we are confronted by new laws which form part of the genetic inheritance of the socialized worker and its hegemony over the development of the capitalist mode of production in the current phase. (Apart from the emergence of these basic new contradictions, however, naturally we cannot forget that there exists in addition the 'other world', or the world of exclusion and hunger: unlike the mass worker, the socialized worker will not forget the excluded.)

Still from a diachronic perspective, on the basis of the above analysis we can identify *a moment of crisis*. This moment is a crisis in the literal sense. It is an economic, political and social crisis – and it often manifests itself as a military crisis as well (that is, a crisis of the new forms which war assumes in an interdependent world). It is a crisis which, as always, affects the system at its weakest points (namely, the countries which have recently been integrated). It is a crisis which penetrates the most sensitive nerves of the structure, namely those relating to the monetary system and to rates of productivity. First and foremost, however, it is a theoretical crisis. That is, *the world economy of the socialized worker* has shown itself to be a radically and totally *antagonistic phenomenon*. That the concept of the socialized worker involved antagonistic aspects is something which we knew already: it was apparent, firstly, when we described the necessity for the socialized worker to counterpose alternative values to capitalist production, and secondly, when we contrasted the socialized worker's ecological Umwelt with the socio-industrial environment of mature capitalism. At this point, however, the antagonism began to make itself felt at the level of the world economy – that is, at the level of the unified world market – and was, thus, greatly radicalized. This radicalism pertained not to a concept, however, but to reality. Similarly, therefore, it is necessary to highlight those contradictions which are inherent in the nature of the world economy of the socialized worker and which thus go beyond the contradictions which are superficially apparent in development. The former contradictions run deeper than the dualism which is the residual production of development: they go beyond the indignation which is provoked by the implacable mechanisms of exclusion, beyond hunger, the degradation of nature and the various forms of totalitarianism which are bound up with these calamities. We partly hinted at these contradictions when we pointed out that deregulation, undertaken in order to integrate markets, had come into conflict – once the latter had actually been brought to a high level of integration – with its effects. And if the most significant aspect of this heteronomy of goals – and thus of the emergence of the crisis – was undoubtedly that constituted by the loans crisis and the crisis of international monetary policies (or in other words, the paradox of a rapid growth of interest rates at a time of low levels of investment), other aspects of the specific contradiction we have been analysing (and which is the product of development and demonstrates the latter's limits) are no less fundamental.

Three, or rather two, such aspects (now that we have briefly mentioned the crisis affecting the management of international loans) stand out. As we have noted, the wearisome, and in some respects, terrible, event of the international loans crisis began in 1982 and principally involved the Latin American countries. At the same time, however, two other major crises began or entered a critical phase, namely *the Middle East and South African crises*. In both cases, what was at stake was the capacity to control, and thus to disrupt, the unity of the socialized worker in areas which are crucial for economic development and exploitation on the world market, namely the oil-producing regions and the legendary region of precious minerals which is South Africa. The instruments used were different from monetary ones: armed blackmail and the territorial expansion of Israel, combined with support for a foul fratricidal war between Iran and Iraq, were the instruments used in the Middle East; while in South Africa we had division of the proletariat along the lines of colour, brutal exploitation, imitation of the Nazi's methods of territorial expansion together with the utilization of enemy labour power, and finally, an attempt to encourage *tout-azimut*, fratricidal wars. In each case the goal was to prevent the re-emergence of a united, insurrectionary subject and to block progress towards the consolidation of liberation movements. It is of interest to dwell on these points for a fundamental theoretical reason, namely that in the above events, the dynamic of the contradiction manifested itself with a violence and a ferocity without equal. These powerful results of the contradiction inherent in the unification of the world economy of the socialized worker are also the paradigms of that structure. Our argument thus becomes twofold: on the one hand reason has given way to the blood of the exploited, and following this line of argument, science cannot but express itself as a perspective of struggle. On the other hand, the scientific significance of this line of research has been amply demonstrated: these regular crises, the pace of events, demonstrate that the unity of the socialized worker forces the implementation of measures of control; such measures, however, provoke immediate counter-attacks – attacks which are equally regular and powerful. Through the socialized worker and the forms of exploitation which its existence reveals, the contradiction is consolidated and its irreducibility manifested. And so we come full circle, both theoretically and historically: the limits of social capital and of subsumption are constituted by the resistance and the alternative posed by the socialized worker. If we have not examined all this from the perspective of organization, this is simply because times are not yet ripe for this operation. We shall say more about this later on, however.

We have thus completed our analysis of the relationship between synchronic expressions and diachronic determinations. Analysis reaches its natural conclusion when antagonistic pressures which are inherent in the concept of the socialized worker develop historically – that is, when they find their material embodiment. Analysis and theory are thus shown to have a genetic relationship with the *a posteriori* and with reality – that is, with the concrete and determinate historical antagonism out of which reality is consti-tuted. It will be objected that given the way our analysis was undertaken, this result, however original in terms of the findings presented (namely, the emergence of the socialized worker after and in opposition to the period of the mass worker), was in some way decided upon in advance. It will further be objected that the result doesn't seem to correspond to that combination of connota-tions (which are as striking and important as they are unforeseen and innovative), which we claimed indicated the catastrophic beginning of the epoch of the socialized worker. In short, it will be objected that we are simply repeating a well-known theme whereby all mystery is uncovered – that with the appearance of the socialized worker, we are assuming that all dialectical laws and their tendency to compose historical syntheses (and thus the legitimation of domination) have ceased to be operative. However, I believe that this thesis is worthy of serious consideration, and that it can, indeed, be confirmed. Besides the other points adduced to support the thesis that a dialectical horizon has finally ceased to be meaningful, it should be remembered that an enormous human prosthesis is presupposed by the structural constitution of the world market such that, at this level, the antagonism becomes extreme. In such extreme circumstances the (at one time golden) rule of development (that is, of the struggle which brings about restructuration etc.) becomes weakened to the point of extinction. When development is all-encompassing, it is impossible to understand what continues to stimulate it; when every expression for value has lost its utility and no longer has any meaning in terms of self-recognition and self-valorization, and society appears as a process of zero-sum development, then the dialectic really has no more place; when differences can only be defined in terms of the determinations of control, then any possibility for a reconstruction having ontological connotations disappears. I am here referring to ontological connotations in the traditional sense, because there exists a new ontology constituted by the historical prosthesis of socialized working activity on a world scale. This constitutes a *redoubling of the world* (and of nature) through social productive activity. To imagine development taking place on this level becomes ridiculous. But in view of the redoubled weight of exploitation and violence which this prosthesis, in its capitalist guise, perpetrates against the socialized worker, it is certainly not ridiculous to recognize that the only, residual, possibility of action lies in overthrowing that domination theoretically and making it problematic and unsustainable. If theoretical criticism and conceptual possibility can then be linked to the force of practice and disruptive capacity, this is another problem. However, the problem of the relationship between theory and practice (whether in theoretical or political terms) can only be confronted by broadening the analysis of how the mode of production of the socialized worker has become world-wide, and by considering its specific forms more analytically, and in more detail. We shall begin to do this in the next chapter.

6

Expropriation in mature capitalism

In the factory, wages were the foundation of the mass worker's community. Wages were the primitive foundation of a primitive community. Production and reproduction, work and consumption were all organized around wages and based on them. Class consciousness was formed as a result of wages and the struggles over their relative value. All this was true of the factory worker, but how do things stand as far as the socialized worker is concerned? We have seen both that the socialized worker is in essence profoundly ambiguous and in what such ambiguity consists. The socialized worker is caught up in the capitalist prosthesis of the world and imprisoned in that doubling of reality which capitalism brought about during, and at the end of, its development. The social dimension of the socialized worker's labour comes to be established within the capitalist prosthesis of reality. The socialized worker's labour is more productive than that of the mass worker. It is endowed with a very high level of productive potential because it is capable of setting in motion the productive potentiality of the whole of society, and of actualizing all the dead labour which resides in it. At all levels and in all contexts, community has increasingly become the foundation of the productivity of labour. Compared to the relationship of domination represented by earnings in the wage economy during the epoch of the mass worker, the earnings of the socialized worker are the expression of a completely new situation. They are the expression of a relationship which is a function of an enormous broadening of productive possibilities: a flower in bloom on a communitary terrain, rich in productive potentialities. Today, capitalist expropriation no longer takes place through wages alone. Given the conditions we have described, expropriation no longer simply consists in the expropriation of the producer, but, in the most immediate sense, in the expropriation of the producers' community. Wages are the expression of individual expropriation, whereas in advanced capitalism, expropriation directly effects the community and the collectivity. Advanced capitalism directly expropriates labouring cooperation. Capital has penetrated the entire society by means of technological and political instruments (the weapons of its daily pillage of value) in order, not only to follow and to be kept informed about, but to anticipate, organize and subsume each of the forms of labouring cooperation which are established in society in order to generate a higher level of productivity. Capital has insinuated itself everywhere, and everywhere attempts to acquire the power to coordinate, commandeer and recuperate value. But the raw material on which the very high level of productivity of the socialized worker is based – the only raw material we know of which is suitable for an intellectual and inventive labour force – *is science, communication and the communication of knowledge.* Capital must, therefore, appropriate communication. It must expropriate the community and superimpose itself on the autonomous capability of managing knowledge, reducing such knowledge to a mere means of every undertaking of the socialized worker. This is *the form which expropriation takes in advanced capitalism* – or rather, in the world economy of the socialized worker. We shall consider the world economy of the socialized worker further in this chapter – this time from a synchronic perspective.

The expropriation of communication represents a mystification of the collective nature of the productivity of the socialized worker's labour. This assumption gives rise to several questions. For example, what is the equivalent for the socialized worker, of the role that 'wages' played for the mass worker? That is, can we identify some factor which can both stand as a symbol of value produced and represent the extent of the socialized worker's expropriation? Communication constitutes the essence of the genuine community in its modern, abstract form. It is the raw material from which socialized labour is constituted and is, therefore, often expropriated, always controlled and sometimes impeded. How, then, is the distribution of values, not only in their monetary, but also in their political form, organized in a society of advanced capitalism? In short, what *are* wages for the socialized worker?

We will provide an answer to all these questions in what follows. For the moment, let us examine how the expropriation of the communication of the community takes place. For the moment we are interested not so much in the articulations of content of the process of expropriation, as in the mode in which this expropriation takes place. Now, in the productive community of advanced capitalism we find ourselves confronted by a primary phenomenon which, following Habermas, we will call 'communicative action'. It is on the basis of the interaction of communicative acts that the horizon of reality comes to be constituted. Such interaction represents a combination of mechanisms, a web of determinatons, characterized by varying tendencies and orientations. It involves genuine structures of meaning. These should allow the fruits of cooperation to be accumulated and thereby make the productive society possible. They *should* do – and in fact, they do. Communicative action provides both freedom and a choice between various intellectual and ethical horizons. Above all, communicative action gives rise to the extraordinary possibility of activating dead socialized labour. Communication is the Direct Current of these relationships. This is why capital tries to gain control of these relationships. Capital adopts a variety of strategies in this connection. On the one hand, it deprives communication of its spontaneous and constructive substance, and as a consequence, reduces it to information – a lifeless, schematic interpretation (which is always equivocal) of reality. On the other hand, advanced capitalism tries to counter proletarian communicative acts (no longer in a defensive way, but from a strategic point of view) by producing various subjectivities which are more adequate to a computerized mode of working than to the spontaneity of the communicative act. *Expropriation takes place firstly in the form of negation, and then in the form of mystification. Finally, expropriation itself becomes a genuine productive process.*

These forms of expropriation are inexorable, resistant and violent. They represent the transformation of the capitalist prosthesis of the world into a negative prosthesis. They are like a flat, glass screen on which is projected, fixed in black and white, the mystified cooperative potentialities of social labour – deprived of life, just like in a replay of *Metropolis*. These forms place before us a metaphysical horizon, terrible in its icy indifference, in which the spontaneity of creation, innovation, the miracle of value, of communication and of communicative and productive activity make no appearance. In this way, capitalist domination carries the impact of its advancement to extremes. Production consists not only in the production of commodities, but in all the conditions necessary for the existence of productive subjectivities. Just as, for the mass worker, capital generated adequate wage-conditions, so today, for the socialized worker, capital tries to establish the social conditions in which communication is to take place. *Communication is to the socialized worker what the wage relationship was to the mass worker.* The establishment of community is both a precondition and the objective of socialized labour. The forms of domination and the types of expropriation of communication typical of advanced capitalism thus represent a very high degree of control, domination and dictatorship. But communication is life. In advanced capitalism, therefore, conflict, struggle and diversity are focused on communication, with capital, by means of communication, trying to preconstitute the determinants of life.

We will now make a brief digression in order to establish two points, the first of which concerns the continuous homology of wages and communication which I am proposing. Now, in order to prevent the argument becoming senseless it is first of all necessary to remember that *by wages I mean, in Marxist terms*, not only that part of the value produced by labour which is given back to the labour force in the mystified form of money, but also that complex of productive and reproductive impulses and desires which are symbolized by wages (and by income in general). I believe that the value of the socialized worker's labour – and thus his/her power – is to be attributed to the substance of labouring cooperation which s/he represents. S/he represents cooperation, communication and created value. One might, therefore, be tempted to say that nowadays, in advanced capitalism and from the point of view of the socialized worker, communication is the substance of value and that wages are a part of this substance. Such an assertion would not be correct, however, because the change of content has also involved a change of form; and this is because the change of content has, as we have repeatedly stressed, been extremely profound, having affected all expressions of value. In short, even though we have a sophisticated conception of wages, one must not confuse these and the values which they represent (and over which, as we shall see, there is continuing struggle), on the one hand, and communication, on the other. In other words, the fact that our understanding of the historical changes (and political agitation) that we are currently experiencing can be advanced by means of the homology of wages and communication, must not be allowed to lead to confusions.

The second point concerns the *distinction between communication and information*. So far, we have seen that the former represents current communicative activity, while the latter is the imprisonment of communication within inert mechanisms of the reproduction of reality once communication has been expropriated from its protagonists. This distinction is imprecise, however, and cannot sustain analysis of the factors which we ourselves have indicated as being fundamental in the creation of the new historical subject. In particular, when one considers the fact that the new subject (and the communicative act) is inherent in the artificial consitution of reality and in the prosthesis or the growing abstraction of capitalist development, this distinction may appear as a category produced by some *deus ex machina*. One must, therefore, be very careful in the use one makes of the distinction between communication and information, occasionally using it, if one wishes, as an abstract, definitional distinction, but bearing in mind that it is quite inadequate for an analysis of the concrete. So much is this the case that in the light of the indissoluble entanglement of communicative activity and computerized accumulation, the distinction may give rise to the suspicion that there is more than one utopian element involved in the emphasis on the independence and creativity of communication. Is communication as such, then, (as value) a pure and simple utopia? No; on the contrary, it constitutes the basic essence of the production of the socialized worker. Precisely for this reason, however, it is to be seen as permeating and enlivening every real determination and as distributing itself widely on the horizon of human artificiality. On the other hand, is information then perhaps pure, empty repetition, a residual fact, an inert substance, a simple detritus? For the same reason that communication is not utopia, the answer is obviously 'No'. It is within this complex structure, then, that expropriation takes place.

At this point, having seen how the various aspects of communicative expression and its expropriation are formally related to one another, we can begin to consider the structure of this process from the point of view of its content. To this end we should make a preliminary observation, namely that the more the domination of the society of communication and of the socialized worker becomes resistent and hegemonic, the more the social basis of production (or rather, the social basis on which expropriation is exercised) becomes united and powerful. As a result, capital sets in motion a very brutal dialectic. (The dialectic is always, and exclusively, a dialectic of capital.) This dialectic represents an unceasing and implacable attempt at subjection but one which is, however, completely inadequate and unsuccessful. This *impossibility of succeeding* makes capitalist attempts at subjection (that is, capitalist imposition of an endless series of experiments, practices and determinations all aimed at producing subjectivity) ever more extreme. We shall consider some of these manifestations of the *production of control* in what follows.

The first and most obvious is economic, or *monetary control* (and repression). Here again we are confronted by an enormous paradox, because in the world economy of the socialized worker, money has lost some of the immediate characteristics of a phenomenon which serves to mystify exploitation. In fact, if production is social, if its value must be measured in relation to the social totality of the production process – and if, therefore, this whole complex appears as an abstraction – then money would seem to provide a good representation of the abstract average displayed by the very nature of value. In this light one might well say that *the central intuition of monetarism* (namely, that money is a reflection of society and of the entirety of exchanges) *is correct*. Money has become – or rather, has become once more – a numerical expression – not individual but collective, not concrete but abstract, not definite but indeterminate. Through its abstract indifference, money corresponds to the quantity of abstract labour that is expressed by the social processes of production. Here lies the paradox. It is a paradox for a certain well-known reason. Already in Walras, the founder of the neo-classical school, recognition of the social dimension of money (in relation to the social dimension of work) had led to the frontiers of socialism. Now, under the conditions of a fully developed socialized economy, the paradox can be unravelled even further: in present conditions nothing would in fact be more logical than a system of a social, average wage distributed equally among all citizens, employed or otherwise. Such a system would not only be morally correct, but from an economic and book-keeping point of view, it would be accurate: in the world economy of the socialized worker, labour takes place on a communitary and uniform foundation. Money can therefore be used to represent directly units of abstract, collective labour. Moreover, this formulation also involves a kind of equality of opportunity for individuals to express labour power no matter how they participate in the cooperative processes aimed at the creation of value. Now, faced with these series of paradoxes which the very development of monetary control has itself brought about, capital has reacted with the violence of one who is exasperated. Recognition of the new function of money as it concerns the abstract characteristics of socialized labour, has given rise to pure reaction. This, then, is the negative aspect: not only is the social character of labouring cooperation expropriated, but its average quality is denied along with the applicability of this quality as a measure. This represents a form of *degradation* comparable to the welfare-state provision: while the idea of the *social wage* is applied in the advanced forms of the welfare state, this is done not out of recognition of the collective structure of labouring cooperation, but rather, in order to provide limited assistance to the poor. And in view of this, any re-examination of the organization of the working day or any major reduction of working hours is, therefore, excluded (or as I would prefer to say, exorcised). Alternatively, the measurement of labour is transformed in a negative way. It is used as a mystificatory instrument of diversity and separation; it is the mystification of expropriation above and against the abstract unification of human activity, communication and cooperation which have been established in advanced capitalism. Actually, the paradox revealed by capitalist attempts at monetary control of the socialized labour force cuts very deep. Capital has realized there is no way out of the paradox that in order to maintain monetary domination of the labour force, it must deny or mystify the very social character which its own book-keeping (monetary control) must presuppose. Having recognized the full extent of the paradox, capital has correctly seen the latter as an indication that its own productive capacity has been exhausted – and it has reacted against this sign of its own finiteness with the violence of one who refuses to come to terms with the inevitability of his own death. From the moment it becomes the numerical expression of a complex of abstract and collective productive quantities, the recompense of a power which is homogeneously constructed and uniformly diffused (at least tendentially), money is used as a repressive instrument. *The result of this short circuit is an extreme brutality.* The sensation of death against that of life, surrounds it.

Again, reflecting on the various functions of money (the various things it stands for and the different realities it represents) we are brought back to the metaphysical interior of materialism, where the dual appearance of community and the dynamics of cooperation, of command or liberation, are articulated and disarticulated and implicate and disclose each other. Already in Machiavelli, and then in Spinoza, in Marx and in Lenin, this relationship constitutes the heart of metaphysics. Understanding it is difficult owing to the complexity of the connections that must be grasped. But it becomes almost impossible, and in any case very tedious when it is borne in mind that this series of connections is in no sense amenable to dialectical solutions. There is no resolution of this conflict. There is only a deep and violent antagonism. Life and death confront one another. The violence manifested by the relationship is inexpressible: only ethical or poetic practice succeeds in capturing it. Such expression leads to innovation, or, in other words, to recognition of the positive or negative appearance of power. In this perspective, Spinoza must be interpreted in the light of Machiavelli and vice versa. Apart from questions of orthodoxy, Marx and Lenin must be read in the light of this relationship and its irresolvability and unsuppressible violence. Contemporary revolutionary materialism exists within these paradoxes, and is measured by them.

The negative aspect of capitalist expropriation of labouring cooperation, generated and imprisoned within the ambiguous, paradoxical and irresolvable situations we have talked about, inevitably spreads and is heightened. If the brutality of social relationships is at a maximum, terror must be extreme. In material terms, *capital's [potere] drive towards terror* is orchestrated by the practice and *ideology of nuclear power*. It is important, even if banal at this stage, to emphasize that the drive towards terror is not a result of some demoniacal quality of capital. Rather, the origin and the mechanism of such a tendency find their origin in the dialectic of capital's expropriation of productive cooperation from which they derive their degree of intensity. Such intensity is greater the more the relationship of expropriation is fragile: in effect, the legitimacy of capital is more difficult to sustain the more the cooperation involved in the productive process has reached an advanced stage. In this situation the legitimacy of power [*potere*] becomes an unacceptable transcendence. The relationship has in fact been implicitly overthrown: the fragile artificiality of power has been confronted by the solid creativity of cooperation. But if power is forced to rule under conditions such as these, then not only are social pressures magnified, as we have mentioned, but – as we have also seen – they tend to bring about a complete breakdown. Power is already undergoing a kind of state of divarication which has both debilitated it and undermined its stability. There is a very particular physical moment – such as when an elastic substance is stretched to excess – when a new state comes about exploding in a qualitative leap. It is just such a moment which our experience and our research now oblige us to consider. This is because that power which has raised the threat of death in order to guarantee continued expropriation, is in reality living in the presence of death.

In advanced capitalism, the *nuclear terror* appears as fixed accumulation, *as fixed social capital*. Examples of this appearance are numerous. After Hiroshima and Nagasaki, the skies throughout the world were from time to time irradiated by nuclear fallout and clouds, both of which served to maintain fear and to remind the whole world of the irreversibility of that singular form of the exercise of power. When, however, the cloud of death that was Chernobyl slipped from the hands of its masters, the power of legitimation evaded the object to be legitimated and with this separation, the cloud merely dripped death. Everybody reacted to this mortal encumbrance. But how could we effectively resist it? Today we live in a delicate balance between life and death and yet are often unable to distinguish between things which are life-giving and things that are potentially lethal. The atmosphere has been poisoned. Does this mean that the nuclear terror is here to stay? Is the fear which has taken root in people's hearts a presentiment of certain death? All this would be true if we experienced nuclear power in the way the bosses want us to experience it: that is, as social capital, as a necessity, or even as wealth, as an irreversible scientific conquest, in any case as a social determination to which we are irremediably tied. But this is not the situation. The image of nuclear power – with its dreadful capacity to terrorize, with its ubiquitous and subtle brutality, with its heaven-like breadth, with its root-like depth, its centuries-long duration and its capacity to induce biological mutations – can be used to combat power [*potere*]. This is possible because nuclear power is lethal and terrible, and thus revolting. I am not saying that this image of nuclear power already *has* been turned against power; I am saying that this challenge, experienced in the shadow of terror, cannot be won without confronting the enormous resistance and the brutal determination of power, and without challenging them on their own ground. If we are to secure victory it will be necessary fully to expose the fact that the foundation of authority [*potere*] in nuclear power is the one and only really fatal disease known to society. Capital is bound up with nuclear power. Capital has employed it and wants to secure its acceptance as fixed social capital. This social foundation, the nuclear terror – whether as capital or as social capital – cannot but be destroyed.

Theorem: when fixed social capital appears as nuclear capital, then its reproduction no longer takes place peacefully. It is neither legitimate nor tolerable. This capital must be destroyed. The dialectic ends here. There remains only the antagonism between a capitalist power existing under the shadow of destruction and the social power of labouring cooperation.

War has always been a fundamental aspect of the capitalist organization of society. From this point of view Hobbes was effectively the expert and the prophet of bourgeois society. The interiorization of war into the organization of society is the fundamental element of bourgeois ideology in the modern age. It is the basic presupposition on which the modern state is founded. We are now living at the end of this historical phase. And as often happens, the origin – in this case, the specific purpose of the social order, namely, the judicial solution to war – has (because of the advanced stage of development) given way to extreme alternatives. War has once more become the immediate back-drop and the over-determination of our existence. *Nuclear power has consolidated this overdetermination and rendered it irreversible.* War is therefore a presence, a permanent horizon and a continuous pressure. Society simply constitutes the background. With the arrival of nuclear power, processes of legitimation have become cruel. Cruelty is now the norm. Fear is no longer sufficient for the maintenance of power.

Fear must be so widespread and intense, that people are stunned by it. Nuclear power tortures the soul. War has become a latent presence in the reverberations of nuclear power which has itself become a fixed point on the horizon of our awareness.

We will come back to all this later on. For the moment we will discuss just one of the consequences deriving from the overdetermination of nuclear power and it is the following. Corresponding to the public character of nuclear power, of its plants and of its threat, there is, in the advanced capitalist state, an enormous spread of secrecy. *The nuclear state is a state founded on secrecy.* Secrecy extends to all organizations of the state and has strikingly increased the number of reserved domains and fenced-off areas of political action. They say that this is necessary for security reasons, and in this they are correct: it is necessary for *their* security. It is necessary for the security of their constitution, their existence and their reproduction; and the fact that their social existence is sustained by secrecy is highly symptomatic. Secrecy – or rather, a principle which at first sight is totally ill-adapted to a society of communication – is in fact a principle which functions so well that it is broadened in step with the deepening of the process of expropriation of social communication. We began with this process of expropriation and mystification of the channels of social communication, of their substitution within a framework of domination: now we find ourselves confronted with a complement of this process, whereby domination appears as the total opposite of communication. *Domination is secrecy.* Expropriation not only mystifies communication and the results of labouring cooperation which such communication produces, it even prohibits communication and destroys its substance. Communication can only exist to the extent that it is selectively used and subordinated to capitalist teleology. The mechanisms which produce subjectivity, therefore, also produce secrecy. Secrecy is a symbol of the capability of destroying the determinations which are constitutive of the processes of communication. The great absurdity of the advanced capitalist societies is that while they claim to be open, secrecy is growing all the time; while they claim to be democratic, secrecy is increasingly protected and defended; while life-enhancing possibilities have grown explosively, secrecy concerning the possibility of death is maintained. This paradox has been carried to its limits, and it is an absurdity which is highly indicative of the great perversity of the political and productive structures characteristic of advanced capitalism.

In other words, in late capitalism, the act of expropriation on which capital is based is aimed essentially at depriving communication of its secret: that creative miracle by virtue of which it is the mode of production of the socialized worker. This secret, once expropriated, is transformed into a mystery belonging to the ruling power. Why does power always appear as something obscure, sacred and violent? In this situation, mystificatory illusion is carried to the point of paradox and the attempt to render power arcane begins to affect its opposite, i.e. the process of communication – and above all, the subject of this process. This act of expropriation, an expression of the 'law of takeover', continues to be the vile act it has always been. The more the social community, the collective subjects, recognize that productive cooperation is the sole foundation of all value, the more ignoble this act becomes. Yet the unsuppressible claims of community are undermining the social relationships of advanced capitalism and putting them under enormous pressure. In short, the world economy of the socialized worker and capital are totally and permanently contradictory; and precisely because of this, revolutionary thoughts, both of a destructive and a constructive kind, are still finding an expression. These thoughts, in opposition to capitalist expropriation, propose *proletarian reappropriation*.

7

The antagonistic production of subjectivity

Having analysed several ideas relating to the current transformation considered as an objective phenomenon, we now want to consider it from the subjective point of view. The subjective aspect (which we shall fully describe in what follows) is absolutely fundamental – the more so, the more the relationship between society and capital manifests itself as a relationship between the state on the one hand, and subjects and citizens, producers and the exploited on the other – as a relationship, therefore, between subjects; one whose complexity depends on the variety of connections, or the depth of the differences, contradictions or alternatives, which make up the nexus between society and capital.

What we want to do, then, is to analyse the dynamics of this relationship from the subjective point of view. What does such an analysis entail? What is meant by the subjective 'point of view'? Does it mean that to talk about subjects in this sense is to establish a substantial relationship and thus to reaffirm an ontological conception; or alternatively, that by itself, the antagonism can be specified only in subjective terms? In order to provide answers to these questions, it will perhaps be useful to establish a few points of reference. *In the first place*, it is obvious that what is being referred to here are not substantial, immutable moments. The subject, the subjects, the ontological relationship and the persistence of the antagonism, all form part of the immediate phenomenology of human experience, and they do not require foundations which go beyond experience. Experience, however – and in particular, the experience which concerns collective subjectivities – is something dynamic. Consequently, *in the second place*, it is obvious that when one refers to 'points of view' – that is, to changing purposes – subjects manifest themselves as 'mechanisms'. (Alternatively – to express it in terms used by Guattari, following Foucault – the subjects will manifest themselves as *agencements*.) Therefore, to repeat, a certain type of substantialist ontology and of antagonistic Manicheism (which are found in certain versions of dialectical materialism) certainly have no place here. They have no place for one good reason, namely, that our materialism is in no sense dialectical. Having said that, however, we are inclined to ask, '*Are these "points of view", then, disembodied?*' And is it necessary to reject not only substantialist ontology but every type of ontology in order to prevent fetishism (revolutionary or otherwise), taking the place of critical reasoning? I do not think so. On the contrary, I believe that the subjective point of view is basically constitutive and that this constitutive process can be interpreted in ontological terms according to an hermeneutic of real determinations. By this I mean that points of view are counterposed in real terms, that the conflict between subjects is something tangible, and that points of view and points of conflict give shape to contexts and frameworks having material importance. Consequently, our kind of structuralism is unable to attain the same degree of indifference as that of a 'process without a subject'. On the contrary, the ontological aspects of subjectivity are established (or rather, produced) through the formulation of points of view, the interlacement of orientations of struggle and the revelation of intentions and desires.

The ontological aspects of subjectivity are produced *in different* (or rather, *antagonistic*) ways. This means that we can identify molar, antagonistic alternatives not only in the genesis of historical personalities, but in the overall fabric of history and society and in the involvement to which the very institutional spinerettes are subjected. History is not the history of class struggles if it is analysed from the point of view of the genetic mechanisms of individual determinations; it becomes such when these determinations accumulate and become social formations. These social formations can be seen as being simultaneously singular, an accumulation of individual aspects, ideological thresholds and machines. Within these general perspectives, new collective singularities come into conflict over the principal problems of life, power and reproduction. Now, the alternatives become molar, dualistic and antagonistic when the conflict is focused on essential aspects of the relationship – i.e. when the conflict is focused on those aspects which force major decisions concerning the existence and tempo of social intercourse. In the present case this means that the alternatives become molar, dualistic and antagonistic when what is at issue is *the problem of the expropriation of labouring cooperation*. In this way one passes from microconflicts to molar conflicts, and the machines which coordinate human activity withdraw to rigid, opposing line-ups. Such rigidity does not affect the complexity of the connections, nor the density of particular histories. Rather, it simply demonstrates the irreducibility of single points of view. It also demonstrates the violence which becomes a natural part of the constructive mechanisms when, through the communication of labouring cooperation, the mechanisms come to be established around problems of expression or expropriation. Antagonism, then, does not simplify, but increases the complexity which constitutes the subjects; and by establishing itself, this complexity creates antagonism. It is a very special form of ontology, one which we can here call a *constitutive ontology*, and which is able to arrive at the formation of collective identities through an accumulation of operations which are always analytic and always creatively efficient. This is what we discover – to conclude this series of observations on the centrality of antagonistic alternatives – at the base of the production of subjectivity. We can add that it is only in this way that we can claim to have an approach which is original or significant in the human sciences. Equally opposed to our method are, on the one hand, the empty abstractions of the idealistic and totalitarian conceptions of science, and on the other, indifferent and cynical pluralist conceptions – where a given subject is no more important than any other, and none are at all important. By contrast, our own pluralism concentrates on concrete subjects, it accepts both dualism and antagonism, it utilizes ideal categories in a differentiated analysis and then uses the results of the latter in the service of an ontological reorientation. Our own ontology finds its roots in pluralism but it rejects the ideal categories of indetermination. It is thus defined by reference to the antagonistic use of the mechanisms and trends which constitute the entirety of the framework (and of the society, state and Umwelt which surround it).

The integration of society and the state is thus formally destroyed.
First of all, then, let us see what form is taken by the state, and
how, as an antagonistic subject, it operates. All juridical constitu-
tions amount to a series of legal provisions concerning behaviour
which are designed to guarantee the legitimacy and effectiveness of
the state's actions and the attainment of its aims. In other words, by
means of the constitution, the state is guaranteed a monopoly on the
legitimate use of violence, where, by 'legitimation' is to be
understood that combination of values, and the network of force
which the state, as subject, tries to establish as the justification and
the substance of its own existence and action. However, it is
insufficient simply to redescribe the legal/constitutional aspect of
subjectivity. It is necessary that the form of the state in advanced
capitalism be revealed as a determinate, historical specification of
tendencies of forces (and of consequent aims and limits). In short, it
is necessary that the state be revealed not simply as the organization
of a context of conflictuality, but also, and above all, as the engine
of expropriation (i.e. exploitation) and as a subject which is thus
specifically opposed to other subjects. We shall therefore pass once
more *from a synchronic to a diachronic analysis* – but this time, with
the sole aim of enriching the description of the articulations of the
state-form.

For example, let us consider the end of the sixties, and in
particular, 1968 which was the conclusive theoretical paradigm of
that decade. Within this historical perspective, what form did the
production of antagonistic subjectivity by the state take? It is not
impossible to answer this question; on the contrary, it is not even
particularly difficult to do so. In its most immediate form, the
answer can be shown to consist in the simple application of the
general principal of the dialectic of struggle, or of that form of the
production of subjectivity which is influenced by the dialectical
mechanism: the definition of the antagonism and of the subjective
compositions which support it, struggles, restructuration, new
compositions and subjectivity etc. As we have already seen,
however, the decade of the sixties, through the reformism which
dominated it – i.e. a reformism which the working class adopted as
its trade union and political programme and as the sign both of its
own spontaneity and of its own organization – produced the
pre-existing crisis of regulation and of the very form of regulation.
After the sixties, the image of the dialectical, reforming state was

followed by the image of the '*crisis-state*' – i.e. by the image of a state forced to have recourse to crisis, and which was therefore a 'consumer' of crisis – as a means of governing. In order to re-establish its domination, capital and its state were obliged to modify not one, but the whole range of their instruments of supervision, organization and distribution of work. This *process of the general restructuration of society* and of the perfecting of the capitalist mode of production, had a specific characteristic however, namely that of not upsetting the subjective determinations and the collective and corporative insistencies which sustained the old order. The process of restructuration was certainly radical, but it was also limited – or one might say, controlled – by the concern that certain elements of temporary stabilization and relative control should continue to be effective. When, therefore – consistently with the increasingly violent and totalizing periods of (the process of) restructuration – the innovative process was revealed in its entirety, then the dialectic came to a halt. Suddenly, but none the less convincingly, the social fabric proved to be dominated by antagonism. It was as if the very dialectical laws which had dominated the findings of the social sciences could no longer be used to grasp reality and subjectivity, and that instead of being interwoven and thus sublimated, they found themselves finally separated in their mechanisms and were thus antagonistic. This happened because the famous period of *reformist restructuration* had been *decisive*, not only quantitatively but also qualitatively, *in the socialization of work*. At this point, society displayed impressive isomorphisms: society reproduced the conditions of the factory; and the places in which direct exploitation took place, together with those in which exploitation was indirect, were continually crossed by transfers of transformative practices. The world of work was completely social, fluid, traversable, permeable and transferable. From whatever point of view one looks at it, this transformation of the centres of productive hegemony, from the mass worker to the socialized worker, is so remarkable, that the dialectic no longer exists. *The relationship between struggle and restructuration has been broken*, because as we have said, it has become socially widespread; it has attacked the organic composition of capital, animating its structure. The relationship has thereby changed its nature, imposing as fundamental (in nature and value) the processes of exchange between manual and intellectual labour, and between labouring cooperation and the communication of knowledge. What, then, is the practice of the production of subjectivity which emanates from capital in this perspective?

The alternative (antagonistic) production of subjectivity by capital is, in this circumstance, nothing other than repetition. What enormous energy it requires! In this perspective, the production of subjectivity means that, both in reality and appearance, the norms of the old mode of production – with its corporative rigidities, its fixed mechanisms and the guarantee of the stability of power – must be imposed on the transformation, socialization, liquefication and mobilization of the productive forces. If, as is soon obvious, this is not possible, and if the neo-corporatist solution is brushed aside, then other means will be found. (At the beginning of the seventies – and in Italy, until the whole of the period of the so-called 'historical compromise' – the neo-corporatist solution was, however, hegemonic.) What is fundamental is to block the political expression of the productive forces – to study them in order to dominate them. In short, with regard to the revolution of the productive forces (which we have described), it is essential to disrupt their *socialization* and to expropriate their *autonomy* (or in other words, their vibrant ability to *communicate* which gives rise to productive cooperation). From this point of view, the production of subjectivity by capital should certainly not create fictitious elements of antagonism. The production of subjectivity is the material to which the antagonism applies itself. The production of subjectivity makes the fictitious elements of antagonism explode and displays them in the foreground. The point, then, is to know them, possess them, and to manage them implacably in their antagonistic form. The production of subjectivity by capital will be entirely determined by the overriding necessity to disrupt the power which socialization places in the hands of the worker and the producer. Given the plan to disrupt subjectivity (which is, so to speak, the work of restructured capitalism), one may ask, 'In what form and in what ways is it developing?'

The mechanisms are complex. Indeed, the point is not to oppose a plan to the structures which emerge from the labour-processes (i.e. to prepare an external alternative) but to infiltrate these processes and to gain control of every change in their expression and of the entirety of the Umwelt in which they constitute themselves. The point is to reconstruct a political cycle where economic cycles have broken down, or rather, where they have lost all capacity to represent and dialectically to contain development. It is necessary to emphasize the complexity of the operations which command the capitalistic production of subjectivity in this situation. In this situation, the paradox is pushed to extremes and the production of subjectivity by capital tends towards the extreme disruption of subjects who are integrated into communal processes of production. Moreover, on the basis of this disruption, the production of subjectivity tends to feign the separation of the subjects.

The powerful origins of these processes – that is, the mechanisms of the production of subjectivity against the socialization of labour and against communication and cooperation – can be located in the present (although signs of their emergence were already apparent at the end of the seventies). There are above all *three instruments used* to break down – usefully, from the point of view of capital – the structural isomorphisms of the social: the reconstruction of the market, segmentation of the socialized labour force, and a very powerful ideological semiotic (of selection, hierarchy and individual values etc.). These being the three basic instruments of the capitalistic production of subjectivity, let us examine each of them in turn. In doing this, one should not forget the anger – and the effort to go beyond (with violence and ferocity) even the natural and historical limits – with which the projects are executed. This is even more the case – as is obvious – the more these projects are obscured by idealism, and are thus effectively inoperative. In short, this is even more the case the more the contradiction attacks the essence of the real (i.e. non-mystified) production of subjectivity and, that is, that production which can be understood from the proletarian point of view in adherence with the movements of the new productive cooperation. To start with, then, let us examine the *reconstruction of the market*. This is a very complex operation. A limited and destructive goal is at once attributed to it, namely the dissolution, or rather, the 'devolution' of the welfare state. Not by accident, in fact, the thousand manœuvres that organize the ideological machine of the 'reconstruction of the market', find an ensured instrumental rationality only in the case of the destruction of the welfare state – and thus, of welfare in all its forms. In the first place, the ideology of reconstruction has a profoundly destructive character – so destructive, in fact, that even the dissolution of those associations often so useful to bosses is sought. The reconstructed market must appear – and must actually be – the very Eden of economic freedoms. But it is not known how to describe these economic realities if not in terms of the negation of the characteristics of the welfare state. None of this should be obscure to us because the welfare state is, in fact, nothing other than the institutional manifestation of the socialization of labouring activity. This socialization involves a relatively instrumental use of political intervention (which usually means *state* intervention). Its aim is to underpin the socialization of labouring activity and on this basis to redistribute the wealth produced by the new productive actors. Therefore, the *destruction of the welfare state* implies the disruption of the socialization of labour. The reconstruction of the market will be a programme of exclusively negative power. (Clearly, even this goal will require the use of instruments and interventions which have profound effects and are of an entirely positive character; the purpose of the operation is, however, mystifying and destructive.) Reconstruction of the market means giving a free hand to the individualistic pillage of social cooperation; it means to promote the ignoble legend of competition and to collaborate in the expropriation of communication. In the second place, at the head of the reconstruction of the market, capitalist ideology places the objective of *segmenting the labour market*. It is not enough – say the theorists of the capitalist offensive – to destroy the conditions of the socialization of the labour force or the horizontal communication entailed by productive cooperation; more positively, it is necessary to establish conditions of separation and detachment, and effective obstacles to the cooperative process. Segmentation – as we have already seen above – is an essential instrument for this goal. It is not sufficient, however: *the dual society*, which is the outcome of this capitalist quest for division, must be capable of reproducing itself as such. It is necessary that successive and continuous motors of division be set in motion. Segmentation thus becomes an ideal horizon, an indefinite process of separation and a regulatory idea. The almost religious – and therefore even more mystified – spirit of inequality among people is inherent in this project. All the objective aspects of social organization, from wages to the family, from employment opportunities to schools and research (and above all the international dimensions such as emigration, immigration, peripheral productive units, peripheral Fordism etc.), must be affected by the spirit of inequality. With this we arrive at the third part of the analysis of the process of the disruption of socialization, namely *hierarchy and its ideological canons*. Destruction of the welfare state and reconstruction of the market, the dissolution of the social nature of labour, segmentation and fragmentation of the labour-market – and finally the dual society and all the other filth which this generates – would have no sense if they were not expressly interconnected within a model of extended reproduction which – to a certain extent – proves to be an independent force and a plan of separation. The capitalistic disruption of the socialization of the labour force and of the communal nature of communication and labouring cooperation is here promoted in terms of extreme mystification and in terms of a radical alternative project. It is promoted as the decision and separate point of view of the class struggle. By this I mean that even capital abandons the cherished dialectic. From an idealistic and typical point of view we thus grasp the highest capitalistic subjectivity. Hierarchical values – which as always, are a conglomeration of traditional elements of privilege and of meritocratic functions – are here imposed, or rather produced and reproduced. In bringing this operation to a conclusion, capital realizes its own antagonistic strategy for the labour force and the strategy which emerges from it. At this point capitalist subjectivity is entirely evident. As is by now clear, its definition has nothing in common with substantialistic presuppositions of any kind. Capitalist subjectivity is a mechanism, a subject constructed by the process, the consolidation of a strategy of struggle and of destruction of the adversary – after having exploited it from top to bottom. This strategy is traced out by the micro-conflict of daily clashes in order to be displaced by exploitation in general towards the definition of large pairs of antagonistic relationships. In this way, the antagonistic opposition is formed on a macroscopic level. It is a molar opposition for or against exploitation, for or against socialization, equality and liberty.

We will now make a final point in this connection. As we have seen previously (and it is something which applies both in reality and to our method) the strategies which run through the social are both rooted in the social and related to the sphere of ideology. Their reality is always and in every case bivocal. To put it in Marxist terms, these strategies belong both to the structure and the superstructure; and they are involved in the combination of relationships through mechanisms of causation which are very articulated and complex. Here, however, we can provisionally establish a kind of law which derives from the observations we made above, namely that the ideological character of the idealistic aspects of capitalist strategies is more heavily emphasized the more pressing the need becomes to destroy the socialization of work and the more this project becomes exclusive and attempts to constitute an antagonistic alternative. To say this is to say that the establishment by capital of hierarchical values increasingly represents a deficit of reality: here the capitalist project no longer mystifies a reality but, observed closely, substitutes mystification for reality and thereby accentuates the emptiness of the world. It also scrapes away the verisimilitude of ideology. *The semiotic of hierarchy and its values* is a very abstract moment. It is not, however, a moment of that abstraction which singularly denies the individual characteristics of labour. Rather, it is a moment of that abstraction which is generically opposed to knowledge of reality. It is a function of command, an articulation of absurd but efficient signifiers. Here the production of subjectivity has become the production of the inhuman. This nazi aspect of capitalist ideology in the period of the socialized worker cannot be underestimated.

In opposition to all this, the workers must initiate an analogous process of antagonistic production of subjectivity. Just as the subjectivity we have been outlining until now is capitalistic, so the subjectivity of the workers must be proletarian. How can it be identified? How can it be recognized? It is difficult to reply to this question. However, we shall try to do so in the following chapter. For the moment, it is of interest to see whether, within the framework of the causes we have analysed, it is possible to recognize mechanisms which allow us to identify the beginning of those processes.

A first point is this: Let us imagine we find ourselves in the situation of an attack on the socialized labour force, such that we are, therefore, confronted by a process of the antagonistic constitution of the capitalist subject and the consequences this has for the workers' society. Now this situation – which is one which was witnessed at the *end of the seventies* – is not linear. There are, so to speak, incontrollable effects (which are perverse from the capitalist point of view, but virtuous from the opposing point of view) which free themselves. The capitalist attempt to break up the productive society sets in motion a variety of forces (such as moments of freedom and experiences of singularization) which, even if they escape the historical continuity of the workers' movement, are nevertheless not easily reconciled with capitalist plans for the market. In developing its strategy, capital is forced to recognize these new singularities but nothing tells us that this journey can be concluded according to the direction established by capital. In reality, these singular moments, although detached from the unity of the socialized labour process and from communicative cooperation (and sometimes ghettoized), manage to produce an effective resistance. They do not know a reconstructive project, but neither do they know – far less accept – the capitalist project. On other occasions in the history of workers' struggles we have found ourselves in analogous situations: the defeat of the struggles was followed by new experiences, often of pure resistance (such as emigration, for example). The defeats, however, were irrecoverable. In the seventies, *the defeat of the mass worker* and its organization was followed by a period of social dispersion and of *very much heightened mobility* in all senses. This *internal migration* along the arteries of society – this mobilization of social energies – was initially a phenomenon of pure *resistance*. It was, however, a very important resistance since it allowed the preparation of materials, conditions and instruments in anticipation of the *reconstruction of alternative or antagonistic mechanisms*. It is important to emphasize that at the same moment in which, in a situation of crisis, capital developed the strategy of antagonistic production, its opposite was also developed; or rather it began to be developed or to take shape as another tendency and as the hint of an antagonistic goal. In this origin there is no longer any dialectic. There are, rather, antagonistic paradigms which from the beginning confront each other and prepare themselves for the action. How does the mechanism subsequently develop?

In beginning to reply to the question I would say that the more the process – on the capitalist side – proceeds from the real to the ideal, the more – on the side of the society of the workers and of productive cooperation – the machine of constitution of the mechanism proceeds from the ideal to the real, and from the lack of determination to the maximum of singularization (or to put it in simple terms, *from resistance to appropriation, from reappropriation to self-organization*). In short this is a journey through the various figures of *self-valorization*. The maximum of ideal insistence is the state of resistance, whereas the maximum of real determination consists in the singularization of the processes of cooperation and in placing them at the service of an effective utopia, entirely subjugated by the singularities – the communist disutopia. We will explain all this later, however. Here, as has been done with regard to capital, it is necessary to remember that the complexity of the process does not detract from the relative linearity – even in the case of the workers' society – of the transfer from micro-conflict to the large molar and antagonistic confrontations of naked class struggle.

What does the movement from resistance to appropriation mean for the socialized worker? It means crossing, almost insensibly and unconsciously, that world of solid values that had been constructed during previous periods of struggle, opposing their residual consistency and the identity which resulted from it, to the active mystification which it underwent in the restructuration. However, this reconnection with a past reality (whose value-determination was enjoyed but which, on the other hand, has now been reduced by the bosses' counter-offensive, to little less than a pure horizon of needs) is not sufficient, unless – and it is something essential – we are able to define, in this past, a deep line, a concrete substratum to which neither the conscience nor the memory attest, but only the continuity of the struggles. And all the modifications, breaks and radical innovations gather around that constructed and re-found base, around that dynamic profile of a subjective ontology. Thereby, every new expression of alternative values is involved in a process which identifies and realizes the productive society as a subject. In order for need to be realized, or rather, in order for the values to be revealed, the connections of sense and meaning from which such values emanate, require a subjective transformation. This transformation is a transformation in which subjectivity is unfurled, through the reappropriation of communication and the experience of cooperation, a *transformation in which the material operation of reappropriation is also a moment of self-awareness*. It is a period in which self-organization becomes the presupposition of an already-known self-valorization – one which had perhaps never ceased (at least in the form of resistance), but which, however, is not open, as it lies in the most profound experience. It is a self-valorization which is organic to the social subject, one which is inherent in the socialized worker (since all its movements are valorizing). Therefore, a semiotic for the antagonistic production of subjectivity begins to be indicated also from the proletarian point of view; between resistance and appropriation, between reappropriation and a new constitution, the process of subjectivization from the proletarian point of view is revealed – in society, within the qualitative transformations that it has actually undergone. To conclude, let us therefore indicate the principal stages of the process that leads to the definitive formation of the alternative proletarian mechanism. Such stages are the stages of an event that we have experienced and that we continue to struggle over. They are the definitive elements of a semiotic of the socialized worker – at least at the level of our awareness of it, in the genesis of its constitutive process. *In the first place*, they constitute an experience of struggle as resistance and as a radicalization of the event of the mass worker; a struggle – articulated, widespread, and deep – against work, on the margins of the mode of production of advanced capitalism; *then*: a qualitative leap, on this basis, towards the irreversible recognition of the social nature of the labouring processes, of the hegemony of the social production in this new form of production; *on the other hand*: a capitalist project designed to dominate this new reality, this very powerful, efficient, brutally repressive project. *In this emergency* they constitute a retreat of working-class consciousness, a relative cancellation of the movement of the socialized worker, as a consequence of the destructive impact of the restructuration and of the repression; the resistance and *the thousand clandestine stories* of a never-destroyed movement, against exploitation, for equality, for the reappropriation of communication and for control over cooperation; *contemporaneously*: the denunciation of, and the struggle against the enemy, by now newly recognized, i.e. against he who arrogates the right of command and of expropriation above and against the labouring communication and cooperation; *finally* – and it is the problem of today – the construction of adequate forms of mass, vanguard organization, in order to lead both the struggle for power and the management of production. Here is how the antagonistic production of subjectivity has come to be organized from the point of view of the socialized worker. In the next chapter we will consider this realty in a historical perspective: we are at an advanced stage in the construction of the revolutionary organization of the socialized worker.

8

Autonomy, from clandestinity to the party

The end of the century is already an immersion in a future which presents itself as the crisis of our recent past and as the announcement of an uncontainable innovation. The crisis is clear: we have defined it as a moment in which the future cannot be explained in terms of the past and in which the actions of the subjects cannot be reduced to the logical canon which is customary to us. As far as the innovation is concerned, it is indescribable: we understand it as a break, as the crossing of a qualitative threshold, as a sudden and violent moment in which the culture and project of reformism come to an end. The innovation can also be historically located in the sixties up until 1968. Then there seems to be pause in the innovation, as if it had subsided in the crisis: for a long period it is not discernible. The consitution continues to develop, however, and then everything which had hitherto lain dormant suddenly reappears. Life manifests itself in history. The class struggle and its innovations – and the innovation which constitutes the *differentia specifica* of the twentieth, as compared to the nineteenth century – are revealed in that guise. *The twentieth century is a transition period.* A large proportion of it is a continuation of the nineteenth century. In it, the twenty-first century begins to unfold. We are living through this transition period and transforming it into an experience which, from a theoretical point of view, is crucial. This is because, in the transition period, we have seen the historical proletarian subject (which established itself as a social subject at the end of the nineteenth century) become hegemonic and open itself to a future which is at the same time unknown and constructed, overpowering and inexistent. The twentieth century has been extremely brief, restricted, congealed and confined within the parameters of a transition period which for each of us may become (if it has not already become) a biographical matter. The biography in question is a biography of struggle, a tragedy or an enormous adventure. It is also, thereby, an experience which can be described in theoretical terms.

The end of the century is already an immersion in the future. The indications of the transition have been particularly striking. Let us consider just two such indications, namely *the cycle/crisis of the dollar between 1971 and 1982* and *the cycle/crisis of the price of oil between 1973 and 1986*. In order to describe these cycles, it is necessary to return to the emergence of the socialized worker in 1968. It is on the basis of the shock brought about by his/her appearance and struggles that, in order to contain insurrectionary initiatives and revolutionary struggles, capitalist initiative attempted to mobilize reformist energies. The dollar, as a result of its fluctuation and its new independence brought about by its detachment from the gold standard in 1971, was thereby thought of as the instrument of a free quantification of capitalist initiative; or rather it was thought of as such wherever it was feasible to implement reformist policies in response to the sudden appearance of the new social subjects. This led to a heightened importance of the role of the dollar and the beginning of an entirely new era for the currency. As the unfettered medium of real equivalence, it was a symbol of freedom and a protagonist of reformism; but as the currency of the principal imperialist state, it was the overdetermination of every historical movement of class-struggle. To what extent can freedom and overdetermination coexist? The recent history of this ambiguous connection demonstrates the crisis of such a connection: the period which began in 1971 with the detachment of the dollar from gold, was ended – or rather was displaced – in 1982 by the Mexican debt crisis. The currency thereby exhausted its capacity to act as the agent of reformism and as the promoter of the enlargement of the world market. The need to control and overdetermine, together with the urgent need to break down all rigidities, presented itself as a paradox. At least this much is certain: that which is perhaps valid for the central countries, is certainly not valid for the peripheral ones. The

Mexicans' refusal to pay their debts thus became an example and a precedent. Freed from gold, the dollar thus began to fall in value and instead of representing freedom and strength, came to represent arbitrariness and disorientation, malaise and uncertainty. The period between 1971 and 1982 (and the subsequent period which is beginning to take shape) demonstrates a development which is typical of a situation of disequilibrium between the dynamics of the mode of production and the forms of control. Why, then, did the extraordinary American initiative of 1971 fail? The answer is that the American government had not grasped the qualitative leap which the determinations of the socialized worker had brought about on a world scale. Where the growing socialization of labour prevented the enormous growth of productivity from being re-subjected to the rules governing interest and profit, there was no possibility of exercising control. Because of this lack of comprehension *the dollar-cycle was quickly reduced* to a 'political cycle', or rather, to an 'ideological cycle'. Reagan succeeded Nixon and the others: the ideological cycle was thereby shown to the masses and the relative rationality of the Nixonian project of 1971 was diluted in the broth of reactionary propaganda. It was the caricature of every instance and event.

Briefly, it seems possible to set out the following *theorem*: The emergence of the socialized worker on a world scale imposes reformism, but at the same time it subjects it to an instrumental use – which in many respects is lacerating – aimed at consolidating its own epiphany and at demonstrating – through the expanded form of reproduction – its own irreversible genesis. Capitalist reformism is thus provoked, used, worn out and beaten. It thus degenerates in a tangle of insoluble contradictions. To an increasing extent after 1968, the crisis of the relationship between regimes of accumulation, forms of reproduction and dimensions of mobility on the one hand, and institutional dynamics on the other, became profound. Only the recognition of the central, unsuppressible and hegemonic reality of the socialized worker was to allow the reconstruction of a progressive political horizon. And since this was not something which the capitalist class wanted, *the problem of the proletarian revolution was put back on the agenda.*

If we consider the 'oil cycle' between 1973 and 1986, we find ourselves confronted, so to speak, by paradoxes which are even more evident than those which we emphasized with regard to the dollar-cycle. In this case too, in fact, a certain reformism – above all, but not exclusively, in the moderate Arab countries – sustained by the high price of oil, was unleashed. In the Arab countries, the political motives which inspired the reformist project were those of determining – through oil-based accumulation – new centres of capitalist expansion. These were intended, on the one hand, as compensation for the political defeat which the moderate Arabs were to inflict on popular and revolutionary forces – Palestinian and otherwise – and on the other, as a cover for the defeat which the same moderate forces were to suffer at the hands of the imperialist powers over the Israeli question. As far as the Middle East is concerned, the oil cycle is thus a highly integrated political cycle of reformist inspiration, one which is regulated hierarchically and structurally. It involves three factors: the offering of employment-opportunities to a hard-working people while at the same time decisively eradicating their revolutionary power; a series of politically moderate nations, enriched by the new – and ever-increasing – price of oil and willing to act, in the medium term, as the element of control as far as accumulation and the maintenance of order in the region are concerned; a supreme imperialist power – and thus an implacable overdetermination – established in the region in order to control the complex ebb and flow of events. Throughout the decade the rest of the world was to pay for the stability brought about by this scheme through proportionate shares of total oil expenditure which was redistributed by increasingly durable inflationary mechanisms. Then, however, the paradox was revealed: in the Western countries, the working class was increasingly less willing to accept the blackmail which was entailed by the above-mentioned equilibrium and the costs and inflation. In the countries of the Middle East, therefore, the contradiction was felt much more profoundly and dramatically – above all from the moment when the Iranian revolution and the desperate holding-back of the Palestinian revolutionary project decisively illustrated the impossibility of combining moderate reformism with a project of imperialist regulation. When – beyond all expectation, and with consequences that are no longer easy to perceive – the whole situation exploded, we were again able to appreciate *the impossibility of combining regimes of accumulation* (even though they may be reformist and even though they may be based on a broad range of determinations) *and conservative institutional and political projects.*

The failure of the project of stabilization after 1968 as a result of the first manifestation of the power of the socialized worker, could not have been more evident. Today *Reaganism is coming to an end.* Reaganism was a strategy which attempted, in the most grotesque fashion possible, to launch the project of a market freedom that might be consistent with, and confined within the framework of the most brutal conservatism. It attempted, in the harshest way possible, to give back to capitalist civilization a new, mystified hope in increased productivity. In taking note of the end of this project, we cannot but be delighted that it will be impossible to stop the emergence of the new subject. The latter cannot be annulled; it constitutes the essence of the contemporary period; it is that immersion in the future that we are already living through. And without doubt, neither the neo-liberal fools nor the systemic wizards will succeed in depriving us of the pleasure of freeing ourselves – quickly, and with a small, brief flash – from all that rubbish which, designed to serve mystificatory ends, has occupied both political debate and library shelves in the last ten years.

The socialized worker and his/her autonomy are, then, at the centre of the debate. This is an attempt to trace that clandestinity of his/her movements which, through a long history, leads back to a strong appearance of surfaces and of powerful innovation. We know the themes around which the productive person of the socialized worker is constituted: the relationship between intellectual and manual labour; the dynamic between centre and periphery, and between North and South, which is reproduced through the expansion of the world market and the disruption of its hierarchies; the tension between production and reproduction and the issue of the social productivity of female labour, which, as a result of the foregoing tension, comes to the foreground; fourthly, the nature-history problematic, or the combination of ecological determinations which production, in its new social aspects, must assume as fundamental; finally, the synchronic dialectic of freedom and equality, between wages and the welfare state which summarizes all the political aspects – both material and ideal – of the development of the person of the socialized worker. Now, leaving aside for a moment the assessments which must be made of each of these relationships, there is a fundamental aspect which must be emphasized, namely that all linear analyses, however they are developed, and including those highly sophisticated analyses relating to the change in class-composition, are of no use in explaining the virtuous synthesis in which the above-mentioned elements and constitutive couples are prepared. Both materialistic explanations from the workers' side and technological ones from the capitalist camp, don't even begin to touch the substance of the problem – which is that of the political autonomy of the new subject and the radical nature of its emergence.

Let us retrace our steps and go over this point in more detail. The conceptualization of the socialized worker at the level of class-struggle is, as we have often repeated, characterized by the *complete restructuring of social relationships*. Social relationships are discovered to be outwardly antagonistic. As a dialectical sequence and a technological causal chain, the sequence struggle-development-crisis-restructuration (and so on) no longer has occasion to manifest itself. The relationship is, instead, accompanied by two tendencies which thwart the social body, crystalizing its tensions. There is no longer any temporal continuity; therefore there is no longer any past or any memory. There are only ontological continuities which are revealed by discontinuity. This discontinuity is a discontinuity in the deposits of composition and in the divergent accumulations of needs and desires when the latter take on a new form. It is also a discontinuity of the ontological procedures themselves. Then there is the revelation, through sudden emergencies – like discontinuities in the historical process – of new events. We are living through this reality and the apocalyptic aspect which accompanies it without reality thereby becoming less gratifying. *The socialized worker discovers that the social relationship is an autonomous foundation*. The concept of the socialized worker is the concept of a political act which establishes an independent political relationship: an antagonistic society as far as power relationships are concerned, alternative with regard to processes of production and reproduction, and autonomous with regard to the subject's and the comunity's aims. And it must be borne in mind that there are no *dei ex machina* which in some way assist the development of the process, or bring about qualitative leaps, or in some way realize the same causality. Rather, the process exists within a free structural horizon, in a domain permeated by a combination of mechanisms which become a system gathered around the central axis of the development of socialized labour. The only radical guiding thread which accompanies this constitution is the political and the autonomy of the political (or rather, the politics of autonomy).

Our problem is one of *establishing the autonomy of the political – not where the political is emancipated from the social, but where the political entirely and independently reassumes within itself the social.*

It is strange to arrive at such a conclusion and to glorify the autonomy of the political after a large part of our political argument and our revolutionary experience has been taken up with a polemic against the concept of the 'autonomy of the political' as it had been elaborated within the Third International and in the Bolshevik Party, and which, here and there, had been taken up again by sad epigoni of that nevertheless glorious tradition. It is worthwhile retrieving the expression 'autonomy of the political' and overthrowing its systematic placement and its historical meaning. In the theoretical situation in which we are acting, *the political* is not, in fact, an abstraction of the social, but is, rather, a *social abstraction.* The political is communication; it is the symbolic; it is the material which establishes social, productive cooperation and allows the latter to reproduce itself and produce value. It is not, then, so much the concept of 'autonomy of the political' (which could usefully be discarded from the tradition) which changes, as the concept of the 'political' *tout court*: a politics which establishes a foundation; a politics which is implicated in the very concept of autonomy. A very impetuous historical process which has pushed the dialectic between autonomy and institutions to the point of explosion – to the point of an irreversible break – now gives us a concept of autonomy which, through antagonism and alternatives, independently establishes the political. Machiavelli is thus rediscovered, at the point he started from, in the social.

However, the critics will retort, *autonomy* was defined as something '*non-political*'. Certainly, it was defined as non-political in the sense that it was opposed to the way in which the political manifests itself in the systems of advanced capitalism. The political = the mystification of the social organisation of work = annulment of the subjectivity which the mechanisms of struggle produce = domination rather than sabotage. Now, however, due to the worker's invasion of society, the placement and the meaning of the terms change: there is no possibility of reserving areas for the expansion of the political; everything is political, and there is a politics of power and a politics of autonomy. While the first remains as we have described it – a dark grandeur subtends its real appearance – the second is an act of recognition which ontologically permeates and establishes reality. It establishes the social by instituting the subjectivity of the project and setting adrift the objectivity of the mystification. In terms of the categories used by the socialized worker, the autonomy of the political is a term which expresses the self-recognition of the social; it is a term which expresses the productive reappropriation of the social; and finally it is a term which expresses the innovative transgression of the social. The political autonomy of the socialized worker = the self-recognition of the subject = the reappropriation of the social = the political innovation of the world.

Above all, then, there is the *self-recognition of the subject*. It would be repetitive to emphasize the process which leads the socialized worker to recognition of him/herself. However, the specificity and the novelty of the problem are apparent once one considers the mechanisms by which, from the state of covertness, the socialized worker passes over to overt action, or rather, once one studies and organizes the covert political movements of the productive machine of the socialized worker. At this point it is necessary to discard a term which historical materialism had taught us to consider as sacrosanct. By this I mean that it is not the material character of the movements which generates consciousness, but collective consciousness which, through its own development, establishes the material aspects of the very movements of the productive figure. This transition breaks with tradition but modernizes materialism. Self-valorization comes after self-organization and not before. Every spontaneous conception of valorization processes is thereby eliminated: the subject presents itself through self-organization and self-recognition. *Organization is the central and basic material element of the constitution of the subject.* In this constitutive mechanism there are no other elements which are as strong or as important. Above all, there is no element, apart from organization, which constitutes the lowest common denominator of the development of the socialized worker. But if organization constitutes the bricks and mortar of the constitution of the new subject, and if organization constitutes and fuels the mechanisms which are the producers of the subject, then – as the synthesis of intellectual labour, of alternative choices and of organizational strength and plans – consciousness is the central element of the productive process of the subject. *To organize militancy* is to develop the contents and the constructive tension of consciousness. There exists no consciousness apart from militancy and organization. The fact remains that what we are here asserting (together with its roots and causes) comes before us – just as ontological determinations come before the movements of action. Everything brings us back to this ontological limit. The experience of the socialized worker began against the great background of class struggle once the cycle of struggles of the mass worker had lessened and once capitalist restructuration had begun to affect the social. The immediate satisfaction of expression and of new alliances; awareness of the social nature of work and of the hegemony of new productive protagonists in the determination of labouring cooperation: all this has been crushed by repression. But it has continued to exist all the same – *clandestinely* – as the framework of resistance. In the normal course of events, repression is dialectical in nature: at the same time as it represses, it recuperates. In our case, however, repression was far from being functional in this sense. It was unable to affect the new subject, and far from recuperating the latter, it underwent its impact. Neither the traditional corporative organizations of the professional workers, nor the favourable market situation of the mass worker's trade unions, nor the subsidies of the welfare state were at that stage able to sustain the productive mechanism: only the new subject was able - through the continual reproduction of its own subjectivity – to do this. In these circumstances, apart from the clandestinity imposed by capital, the organization was formed and reformed. It is not possible, in this connection, to make any fine distinction between the inexistence of the political organization as compared with the productive organization, because while in general this distinction is only a fine one, in the case of the socialized worker it is, as we have seen, false. Then, when the new circumstances push the subject into the foreground, the complexity and the profundity of the movements of organization and con-sciousness will come to be revealed. One final point: what is happening within the clandestine processes of the socialized worker, does not necessarily constitute a memory. Sometimes, indeed, when one lives through phases of overt struggle, the memory may be one of defeat and of the thousand-and-one underhand or mistaken methods which the clandestine struggle involved. No, this is not the point: self-organization precedes memory. Apart from memories, there exists for the new subject an ontological permanence, an advanced unconscious and an accumulation of experiences. The reappearance of overt struggle reorders and imposes these latter as the matrix and perspective of self-recognition. Thereby, apart from memories, through the constitution of the new subject, the genetic process continues: not in a fetishistic way, but in a creative manner. And when the new subject emerges, it carries with it all the experience of the past. The whole of existence is comprised – as in a Leibnizian cosmogony – within the new subject. It is for this reason that existence begins with self-organization. That is to say, existence begins again where our ancestors left off. To start again from the beginning is never to turn back.

The reappropriation of the social is the second term of the new synthesis. Once again, implicit in this term is the autonomy of the political, i.e. the autonomy of the ontological political which we said above was becoming overt. The sense in which the autonomy of the political constitutes a point of departure should now be entirely clear because the socialized worker does not recognize disparities which cannot be related to his/her project – which cannot, in other words, be placed in the service of his/her will to knowledge and power. All this is possible because the social – to the extent that it constitutes the fabric of production and does not recognize transcendence with regard to work – is entirely and fully penetrated by the socialized worker; it is penetrated according to determinations, tensions and constitutive mechanisms. Therefore, that which is set in motion – namely *the reappropriation of the antagonistic social nexus* – is a genuine mechanism of reappropriation. Several points need to be made at this stage. In the first place, this process of reappropriation is dominated by the self-recognition of the subject in the sense that the ontological tension of the constitution promotes equality between the components of the constitutive process (or at least, promotes their equality as elements which are equally necessary for the constitutive process itself). The reason for this is obvious. In the constitutive process, diversity and difference are accompanied – in a horizontal and transversal manner – by the law of unification, aggregation and recognition. Even from the formal point of view, diversity exercises a fundamental influence with regard to the aggregation of the components of the new subject: in the sense that the transversal nature of the cooperative relationship is fundamental in this connection. Equality is the unifying criterion of the freedoms, behaviours and activity of the subjects which constitute the new productive protagonist. In short, equality is effective within the machines, mechanisms and forms of the constitution. On the other hand, however, equality is also a force which is turned towards the outside, one which is decisively organized for the resumption of control, i.e. for the expropriation of the expropriators. This is the second point which needs to be made, and it is important to emphasize it. What it amounts to is that reappropriation is an entirely material process. It is a reabsorption of the social by the political – a process which cannot be obstructed save by the diversities and pauses which manifest themselves in the transition from a formal possibility to the historical determination. This means that *the productive too must be incorporated within the political*. In the person of the socialized worker and in the strength of his/her hegemony over the whole of society, the productive is already formally incorporated within the political. The productive must now become incorporated in real terms in the sense that productive organization, being at the same time *social* organization, must become identical to the organization of the socialized worker. *The party of the socialized worker is the subject of production*; it reabsorbs social production within itself. Expressed briefly, the third point we wish to make is this: through production, *the egalitarian substance of the subject* necessarily becomes social. The egalitarian premises of communism's organization of society, of production and of the state, at this point become possible. Equality then reigns everywhere: as an element of the reappropriation of production by the social subject, this premise is also the indication of a very radical democracy.

We thus arrive at the third point which interests us, namely at the description of the *innovative transgression of the social* which characterizes the constitution of the proletarian subject and its organization. Here the issue of antagonism, which we have so often recalled and re-elaborated in these pages, once more becomes central to the argument. This is because self-recognition and the process of social production which the new subject appropriates to itself (to the point of wanting to identify itself creatively with its forms), become the motors of a continuous process of innovation – and this from a point of view different from the one characterized by the simple definition-constitution of horizons of values, alternatives and theoretical innovations. Here, once again, the problem becomes a practical one: the process in which we are involving ourselves is a process of disruption, of transformative determinations and of constitutive mechanisms. At this point the constitutive ontology opens out onto the margins of the non-being; it tends towards that new reality which does not yet exist. Paradoxically, until this moment, the revolutionary process was aimed at the restoration of the given, i.e. at the restoration of what had already been constructed – which repression and restructuration had tried to hide; now the revolutionary process reassumes the characteristics of transformative violence. As the power to identify and define individuality, the terms of antagonism once more become crucial. Leninism and violence once more become of contemporary relevance. It might be asked whether this does not contradict that superabundance of democracy that has hitherto been displayed by the constitutive process. But why should it be so? The self-recognition of the subject and the reappropriation of the supporting framework of the social constitute a democratic process of the organization of production and an exclusive determination of the latter against the subject's enemies – or rather, against all the political and natural limits which the historical process, capitalist domination and production for profit have consolidated against the movement for liberation. Here, autonomy of the political is a concept which more closely approximates the traditional conception: this is possible to the extent that the social has been absorbed into the political and the political consequently transformed. The socialized worker is no longer simply a product of the history of capitalism, neither is s/he merely the necessary condition for production *en general*. S/he is, rather, a subjectivity which underlies every innovation and which is stretched out as the egalitarian fabric of all socialization. S/he constitutes a subjectivity which produces power through every productive community. Thereby s/he legitimates his/her own *right to the revolution*. Revolution is knowledge and power: the problem of the legitimacy of the revolutionary process is not an abstract one; neither is it a simple piece of juridical nonsense. Rather it is the expression of hegemony; it is the identification of an antagonistic relationship; it is destiny. Between clandestinity and the party, autonomy thereby establishes a complete scheme of organizational, productive and revolutionary potentialities.

The mechanism of hope is linked to that of realism. Once the proletarian social subject has greatly increased its penetration of the real, then we know that the revolution is possible. Utopia is thus accompanied by the certainty that reality is oppressive though under control. Let us call this situation 'dystopia'. This means that we have reached the threshold of victory and that the causes which inspire us are irresistible. It also means, however, that victory will require the employment of new and terrible forms of violence; that it will require the direct organization of the social, the reappropriation of production and the establishment of a new social and productive order. We know that all this is necessary – and yet we do not want it. But it is not something we can decide about. We are at the mercy of the joyful excesses of knowledge and of the community.

PART 2

9

Letter to Félix Guattari on 'social practice'

October, 1984

Dear Félix,

I have been asked to make a contribution to your meeting in Montreal, and I am happy to devote some thought to it. But I don't like the idea of a manuscript which I could entrust to the post for that far away meeting: it would seem dry and pretentious. So, on second thoughts, I've come to the conclusion that the best thing to do is to ask you to read this letter at the conference – the latest of those I have sent to you, and which concerns, as usual, our study of 'social practice'. In this way you will be obliged to intervene, to clarify the discussion's presuppositions, and, perhaps, to polemicize with the others – and with myself. This is how my dry and distant contribution will become living and immediate – as immediate as is my desire to resume, after several years of forced absence, a productive discussion with all the comrades.

Now, it was obvious that, having outlined several very general programmatic elements in 'Les nouvelles alliances', you and I would have to pose the problem of social practice. Programmes must, in fact, be realized, otherwise it is pointless to enounce them. But it is also true that a theme such as that of social practice has been subject to such a degree of discredit and irony in recent years – such are the renegades! – that one is obliged to ask oneself not only if a social practice, a subversive and transformative militancy, are still possible, but even if a programme is formulatable and a revolutionary discourse communicable. In order to understand it – and, if necessary, to quell any doubts – let us examine the matter more closely.

On other occasions I have been convinced that the two possibilities – that regarding the programme and that regarding practice – were linked by way of a single test: if practice must verify the truth of the programme, still, the programme is formed only to the extent that the subjects realize it. When I was young, we used to call this virtuous circle 'with-research' and in concrete terms we made it live in the class struggle. In the sixties, in the large factories, with the workers of Fiat or of the chemical factories, we had a single method of verification – immediate practice: the truth of the rejection of work was to bring the plant to a halt. Our arrogant scepticism about the ideology redeemed in practice an incontrovertible criterion of truth. The truth was indicated in its obviousness. How Wittgensteinian our workers were!

It would be easy, today and in this regard, to repeat that frank, and perhaps a little brutal, *verum ipsum factum* – but not realistic: it seems unlikely that the problem of social practice can be resolved by this repetition – neither by this theoretical repetition of a method, nor by that fantastic and felicitous practical memory. A method is not an instrument that can be indifferently applied. On the contrary, to tell the truth, the methodology exists only as the outline of a hegemonic subject, of an emerging truth, of a triumphant historicity. It is for this reason that they turn out to be so incredible – those who, afflicted by today's lack of resolve and the undoubted fading of the collective memory, feign critical adolescence and acne of their no-longer beardless skin, and imagine innovative happiness from within the linear rhythms of the consciousness and indefinite openings. . . Contrariwise, one fact is certain, namely that we have been defeated, and that this defeat has an ontological significance as important as that of the wealth of needs, desires and intelligence brought about by the transformation of consciousness in the revolutionary struggle. Now, let us ask ourselves, does the gravity of the defeat annul the significance of the transformation? I don't know. However, let us see. We have been defeated. We must start again. We must avoid reminiscence and realize that there is no possible repetition of the event. Even if everything were different, it would not be a case of Ulysses returning to Ithaca, but rather of Abraham marching towards the unknown. This defeat represents a solid barrier, an obstacle that will be removed from the road to consciousness and social subversion only by means of an enormous critical capacity. There remains but to reconsider the defeat – its causes and the ways in which the enemy has beaten us, remembering that there is no linearity to memory: there is only ethical survival. Before me I see industrial modernization, the rediscovery of profit and the reinvention of the market: *dura lex sed lex*. We have been defeated. The culture and the struggles of the sixties were defeated in the seventies. The eighties have witnessed the consolidation of the victory of capitalism. It could be, then, that I am an archeological remainder, that the defeat has been more important than the transformation that we have witnessed – if it were not. . .

If it were not that, there could be no modernization that avoided the places in which we were present: for the enemy our defeat came before his project, it was the formal cause of their modernization. But what can tie our negativity to their affirmation? The fact is that modernization is only the resumption and powerful mystification of what we were, of the knowledge that we used to possess. A few examples. In the first place, from the negative point of view, the restrictions to the exercise of command that we were building up had to be broken, and the demand for the guaranteed wage – based on the growth in effective demand and, by that time, uncontainable desires – rejected. Still in the factories, from the positive point of view, the bosses had to establish a new organization of production whereby submission to authority would be rewarded by 'less work'. Automation is freely invented by the knowledge that springs from the rejection of work but is, on the other hand, applied in order to break and mystify the generality of this proletarian and labouring need. In the second place, in society, through an attentive, articulated and intelligent manipulation of 'public expenditure' we were organising a new model of the social working day. In order to modernize, they also had to beat us on the social level, through inflation, through the renewal and the tightening-up of the rules of exclusion (repressive, hierarchical, functional, etc.) – but at the same time they had to submit to great processes of 'tertiarization' and the socialization of the entrepreneurial capacities – and that obliged them, consequently, to exercise generalized control through information technology. In this ambit a completely unresolved power battle is still developing. The computerization of the social is freely invented by the positive, labouring and proletarian utopia, concerning the length of the working day wrested from the control of the boss and verified, instead, within the horizons of labouring cooperation; but it is contrariwise applied to break the pressure of this need and to exploit capitalistically the power of social labour (of the labour that freed itself from a parasitic industrial territorialization and that reveals itself as social universality). Finally, wherever the struggles and desires for liberation stirred, we witnessed a similar mechanism: of oppression of our power and of mystification of our knowledge – a ferocious and bloody dialectic beneath which we have been ground.

To retrace the inherent characteristics of this enemy dialectic does not imply – if ever it is necessary to do so – that one should forget the defeat that has been inflicted on us – on the contrary, it means one should appreciate the intensity of it. It does not imply an impossible restoration of the past, but on the contrary, a confrontation with the new totality of the machine of domination. Totality is always that of the enemy: a totality that reclassifies the elements of concrete history and shapes them in the functional circularity of command. We possess some important, and at times fundamental, components that the machine of domination, however, now reorganizes in the new totality. Our memory can sometimes scour some of these elements – but after and in defeat, our knowledge is without power: within this powerful mystified world that opposes itself to us, within this scene of things and of commands, it is unable to cope. In order to begin living and organising the knowledge again we must, therefore, break this new totality. In order to give power again to our particularity, we must tear our segmented being from the totality in which it is imprisoned. If the totality in which we are gripped is not destroyed, there is no declaration of our contingency or of our particularity that can – as it has on other occasions – be applied to the reconstruction of the world.

The destruction of the limitations imposed by the totality thus poses itself as the first act of social practice – not because of a hankering after the past, nor because of nostalgia for angry, anarchic convulsions, or for the jesuitical bolshevik professionalism, nor, finally, in order to participate in a new Bacchian rite which, in seizing the heart of the state, both destroys it and appropriates it; but on the contrary, because this destruction is the only way to escape from the prison of the totality and to be free as segments, as particularity. It is on this act of destructive freedom that every constructive social practice can alone be founded.

Reformism, revisionism, socialism (in brief, all the ways of indicating that which, in the real movement, is opposed to communism), have all worked towards the negation of the link between liberation and destruction. From the social democratic crushing of the innovation concerning the continuity of values, to the Stalinist terror of the bureaucratic reduction of liberation to emancipation – in every case the relationship is denied and in place of its potentiality, monstrous consequences are presumed to follow. It is not surprising that nowadays the concept 'Left' carries little weight or significance given that one of its fundamental constitutive elements – the connection, precisely, between liberation and destruction – has been set aside. The concept of 'Left' is a concept of war: how can one claim to forget its destructive dimensions, how can one disavow the tension of power that upholds the will to liberation? Still more paradoxical, then, is the fact that the great increase in our ability to understand power – its extension described by Foucault, its molecular penetration described by our closest teachers and comrades etc. etc. – has been imputed to us and almost used against us: as if the awareness of its complexity, instead of making possible a higher destructive capacity, were a maze from which we could no longer extricate ourselves. Why should the ability to dominate complexity not be added to the knowledge of the transformation – respecting the singularities that compose it – against the necessity that is instead typical of the enemy power, of the forces of conservation, to destroy every single cause of liberty and life?

There is, besides, a kind of reluctance, of ontological diffidence – when it doesn't manifest itself as an ethical allergy – about destruction even in the closest milieu of our friends and comrades. Communism is, in fact, justly imagined as an enlargement of being. (And if we had not always been convinced of that, feminism would have enjoined it as an ultimatum.) But this reluctance is unjust because the destruction that communist liberation demands does not disfigure the surfaces of being. In this respect, I like to compare our type of destruction with the functions of philosophical doubt in the history of thought. Doubt, in fact, did not abuse, but discovered, the horizon of being: doubt in all its forms – from

Socratic ignorance to Cartesian doubt. But what destructive force it simultaneously introduced into the struggle for critical transformation! Let us look at Cartesian doubt. In the seventeenth-century world of the affirmation of the bourgeoisie and of the birth of the modern state, where ideas have reality, traditions have power and magic still constitutes a solid horizon – there, doubt is not only a science that affects ideas, but above all a practice that cuts into their concreteness, their mechanical existence and their material consistency. Doubt is a social practice destructive of things, not simply of spectres and of unreal ideas – destructive to the extent that it affirms liberty. It is not a suspension of reality but a power against the mystified form of the real, against the overbearance of power and of its illusory forms – faiths, errors, falsity, and all the 'idols' of consciousness. There can only be liberation, ethical existence in truth, from the moment of the destruction of the prison of knowledge.

The *posse*, therefore, comes before the *nosse*. It does so in all circumstances – in the case, for example, of the boss who, in order to dominate us, in order to deprive us of knowledge, must found all his dignity on power. The *posse* is, for him, the material condition of the *nosse*. But the *posse* is also the condition of the *nosse* in our case – the formal, rather than the material condition, but not any the less effective for that. Every time we are deprived of knowledge, this happens because we are defeated on the terrain of power. Certainly, our relationship to knowledge through power is not something vulgar – it doesn't have the arbitrary and blind significance of anticipation, or better, of the continuous overdetermination of knowledge: such is, instead, the quality of the relation that the boss has had with being ever since the supersession of the law of value and with it, the progressive function of capital. Rather, in the concept of the transformation itself – which forms a bridge between destruction and liberation in transformative social practice – the relationship between knowledge and power is full and very fertile. I like to play with the ancient couplet 'rational/irrational': in this metaphor the capitalist anticipation of the *posse* by the *nosse* is irrational; the proletarian relation is, instead, rational. By 'rational' here is understood that form which produces its own content. From the proletarian point of view, the *posse* and the *nosse*, destruction and liberation, are formally coterminous and mutually determining. The formal contemporaneity of knowledge is the condition of the material anticipation of power: in proletarian action, knowledge thus legitimates power, it makes it just. (N.B. Analogous reasoning can be employed with regard to the temporal dimensions of the anticipation of power by knowledge, and thus of the range of ontological qualities that temporality assumes from the point of view of capital and from that of transformative social practice. With regard to all this my work *Macchina Tempo* can usefully be consulted.)

Let us return then, my dear Félix, to the determinations of our enquiry into social practice. Starting from the beginning, let us develop several presuppositions. In the first place, if destruction is the internal condition of liberation, if the idea of a dynamic is fundamental to the definition of the concept of the transformation, the process of social practice does not, thereby, consist in a simple flux. On the contrary: we cannot consider social practice except as a notion of *consistence d'agencements*, or of investments and of social obligations. However, on the one hand this consistency is entirely ontological and does not provide for, or hold possible, superstructures or overdeterminations; on the other hand this ontological consistency is the interlacing of structural phylums and of dimensions each time specifically territorialized. The specification is given according to the historical series of the development of the forms and of the phases of the social organization. Now, within this framework, what does it mean to specify, determine, the connection between destruction and liberation, between power and knowledge? How is this relation represented when we descend from the very general discourse, to the concrete level of our society – to the determinate horizon of our ontological field – and confront the machinal and deterritorialized consistency of the institutions and of the statal, repressive, capitalistic *équipments collectifs*.

We can tackle this problem from two perspectives. The first is that of the structural organization of the state – and here it will serve as an example; the second is the specification of the organization of the process of liberation. Now, in both perspectives, the problem is constituted by the multiplicity of the senses in which it is possible to define the complexity of the social segments, and of the ontological and material functions which, converging, being synchronically interlaced, and accumulating historically, come slowly to form a structural totality.

It is evident – as you yourself maintain, Félix – that in talking about the state, for example, one is talking about a complex and stratified ontological dimension which, internally, comprises a series of levels that from time to time have been available for the territorialization of domination. These segments not only make up the state, but are produced and reproduced in subjectivity itself. Therefore, it is highly problematic to talk about the 'extinction of the state', and decidedly absurd to talk – other than metaphorically – in terms of its destruction, pure and simple. One can certainly always conceive of a new kind of formation of the social segments in the state – a formation which is more open in the sense of being composed of phylums which are deterritorialized to a greater extent and which have broken with capitalist policies of reterritorialization. However, all this requires an historical accumulation, which is both permanent and solid, of ontological experiences.

If we now take up the problem from the point of view of society and the social subjects, it can be understood how analagous processes take place, in parallel with those we have described on the level of the state. By this I mean that through the state and its stratified structure we can grasp the problematic development of experiences of organization in society and the accumulation off *équipments* which are addressed to the organization of social labour. Thereby, in the consciousness of the social subjects and their mass actions, we can trace elements of solidity and composition: experiences of struggle, victories and defeats, liberation and organization – but above all the history and the phylum of that knowledge of liberation which this entire broad development has nourished.

There was a time when, in the field of Italian and European workerism, a distinction was made between the technical and the political composition of social classes. This dual approach was merely analytic: the definition was in fact absolutely compact and its articulations were rightly verified in terms of the dimension of lived experience. However, there is an important affinity between the methodology of workerism and the more advanced methodology of historico-social investigation. By following the historical events surrounding the development of the organization of the working day, of the labour-market and of the structure of production and reproduction – and above all, by following the events surrounding the cycles of struggle – a description of the evolution of forms of class consciousness was successfully developed within the field of workerism. I consider this description to be unsurpassed and unsurpassable. This old piece of research has, then, now been confirmed. Even the history of the party (or in other words, the history of the continuous dialectic of class consciousness between the institutional *équipment* and the revolutionary *agencement*), in its anarchist, social democratic, socialist and Leninist forms was explained in terms of the evolutionary direction of class composition. It must be made clear that through this evolution, a genuine accumulation, a subjective dynamic of classification and of selection – of constitution – was discovered. All this became fixed in consciousness and past experiences of organization became the critical material for the continually renewed project of liberation. In this light, Leninism has effectively gone beyond anarchism and social democracy (which were Leninism's immediate antecedents and adversaries), reducing them to the segments of a new organizational form, salvaging them and reclassifying them as part of that original *agencement* which Leninism itself constitutes.

It is obvious that today, in the same way, should the struggles for liberation reach a critical stage, the worker of automation and social computerization would, in the new social form of organization and liberation struggle, understand and go beyond Leninism. Leninism is associated with liberation in the same way that anarchism is associated with Leninism. Within the new perspective of organization and struggle, Leninism is certainly an element to be overcome, and yet it will always be present in the *agencement* that we are going to prepare.

We can thus return to the discussion about the relationship between liberation and destruction. What can and must the destructive moment consist in at the current stage of social practice? It must consist in a dismantling of the state totality in which the segments of social and productive life and proletarian knowledge are about to be reorganized after the defeat of the 1970s. To defeat so-called modernization is certainly not to deny the importance of the technical and material transformations through which such modernization comes about. It is, rather, to remove them, to free them from the totality and to allow them to act against the overpowering end-state which capitalism today wishes to impose, to act against the ordered reterritorialization to which they would thereby be subjected. Destruction involves setting in motion a process of the general dislocation of the complex of components of production and reproduction. Certainly Leninism cannot be the basic driving force behind a social process of these dimensions and at this level. Leninism is devoid of these dimensions and these qualities from the start. It is estranged from the revolutionary needs of a social, productive class moulded by a hegemonic consciousness, and for this it can be broadly criticised. But besides criticism, let us be careful not to treat Lenin like a dead dog: Leninism stands, and will always stand, as a powerful reminder of an inescapable task of the class struggle, namely to destroy the totality of the enemy's mechanism of domination. For those that desire liberation, this is a task which must be continually reaffirmed. The overall dislocation of the framework of liberation thus involves, as a central experience, the destruction of the totality.

At this point we can begin a new series of reflections. To start with, let us remind ourselves of a few points. Today we are living through a period of defeat; let us never forget it. Alternative social practice (which in itself nourishes the theory of destruction) has little room for manœuvre. In fact such practice often tends to come to a conclusion within the framework of the totality produced by the ruling powers. And yet paradoxically, the ruling powers' awareness that they are confining and imprisoning , within the framework of the totality, others' rather than their own knowledge – knowledge which is not prepared for mediation, which is bitter and often unsuppressible – is very high. Certainly, the precariousness of domination is revealed not so much by the resistance of the oppressed, as by the fragility of the relations of domination. (Many dimensions should be analysed in this connection: the circulation and velocity of the mechanisms of consensus-formation, first of all, and the temporal dimension of legitimacy – but we will deal with all this on another occasion.) This objective aspect of the crisis must not be underestimated. The level of synthesis of domination and the degree of intensity in the enemy's capacity to produce subjectivity, are objectively minimal. The enemy's totality is unable to become organic. However – and here we come to a new series of reflections – this is not enough to establish a theory and practice which comprise a new notion of the 'Left'. In other words, it is not enough to conceive social theory and practice once more as basic activities, as an instance of the destruction of the opposing totality, or as an intervention in the objective contradictions. In short, social practice must be more than merely a theory of the crisis. Rather, it must also consider the ontological dimension and develop the constitutive tendency.

Now, when we destroy the ability of the enemy totality to contain, under its own domination, the knowledge of the exploited, in that very moment we acquire the ability to express the strikingly segmented character of theory, the unsuppressible particularity of desires, the entire transversal fabric of the *agencements*. Naturally, therefore, the entire weight of our social practice is involved in the destruction of the enemy totality. This is not because the act of breakage is something which is ontologically prevalent in the logic of social actions, but simply because the break gives rise to a large possibility for expression. Social practice is revealed as the exercise of liberation of desirous segments. When these expressions are revealed in their entirety, the machines of war – which can continuously dismantle the totality and which can turn this destruction into a constitutional fact – are set in motion. The concept of the party and of the 'Left', not simply as a machine of war but as the fullness of the expression of the segments and of these positive acts, can consequently be defined.

A series of historical processes of great significance which have developed in recent years are now making themselves felt and we are all aware of the great novelty that they represent: I am referring to the experience of Solidarnosc in Poland, the development of the Green movement in West Germany and – though much less organized and still in need of critical examination, yet very important for analogous reasons – a series of other new movements (such as the Autoconvocati in Italy, the Spanish struggle against NATO and the British miners' struggle). As compared to the organizational traditions of the workers' movement, the characteristics of these movements of organization and struggle are completely new. They cannot, therefore, be related to our history and our tradition. These movements illustrate both the ontological experience which the breach in the totality involves and the liberation of an energy which is permanently directed against the totality. Through an analysis of their composition, it would not be difficult to establish the material foundations of these political formations of the exploited class, but it is not necessary to do this here. What is more important is to emphasize the extraordinary innovation which all this illustrates. All the movements we have referred to have emerged after a deluge and it is not a bad idea to begin to realise that after a deluge not only does the world continue to exist, but that, in fact, such a calamity makes the soil highly fertile.

Let us see what the original characteristics of these movements are. In the first place they are movements of society; in the second place, they are not reformist movements, but movements of a different kind. Therefore, they are transversal and alternative. Their aim is not to take possession of the totality, but to destroy it; and in destroying it they affirm the independence of their knowledge (as well as its richness and its great multiplicity) and the influence of their power. I do not know according to what laws the presence of these movements gains its solidity; if such laws exist, however, it is necessary to discover them. I would like to throw down a hypothesis in this connection: the transition from fluidity to consistency, from movements to the party, depends essentially on the physical power of the masses and the degree of intellectual radicalism employed in establishing the relationship between the power of the new knowledge and destructive capacity. My impression is that the degree of solidity and of organizational stability – of ontological irreversibility – of a movement of struggle can be estimated (and possibly definitively established) only when it recognizes itself as the machine of a radical shift of the terms of politics. For the first time, as happens at the end of a utopian process that has developed for too long, paradoxically the autonomy of the political has taken shape as the independence of the social and as the rejection of the state.

Modern liberalism and the Right have understood many of the current determinations of revolutionary knowledge. As a result they have tried to mystify it and in this way we have witnessed the festival of the 'nouveaux philosophes'. There is really nothing *laissez-faire* about the alternative politics; on the contrary, that we should demand the total collectivization of the means of production, seems to us to be something obvious and banal. This is not the issue, however. The issue is another one, and it is very important. Freedom is the position of an essential diversity in a world where every possibility for conditions of freedom has otherwise disappeared and been absorbed into the totality of the ruling power. Only the irruption of difference – of an alternative ontology – within the institutional sphere of the political can thus permit the re-establishment of a sense of liberation and hence of a transformative social practice. In the philosophy of knowledge and science, in aesthetics and in all structural/functional systems, the emergence of a cataclysmic element – of radical difference – becomes, to the same degree to which humanity's horizon has suffered the totality, a fundamental moment. Only a subversive politics is unable to produce this excess of truth. And yet only subversive politics has repeatedly succeeded in providing an image of totality (which was not one of closure but of radical innovation) and thus in anticipating, in illustrating, the concept of cataclysm: in the absence of the cataclysms represented by the events of 1848, 1870, 1917, 1968. . . and so on, science would never have discovered the cataclysms of thermodynamics. The problem now, however, is to work up to a cataclysm. Saying this, however, involves many large issues that we are unable to resolve. Yet we must resolve this problem: namely, how to constitute ourselves as a cataclysm while working up to it, how to constitute ourselves as a totality without being such, how to constitute ourselves as a destructive opposition to capitalist and state totality without becoming its homology. What is needed is a radically democratic type of subversion where organizational forms have the impact of Leninism and the freedom of autonomy. Social practice must be an *agencement* of singularity – while avoiding the fetishism – whether this be called the 'general will' or the 'common good' – which intervenes to annul difference and turn it into a mere cog within the cosmos of exploitation.

To conclude, Félix my friend, a terribly powerful social practice of the enemy comes to mind – one which I have felt personally and which has contributed to our defeat. I am referring of course, to terrorism. It can be characterized very simply: it is a monstrous event – the mystified translation of state violence and of its empty fiction of totality, the unilateral, mystical blitz which drowns liberation in destruction, removing the dynamic and gentleness of the relationship once more. Yet terrorism has been a scandal and it will still be such unless we are able to avoid its monstrously scolding us with that which we are unable to be, namely people who rebel *sans phrase*; people who reconquer freedom and who make the break – which had been blocked by the ruling powers – effective. Terrorism has been able to accuse us of not being free, of not being David, but rather of being sheep before Goliath. We will be able to invent a new life from which both terrorism and state violence are banished only if we return to a militancy which is able to pose the completely radical problem of alternative values and methods. We will be able to do this only if our social practice is taken up by several thousands, several millions, of Davids.

The *posse*, it was said, came before the *nosse*. We will be accused, Félix my friend, of being fascists if we say such things. Let people say what they will, however. As far as I am concerned, I would be prepared to make things even worse (even to the point of bad taste and vulgarity): to say that love and only love can determine the connection between power and knowledge. From the depths of this shameful confession of irrationalism, I will bring some old friends to give me justification. The first among these is the good Spinoza, given that he too, in making reference to the maxim of the great philosophers of the Italian renaissance, believed that love lay between power and knowledge. Then, however, there is the eternal supporter of Goethe – Lenin: 'In the beginning there was action'. Let's get a move on.

A hug to everyone,
Yours,

Toni

10

Journeys through civil society (In memory of Peter Brückner)

1   The power of civil society is presented in Hegelian philosophy as the essential foundation of the theory of the state. If civil society is, in fact, the very foundation of the dialectic, then civil society is the permanent revolution – which dialectically poses the need for, and thus the legitimacy of, the state. In Hegel, the revolution is, in this sense, the very basis of the state. The 'taking of power' by civil society, is the realization, the negation and the sublimation of this. It is enough to have gone through Hegel's writings – not so much his youthful works as those of his early adulthood (during the Jena period) – to see this essential feature of the Hegelian system: the *Philosophy of Right* of Hegel's maturity does not repudiate it, but simply deprives it of all its potentially subversive effects. It is, however, true that this act of deprivation is successful, so that in Hegel's mature works, what had been a revolutionary dialectic is transformed into a veritable theodicy – in the *Philosophy of Right*, in fact, the revolution (i.e. the movement of civil society) in founding the state re-establishes order. At this point, the state is able to become an element of the philosophy of history – it loses all qualities of dialectical changeability, every vestige of negativity and all ontological potential in order to place itself within the perspective of divinity. The revolutionary legitimation of the state is surreptitiously expelled and substituted by the latter's metaphysical legitimation.

Hegel's argument is not, however, imprecise. The revolutionary establishment of the state theorized by Hegel is qualified by the bourgeois organization of civil society. The mechanism of revolutionary legitimation is reproduced by the dialectic of social labour as capitalist society begins to organize it – its organization is what capitalist production (in the Jena writings), bourgeois society and its alliances (in the Berlin philosophy) bring about. In Hegel, then, the dialectical process of the establishment of the state starting from civil society, follows that rhythm of progressive vertical organization which the history of the capitalist revolution prefigures as its own necessity and as its genuine 'idea of reason'.

By submitting the dialectic to a materialist analysis of classes, Marx struck at the heart of the Hegelian conceptions of civil society and the state. At the level of a horizontal analysis of the balance of forces between classes, Marx indeed emphasizes the essential insolubility of the dichotomy which capitalism determines within the relations of production. Consequently, the dialectic of the capitalist revolutionary project is also insoluble. Starting from civil society, this project aims at organising in a vertical system in the form of the state, the value and the specificity of the capitalist organization of production. Under no circumstance, then, is capitalist progress able to establish anything more than progressive revolutionizing thresholds. The same revolutionary state does not, and never will be able to bring the movement of civil society to an end. Civil society becomes divided and not sublimated. Sublimation is ideology, pure and simple. It is the collapse of science into mythology. Every theory of the state is theological. Revolution has hitherto only perfected the state; the point, however, is to destroy it. But this destruction is internal to the dichotomy by which civil society is organized; it exists within its horizon.

2   The conception of 'taking power' and the vertical organization of the decisive mechanism of the capitalist dichotomy of society in relation to the state, typical of orthodox Marxist-Leninist conceptions, represent a genuine restoration of the Hegelian dialectic. The so-called 'crisis of Marxism' is thus essentially a crisis brought about by the attraction of revolutionary thought (and of the Marxian reading of the revolution) in the field of Hegelianism-Leninism. Marxism's crisis with regard to theories of the state, therefore, is due to the fact that Marxism has as a consequence been transformed into the old art of legitimation of the state. It is not, however, legitimate to attack Marxism from the right – caught in

this cold current, Marxism has lost its critical edge and has become the philosophy and logic of capital. Criticism can only come from the left, so to speak – i.e. from within the perspective of transformation, from the sympathetic and innovative point of view of the revolution.

But is this possible? Is it yet possible to submit Marxism itself to Marxist and revolutionary criticism? I believe that it is possible and I believe, moreover, that to begin with, criticism must be focused (as it was for Marx) on that specific aspect of the Hegelian tradition in which civil society organizes vertically in the direction of the state, the solution to its own internal dichotomy. In this regard, materialist analysis in the first place demonstrates the impossibility of any solution which is not consistent with the actual, determinate configuration of classes and of their struggle. This means that civil society is still dichotomous and that the conflict is essentially irresolvable. At this point, however, the analysis must be integrated, in the sense that, contrary to the reaffirmation of the Hegelian version of the theory of the legitimation of the state, not only can the presupposition of the elimination or the solution of class conflict no longer be conceded, but, given the existing state of experience and research, the form of the vertical organization in which the elimination or solution of the class conflict would arise, is equally inadmissible.

Let me clarify this point. A basic characteristic of contemporary capitalist societies is the real subsumption (that is, the submission) of civil society within global capital. This phenomenon normally manifests itself in the form of the state. As analysis has revealed, the initial situation has thus taken a leap forward, the analytic base has shifted. The leap forward is a global one involving all the defining characteristics of civil society as such. Indeed, real subsumption reveals the social dichotomy not simply within civil society, which in any case is impossible to isolate in this situation: rather, it reveals the dichotomy to us within that determinate complex which is constituted by the new composition of civil society and the state. This compound thus becomes the exclusive object of analysis. Any other approach has a merely philological value. The problem of the governability of this complex society-state is the same as the problem of the orderly reproduction, or the revolutionizing, of this complex. In this perspective, the dichotomies of society therefore tend to become completely horizontal. The so-called doctrine of the state – if one still wishes to use this outdated terminology – can no longer concern itself with the notions of 'sovereign and subject', but only with 'power and countervailing power' – bearing in mind that while power and countervailing power may be treated as inter-changeable terms in a formal analysis, they certainly cannot be so treated from the point of view of political analysis. As a consequence, the themes of legitimation 'at all costs' become formal and circular, while the materialist themes of revolution, and in general, the political themes of governability, become the capacity to grasp the dichotomy on a completely horizontal terrain. I call this 'horizontal' terrain, the terrain of war. A theory of the state or of revolution must assume a terrain of war to be normal. Politics and the process of constitution are the continuation of war by other means.

3 If the social dichotomy has been shifted onto the level of the society-state complex, if it is impossible to conceive of vertical solutions to the conflict (unless – as often happens due to the precariousness of theoretical frameworks of legitimation – recourse is had to catastrophic overdeterminations of the situation), and if these conditions are actually operative, then the only strategy possible would seem to be one of trying to stabilize the conflict. It seems to me that both in the field of jurisprudence and in the field of the constitutional and political theory of the state, approaches of this kind have recently been tried out.

In the field of jurisprudence, contractualist versions of the theory of legality are very fashionable. What is characteristic of these approaches is the dissolution of all abstract and general definitions of law. Legal principles at last have the advantage of a secular state: however, they pay for this secularization by assuming the impreci-sion of forms of domination which do not contain within themselves the (more or less mystified but nevertheless powerful) legitimacy of a formal rationality.

In the field of constitutional theory, corporatist versions of political bargaining are in vogue. Indeed a disinterested analysis cannot but recognize that the constitutional functioning of the advanced capitalist states effectively consists of a network of corporations and corporatist coalitions. The material constitution composed of these forces overdetermines the formal constitution, or rather underdetermines it and brings about a crisis in every nerve centre of its functioning. Neither, given the vitality of the corporatist forces, is it possible (as it was in the thirties) to think in terms of on-going reform of the formal constitution – such as to adapt progressively to it the convulsions and changes of the principal protagonists and to the insurgence of the material, corporatist constitution.

In German philosophy, and by Gehlen in particular, this latter circumstance has been acknowledged and characterized under the heading of *Posthistorie*. The definition of *Posthistorie* combines both the material character of real subsumption as something current and historically irreversible and (consequently) the crisis of the traditional organization of the legal and constitutional system. An attempt is therefore made to confront this new situation starting from a plausible analytic framework of social action. The sole aim of the theory is evidently that of establishing criteria for the stabilization of the conflict. The complexity of reality cannot but be contained and controlled: in *Posthistorie* the state exits from history in order to enter in the 'modern' that is – in the definitive crystallization of the forces of historic production. I will therefore postpone analysis of Gehlen and his school until I come to Luhmann in order to clarify further the topics I am referring to here. It is, however, clear that these theories succeed in revealing the horizontal organization of state-society relationships only to the extent that they mystify the permanence of the dichotomous element that nevertheless characterizes the new state-society complex.

On the other hand, the hypothesis that the horizontal organization of the conflict constitutes the basic form of the dialectical relationship within the new society-state complex, does not seem to me to be able to hide the dichotomous essence which, from a Marxist point of view, must nevertheless be attributed to the relationship. Indeed subsumption does not abolish the dichotomous nature of civil society, it only eliminates the possibility of resolving it by organizing the solution to the conflict vertically in the direction of the state. In effect, from within the perspective of the new relationships, social antagonism and the desire for transformation and revolution make themselves felt more powerfully and clearly. The class struggle is not determined.

Peter Brückner is perhaps the author who, on the very edges of the Frankfurt school and above all within Gehlen's anthropology,

174   *Journeys through civil society*

has best shown the new characteristics of the concept of 'revolution'
within these new dimensions. The class struggle has not come to an
end but has been displaced onto a terrain which pertains to the
human totality. Real subsumption and the horizontal organization
and mass character of social relationships deny the very possibility
of formal control and emphasize the material nature of human
social relationships.

4   If we assume a flat horizon which is neither overdetermined nor
overdeterminable, and which is permeated by antagonisms which
tend to take on the shape of a dichotomous relationship having a
material foundation, is it then possible to identify means by which
the conflict might be stabilized?

Apart from the abstract neo-contractualist models, apart from
the vulgar prescriptions and practices of neo-corporatism, and apart
from the mystificatory distortion of functionalist and social-action
theories, it seems to me that from the point of view of a proposed
constitutional settlement of conflict, the only useful theoretical
framework is the one offered by federalism. In federalism, subjects
are portrayed as autonomous entities which come together (in the
present case they work for the reproduction of the system) on the
basis of equality. Therefore, there is no contract between subjects,
nor the possibility of a constitution which nevertheless recognizes
and equalizes, in general and abstract categories, the rights of single
and collective bodies: there is, rather, cohesion between the
subjects and an agreement to be evaluated in the light of the defence
of the characteristics of the single subject and of the conservation of
the collectivity. This, however, is not the place to illustrate the
extent to which the constitutional materialism of the origins of
bourgeois society in the seventeenth and eighteenth centuries was
comprised by these theories of federalism. What is principally
fascinating about this theoretical framework is the conspicuousness
of the subjects that come into play, the irreducibility of their
constitutional presence. The framework is precisely that of the
organization of a state of war.

In all probability, then, in this phase of the class struggle, the
basic problem is that of the constitutional stabilization of the class
struggle. But if this is the goal, it will be necessary to identify non-
mystified criteria which allow the boundaries of the sphere of action

of the subjects to be taken as a basis for reciprocal regulation between subjects.

The fact remains, however, that the development of means to establish order and consensual agreements designed to stabilize conflict can only take place on the basis of a prior recognition of the equality of the subjects. Is this possible, however? Or is it not the case that disparities are still so apparent as to make this and every strategy of stabilization unworkable? In particular, do there not exist forces which still aim at the restoration of ancient equilibria and ancient relationships of accumulation and capitalist reproduction, and which to this end, are even willing to have recourse to means of overdetermination which are destructive of the relationship?

It is obvious, however, that today, a period of stabilization is in the interests of the proletariat. Indeed the social revolution of which the proletariat is the carrier, is advanced through stabilization. On the other hand, stabilization is not in the interests of the traditional wielders of domination because, as they are very well aware, it is through stabilization that the social revolution is carried forward – even though the latter may not manifest itself as a political revolution.

It is thus in the fundamental interest of the proletariat today to impose stabilization and to ensure, through the struggle for peace, that the social revolution is taken forward. This interest is articulated by the means and the campaigns to deepen, uncover and enrich the proletariat's own subjectivity. To consolidate this inheritance through peace, and to tie this maturity to the social revolution is today to carry out a genuinely constitutional act. In this way civil society, which will no longer be bourgeois, but proletarian, will be rediscovered – not with the aim of establishing over it a new state which will sublimate it, but probably with the aim of destroying this monstrous bourgeois and capitalist fetish and succeeding, as a consequence, in devolving all its various functions to the community. It is beyond doubt that this is a utopia: but it is a utopia that is progressing and unfolding on the terrain of being – so much so that the enemy must assume it, even though in a mystified form. He himself promises a society which is peaceful and technologically equal – and therefore without classes. But to think that technology rather than the act of human transformation can eliminate classes is the worst of all utopias. The fact is that social movements can never be crystallized, can never become institutions and can never be reduced to a technical apparatus.

Within this new framework, new constitutional manœuvres are being tried. (In order to appreciate that this problem is a real one, it is sufficient to examine, for example, Johannes Angoli's contribution 'Zwischen Bewegung und Institution', *Tageszeitung*, Berlin (18 February 1983), on the role of the 'Greens' in the German *Bundestag*.)

11

State and class in the phase of real subsumption

1. STATE AND CLASS

1.1 *The relationship between the theory of the state and the theory of class*

There is no relationship between the theory of the state and the theory of class in the sense that while the theory of the state is a theory of domination, the theory of class is a theory of self-valorization (*Selbstverwertung*) and proletarian independence. This does not mean that the state is not an instrument of the ruling class or a monopoly on the legitimate use of violence etc. etc; it means only that these characteristics no longer have anything in common with the movements of the working class. We have been used to considering state reformism and the activities of state organizations in general as a response to the movements of the working and proletarian class. There was such a connection during the period of the liberal, and 'planning' state, but today this relationship no longer exists. On the basis of the theory of class it is not possible to construct any framework for understanding the development of the state. In this sense – in terms of its fundamental nature as the autonomous producer of an order which is functional for the mere reproduction of the ruling class, i.e. the exploiting class – the state has isolated itself. The mechanisms of exploitation are essentially

This article is the product of a discussion, with the comrades in Rebibbia prison, on topics proposed by the journal *Kapitalistate*.

administrative in nature, and their purpose is the simple reproduction of the power-machine.

1.2 *Location of the proletariat and use of the two-class model*

The proletariat exists wherever labour is exploited; it therefore
exists throughout the whole of society. We live in a society in which
productive labour is equally distributed among all sectors of
production. The distinction between productive and reproductive
labour – between production and reproduction – not to mention the
distinction between production and circulation, is completely
untenable. Exploitation must be analysed in the light of the real
subsumption of society within capital – i.e. of the entire society
within the state. What is most widely read here in the prisons, is the
'unpublished sixth chapter' of *Capital*. The basic protagonist of
the communist revolution is the social subject of exploitation: the
socialized proletariat, i.e. the metropolitan proletariat. The two-
class model may be retained – save for the fact that it may not be
conceived of in spatial terms. There does not exist any spatial
division between the exploiters and the exploited as is the case with
the traditional 'factory model'. There only exists a division which is
wholly internal to exploitation itself – which concerns the working
day in its entirety and expresses itself in the struggle (involving the
whole of society) over the issue of the appropriation of time. The
two-class model is a temporal model which counterposes exploited
time and free time. Consequently, it is obvious that the two classes
entertain not dialectical, but merely antagonistic, relationships. In
the organization of the working day, the relationship between the
quantities of necessary time and surplus-value time has lost all
proportionality. At most, it is measured in monetary terms, i.e. in
terms of money wages – as the concept of real wages no longer has
any meaning. Where is the proletariat? The proletariat is everywhere, just as the boss is. But this simultaneous ubiquity means
only that each in turn experiences the weight of power. In the epoch
of real subsumption, the spatial interpretation of exploitation no
longer has any meaning. In the working day, exploitation has a
temporal meaning.

The only real problem as far as use of the two-class model is
concerned, is that of identifying those courses of action which,
through proletarian independence, are conducive to the unity of the
revolutionary subject.

1.3 *The state and class-structure*

Abstracted from dialectical relationships, the class structure must be viewed from within the perspective of that domination which is aimed at the reproduction of the capitalist system. At this point, therefore, what must be proposed is not a theory of the capitalist mode of production and of the division of labour, but, quite simply, a theory of administrative functions and types of domination. Capital and its state do not substantially shape classes, but they identify them and give life to them within a process of reproduction. Neither can we properly speak of classes in this respect. In fact, what the state has in its favour is a relative disaggregation of society in the face of totalitarian mechanisms of reproduction.

The state wages a fierce battle against any form of aggregation of the social forces of production. Its only power to shape consists in the work of disaggregation which it carries out. What one is dealing with, therefore, is a negative relationship. The content of the work of symbolizing social reality carried out by the state, is a continually renewed attempt at segmentation.

The state is not able to absorb the innovatory initiatives which emanate from the exploitative society: it is able merely to register them and to insert them into an abstract and symbolic framework of the legitimation of domination. The state represents itself in images; it is a film, a television, an information mechanism which passes before the concrete existence of the working class and its various fractions. The state is the pure mystification of domination: it cannot exist other than as efficient mystification. The state, then, does not shape classes, but it represents them. None of the problems concerning classes has anything in common with the way in which the state speaks about them. The state is the form of this unreality.

1.4 *Socialist society and Marxist analysis*

It is not at all clear why Marxian analysis should not be applied to the actually-existing socialist societies. But while it is not clear why the revolutionary method should not be applied, it is, on the other hand, clear why the Marxist method should be applied. The so-called socialist societies are backward capitalist societies. In some of the socialist societies the processes of real subsumption have not yet been fully developed. There still exists a certain margin within which class struggle of a traditional kind can take place. Typical in this regard is the Polish case, and the comrades fighting there deserve our complete solidarity. Application of the Marxist method to these societies has two advantages: the first is that it provides us with a composite image of the development of the societies based on the exploitation of wage-labour; the second is that it places before us various alternative shapes that this model may assume.

Today, in particular, the socialist societies seem to be tending towards discarded models of the development of Western capitalism and, that is, towards the predominance of military structures in the supervision of exploitation. This derives from the high level and the violence of the class struggle in these countries, which in its turn is due to the conflictual relationships among imperialist powers in which these societies are caught up.

2.   THE STATE AND POLITICS

2.1   *The theory of the state and socialist strategy*

The relationship between the theory of the state and socialist strategy appears in terms of demystification, or in other words, in terms of a negative theory. Just as the problems and issues touched on in the first section must be considered in relation to the Marxian transformation of real subsumption, so this second group of questions leads back to issues of self-valorization and proletarian institutionalist. Now, once the job of demystifying the state has been carried out, one can nevertheless ask oneself if the amplified theory of the state is in some way useful in defining the mechanisms of socialist strategy. Posing this question is the same as posing the question of how necessary power is, in the establishment of socialism. But the reply is not simply of necessity abstract – it is absolutely impossible to give, since there can exist no homology in the way in which power is conceived on the two sides of the class struggle. If one wants some help, then, rather than to problems of *Staatslehre* it is necessary to address oneself to the particular themes of the *law of nations* or to the history of the conflict between Church and State: this raised the problem of external and mutually independent powers and their conflictual proximity. Some people believe that neo-contractualist perspectives can be useful at this point inasmuch as they allow one to understand and systematize those zones of intersection among the various spheres of power which emanate from the classes. But one has the impression that these perspectives are no more than allusive, unable, that is, because of their formal nature, to capture the sequences of strategies and countervailing powers that have been historically developed.

2.2   *The traditional socialist model and the new movements*

The traditional model of socialism is an ideology of productive labour and its social organization for the purpose of accumulation. The revolutionary content of the consequent democratic appearance – *as is also true of progressive liberation and ecological movements* – poses problems which can no longer be resolved within the historical-theoretical framework of socialism.

The subjects of the revolutionary struggle have undergone radical change: the content of the liberation struggles have reabsorbed and transformed the content of the struggles for emancipation. Thereby liberation becomes liberation *from* work rather than the emancipation of work. From this point of view, the new generations that are engaged in revolutionary struggle are *memory free*. But this does not mean that the revolutionary process is devoid of principles. On the contrary, through the fundamental rejection of existing forms of social organization, and through the experience of communitary and social struggles, the revolutionary struggle takes shape with a radicalism which is rarely perceived. The principles are born through the development of the struggle and among them one must above all pin-point the aim of improving the quality of life and of combatting and destroying all attempts to subject life to death. The issues of equality and socialization of the mode of production which are peculiar to socialist existence are adopted in a way which is not particularly problematic because it is clear that equality and socialization (*Vergesellschaftigung*) are not essential objectives (indeed to a large extent, they are not even any longer objectives), but conditions imposed by capital, ones to be reconquered by a practice of liberation.

2.3   *Redefinition of the concept of socialism*

By the term *socialism* we understand a society organized on the basis
of an ever-more complete planning of social labour, ordered for the
purpose of capital-accumulation, and thus structured according to
economic and physical forms of state coercion aimed at obliging the
population to work. We also understand by socialism a society in
which the division of labour exists, even though such division of
labour is linked to problems concerning the reproduction of society
and its organization, rather than being a necessary function of the
nature of work and production. By *communism*, on the other hand,
we understand a society which has freed itself from the necessity of
labour: thus, a society in which collective organization is aimed not
so much at the accumulation of labour as at its reduction – and at
the simultaneous liberation of all human energies and at the
complete and general utilization of time for invention and for the
struggle against disease and death. In the current phase of the class
struggle, the distinction between socialism and communism is
absolutely fundamental. Socialism no longer has an independent
existence as a historical necessity. Rather, it has been absorbed into
and moulded according to the forms of developed capitalism; that
is: either according to capitalist socialization (*Vergesellschaftigung*),
or according to the authoritarianism of actual socialism. As
implemented by capital, socialism is one of the guises in which real
subsumption manifests itself. In the circumstances of real subsumption, however, proletarian independence manifests itself as
the demand and struggle for communism. The conditions necessary
for this struggle are given by the substance of self-valorization
(*proletarische Selbstverwertung*) and in the autonomous processes of
proletarian institutionality (*Institutionalisierung*).

2.4   *The relationship between class struggle and the state*

We can explain the class struggle not as an aspect of a complex
dialectic of continuous restructuration (indeed the formula of
proletarian struggle *versus* capitalist restructuration is a relationship
that no longer exists in the circumstances of real subsumption) but
as instances of the appearance of needs and initiatives of appropriation. The state finds itself regulating the flows of the production
and reproduction of wealth. The proletariat, in its various forms,
strata, movements and so forth, attempts to appropriate an ever

larger and more significant share of this wealth; and not only of wealth: but above all, of freedom and of time. The struggles do not have a mediatory function – just as state domination no longer has a mediatory function. Mediation is dead. The production of goods takes place through domination. The relationships between production and reproduction, between domination/profit and resistance/wages, cannot be harmonized. Capital, through its state (and today collective capital cannot exist other than in the form of the state), overdetermines and attempts to construct functional social relationships which serve the framework of capitalist imperatives, but which have nothing further to do with the independence of the processes of self-valorization. Struggles *within* the state are always struggles *against* the state if the subject that initiates them is the proletarian subject. The very administrative procedures of the state can today be studied according to a logic which is one of separation: a logic which conceives the relationship as the conflict of countervailing powers. However much validity (that is, validity in terms of the existing order) they may have, juridical and administrative acts are potentially totally ineffective: administrative acts become effective only when the countervailing power gives its assent to them. 'Within and against' are not, therefore, exclusive determinations, but are, rather, the determinations of a single road along which the proletariat travels in the construction of its own independent institutionality.

2.5   *The movements and the constitution of the revolutionary subject*

The only political struggle which the proletariat must today carry forward is the one within itself. This is a struggle which must lead the proletariat to bring about unity between antagonism against the state on the one hand and the multiplicity of the movements and causes by which this antagonism is expressed on the other. A sort of materialistic *Vergleichung* must be developed among the manifold class expressions. United against all forms of exploitation, this must be done with the awareness that the search for unity necessarily takes place on the terrain of antagonism – and, therefore, in the presence of the class enemy – but also with the awareness that this type of unity does not take account of the complexity of the expressions, the behaviours and the needs of the proletariat. In short, it must be done with the awareness that the 'wealth of the proletariat', to modify Adam Smith's phrase, cannot be reduced to the sole function of exercising countervailing power but must equally be expressed in the form of the varied and multiple social power which it constitutes. The process of the internal constitution of the proletariat, through the multiplicity of its stratifications and its needs, is today the most fundamental problem of a politics of class, however this might be conceived. The constitution of the revolutionary subject, through its manifold expressions, is today the real problem of hegemony.

3.   THE STATE AND THE PARTY

3.1   *For a redefinition of the marxist theory of the party*

The Leninist theory of the party (and in general, those conceptions of the party of a Third-International stamp) maintain that the party is the representative of the working class and thus external to society in a twofold sense: in the first instance because the party is the conscious and responsible vanguard (so that its externality with regard to the class comes about in terms of representation), and in the second instance because the party of the working class conceives of society as something external to the working class. Now as a result of the transformation which subsumption has brought about, the working class is not external to society, but rather, is bound up with all the segments of the productive power which is dispersed throughout society. We call this new subject the socialized worker or the metropolitan worker. What is the role of the party in the light of the new reality constituted by the revolutionary subject? We can immediately say that the party cannot assert itself as a representative: this is not possible given the social composition of the proletariat. Even less so can it assert itself as the vanguard of the working class before social labour. The problem which this double negation of the traditional theory of the party raises cannot be solved other than in practice, i.e. through continuous experiences of organization and struggle.

In all probability, the party will be able to be born again only as the organizer of countervailing power, and thus as the collective social agent of communist organization. In any event, the establishment among the masses of proletarian organizations and openings for countervailing power and proletarian institutional structures which lead towards communism, is the party's sole present-day task. As an instrument of the transition, the party must disavow any role as a representative of a general interest of the class, and instead must assert itself as the capacity to organize and satisfy particular class interests.

3.2 *The role of the 'communist' parties*

In Eastern Europe as in a large part of Western Europe (the difference is not one of quality but of quantity) the party is purely and simply a function of the state. In the countries of Eastern Europe the party is the master: the master of the organization of work and thus the agent of social exploitation.

On the other hand, in Western Europe, and in particular in those regimes characterized by an extreme parliamentary pluralism, the party system has by now become a neo-corporatist system having a very heavily bureaucratic and repressive valence.

This matter concerns the so-called West European communist parties whose relationship with the working class is becoming ever more limited and reduced to the defence of those traditional and reliable strata constituted by the factory proletariat. Revolutionary thrusts emanating from new movements are taken up only to the extent that they can be accommodated within a framework of political compromises of a corporatist kind. The ideology of work and productivity have led the communist parties of Western Europe to line themselves up, without a single reservation, in favour of nuclear energy. As far as the youth movements are concerned, the West European communist parties have played an equivocal role between repressive acts and attempts at ghettoization. As far as they are concerned, the environmental question consists merely in campaigns to clean up the cities. The work ethic has done its greatest damage in terms of repressive policies against social deviance. The prisons are full of people who have been marginalized by the urban exclusionary regimes. In short, the so-called communist parties have often been the principal sources of conservative and reactionary ideology. This does not imply that the communist parties do not still comprise a large mass of the proletariat. Their role, however, is fundamentally one of the corporatist regimentation and control of these forces. The role of the communist parties in the management of industrial restructuring and in the 'battle against inflation' is perhaps exemplified – in terms which only with difficulty can be called other than Reaganite – by the brief period of the historical compromise in Italy. The socialist parties, principally in France and Germany, have attempted to initiate a dialogue with the new movements. From here – that is, from here in prison – it is difficult to assess whether these manœuvres have had anything more than an electoral purpose.

3.3   *The relevance of parties in the movement for communism*

The fundamental reality which must be presupposed is that given by the significance of the parties for the state. The parties are financed by the state as stable elements of its make-up; the parties have a direct hold on the mass media, and a centralized bureaucracy guaranteed by the powers of the state. The parliamentary regime does not exist in either a pure or an impure form: it has quite simply been substituted by the party regime. In this situation there are two possible roads to the transformation: either the one that passes through the creation and consolidation of countervailing powers (countervailing powers which are also and above all directed at the parties and at the participatory activity which they exercise in framing the state's will), or the concurrent one of *Sprachlosigkeit*, of the absence of legitimation or of passive legitimation. In the Italian tradition of Gramscism, one speaks of 'passive revolution' in the sense of a revolution from above which the masses undergo passively. Today, it is perhaps appropriate to use the expression 'passive revolution' to indicate a passive process of sectional movements of the masses which imposes a revolution from below. The general opinion is that the parties are both weak and strong – in the sense that while their power is entirely guaranteed by the activities of the state, in no case do they function as transmission-belts for any kind of 'popular will': they are shabby machines of mystification.

4.   THE STATE AND POLITICAL POWER

4.1   *The state form and the historical determinations of its strength*

In tackling this problem it is perhaps necessary to recall a basic conviction, namely that the state is the form in which the process of extracting surplus value takes place. If the 'relative autonomy' of the state had some kind of meaning during previous phases of capitalist development, any kind of autonomy of the state and of the political is inconceivable during a period of real subsumption. In the countries of actual socialism, owing to the insufficient development of capitalist production, there is probably still room for relative autonomy of the state and of the socialist project, but this is absolutely impossible in the advanced capitalist countries. The strength of the state is thus, in the first instance, the strength of the collective capitalist. In historical terms, the state's strength can be explained only on the basis of the dialectic with the workers' struggles which pushed capital in the direction of subsumption and led the state to embody it. Today, in the phase of subsumption and the reappearance of its antagonism, the concept of 'strength of the state' has reached a crisis. The theory of the dialectic has come into conflict with the theory of war. The state is one pole – and only a pole – in a reality of war. Its attempts to symbolize the world of social production, (and through symbolization, functionally to segment it), have encountered an ever-increasing resistance which extends to all the bonds of social production and reproduction. The historical explanation of the strength of the state must take full cognisance of the latter's real weight: a process that has been interrupted – the last dialectical act to be performed. The dialectic is not a law of actual development, neither is it a metaphysical law: it is quite simply a law imposed by capital. Communism proceeds to its supersession. And therefore, already, through the conduct of the war and new organization, the most basic law is that of war; the strength of the state is, however, always that of a pole – and one only – of class relationships.

4.2 *The relationship between formal, legal and political rights and the progressive struggles of the class*

Legal and/or political rights which are formal and/or informal but effective, are not simply functions of capitalist development even if they have been influenced by it (and even if they have, as a consequence, rightly been demystified). However, because of the new composition of the class, even these formal rights correspond to unsuppressible, material needs. Democratic battles are thus consubstantial elements of the working class in its socialized form.

Progressive struggles create opportunities for the new institutionality of the class: it is necessary to contest the idea that the struggles may end in integration. Integration only arises from the absence of struggle. The not unimportant effect of self-valorization is inherent in the struggles. The equilibrium which may be re-established after the struggles have taken their course does not leave the balance of forces intact. A theory of the total integration of the struggles can never carry any weight. A state of peace cannot be established on the basis of the same equilibria and the same relative shares in the division of wealth that pertained before the struggles. As an ideology of the maintenance of equilibria, Keynesianism played a role which was advantageous to the working class. But Keynesianism is finished. Today the problem is that mutual and antagonistic one of indicating in creative terms, the appropriation, not only of wealth, but of the temporal being of society, by the two sides in conflict.

4.3   *Legislation and law in capitalist and communist society*

The role of legislation and law cannot be other than that of forcefully overdetermining progress towards communism. Inasmuch as this process is carried forward, it is reasonable to think that, together with the state, the role of law will also wither away – provided that one does not have a mistaken notion of what law is: that is, as the simple reflection of organization rather than the overdetermination of the social. But laws are norms, domination and surplus value transformed into will – in capitalist development, their contents are arbitrary and reduced to simple concepts of validity. Kelsen is the unsurpassed representative of the development of bourgeois law in its formal and normative aspects. The working class cannot call law by names which are different from the ones used by the bourgeoisie. They can only destroy bourgeois law. There remains the case of agreement and contract. During the period of the transition and the new passive revolution which we are living through, contractual agreements may be important. But they should be reduced to the descriptive level and to the theory of international law (*law of nations*) rather than to currently existing public law. From this point of view, actual practice completely supersedes law. What is important in this respect is not to get things mixed up.

For example, let us consider the widely used term, 'new laws'. The means by which law is created are bound up with the very notion of the state, whether capitalist or socialist. Every creation of a law by the state is, at the same time, the creation of its negation. Capitalism creates new needs, behaviours etc. which must be *controlled* to the very same degree that law *establishes* such needs and behaviours etc. This is obvious, and does not seem to create any difficulties for the maintenance and reproduction of capitalist domination.

If by 'new laws' it is understood that through their recognition new elements of conflictuality are likely to be induced, this too would seem to be fairly obvious. It is no coincidence that the capitalist machine of the production of law is, at the same time and to the same degree, a machine which is organized for the solution of conflicts, i.e. one which is functionally organized for the reproduction of the capitalist state. The problem, then, is not one of new laws, but rather the tendency of the proletarian countervailing powers to concretize themselves and become hegemonic. The real problem is that of the collective demands that are beginning to be raised and which cannot be contained, save for brief periods, within juridical systems. It is clear that in this sense – that is, within a framework of new contractuality, on the basis of a series of relationships which are not so much juridical, as relationships of force and of forced settlements – a lot of new laws are produced. But it is very dangerous to use legal terminology to describe these collective demands. Contemporary Italian history is rich in relevant examples: both as regards the effective valence of the demands of the proletarian subjects (whence the impossibility of limiting them by law and the habit of taking them on as such; for example, limitation of the right to strike and control of the trade unions) and as regards the exceptional production of norms to obstruct new systems of power (for example, the celebrated workers' statute).

4.4 *On the role of violence of the state and against the state*

The current role of violence against the state is difficult to establish; and, in the absence of a theory of proletarian organization and countervailing power it is also difficult to establish the general role of violence. The exercise of violence against the state has effectively become as widespread as is the exercise by the state of violence against the subjects. It is difficult to imagine a fatal moment of an unleashing of univocal violence which destroys the state. If the theory of the countervailing powers and the direct organization of the proletariat has any meaning, then violence must be related to the rational action of proletarian organization and countervailing power. Given the complexity of the social organization of the proletariat, the ideologies of armed insurrection do not hold theoretical water. The processes of the current transition will develop within a time-period that cannot be the 'now' of insurrection. Rather, the relevant time-period is that necessary for the unsuppressible trend of proletarian power to consolidate itself and at the same time to appropriate wealth. The point is not only to destroy, but above all to build.

The absence, among the topics proposed by *Kapitalistate*, of any reference to the themes of proletarian self-determination and new constitutionalism is to be criticized. These are perhaps the principal topics on which revolutionary criticism and imagination is exercised today. The basic problem seems to be to succeed – even by means of comparative discussions – in identifying how proletarian self-valorization can become open institutionality. There are many processes that we are trying to follow and to describe. But in this connection we need to arrive more closely at a complete theoretical framework.

The topics on which we should concentrate attention would seem to be: on the one hand, the failure of both the reformist strategies (such as those of most of the European communist parties) and of the insurrectionary strategies of the communist left; and on the other hand, the consolidation of practices of countervailing power, by means of the enormous struggles of the movements and the active strata of the working class.

12

Some notes concerning the concept of the 'nuclear state'

There exists the state and there exist production cycles in the provision of nuclear energy and atomic weapons; but does there exist a specific technical-theoretical entity that can be said to be a 'nuclear state'?

Of course from a descriptive point of view, it may be noted that a series of specific policies have been developed in connection with the relationship between the state and nuclear arms/energy, which concern not only the strictly military- and energy-domains, but also the domains of economic and financial policy, policies for the planning of industrial conversion and restructuring, regional policies, public order policies and the activities of the secret services, not to mention of course, foreign policy, foreign trade and industrial supplies, scientific and outer-space policies etc. etc.

However, even supposing that the complex of new relationships and activities induced by these policies has tended to bring about a qualitative leap, or even believing – as it is more natural to do – that the development of nuclear energy has led, more modestly, to significant changes in the existing mode of production, nevertheless, it does not seem to me that it is possible for this reason alone to consider the nature of the state as having been modified and therefore that it is justifiable to introduce the specifically new concept of a 'nuclear state'. When the principal source of energy was switched during the first half of the present century from coal to electricity, quite rightly this was not thought to have led to a change in the form of the state, even though many of the relationships between types of production and state activities were affected by the transformation. Electricity continued to be a technical aspect of production – and Lenin was able to marry it with the Soviets just as easily as capitalist governments were able to employ it in the development of the monopolistic corporations. The technical transformation was, therefore, something relatively autonomous.

If we want to establish what is entailed by the notion of the 'nuclear state' we must, then, apprehend a particular concept, one which specifically describes the relationship between the type of energy and the form of the state. We must, in other words, provide an answer to this question: 'Through the development of military and energy policies associated with the use of nuclear power, have there been substantial modifications, both in normative and in constitutional and political terms, such as to affect the nature of the legitimation of the state?' That is the question.

Let us first of all examine the matter from the normative point of view. And let us ask ourselves: what is involved in the concept of legitimacy in a democratic state? Our reply is that legitimacy is a constitutionally guaranteed relationship between the legal exercise of violence on the one hand, and on the other, the consensual and democratic formation of both political directives and the organizations retaining a monopoly over the use of violence. This means that between the organizations of government, and the processes and subjects from which the formation of the political will derives, there must exist a certain balance which is overseen and/or re-established by organizations having constitutional jurisdiction, and which is regularly put to the judgement of the popular will through the collective subjects which organize it.

Let us ask ourselves then: does the development of nuclear energy and the manufacture, stock-piling and possible use of nuclear weapons affect the concept of democratic legitimacy and its constitutional implementation? Does it modify the relationship between the legal exercise of violence and the formation of the popular will?

It seems to me that the correct answer to these questions cannot but be positive: democratic and constitutional relationships are changed by the development of nuclear energy and the development of policies of nuclear defence because the latter remove all limits on the potential effects of the legal use of violence and render the relationship between it and the mechanisms of the formation of the political will, a highly unequal one.

In periods of social and political crisis (or, if one prefers, of heightened class struggle) these dynamics of separation become acutely apparent – independently of whether we analyse them theoretically or describe them empirically.

We have not yet talked about the concomitant effects of the development of nuclear energy – that is, of the effects of fall-out and ecological destruction. While in no sense secondary, these are not of immediate relevance to the concept of normative legitimacy – even though it could be objected that the conservation of natural resources and the protection of the conditions of biological reproduction are included among that combination of values which the constitution (any constitution) scrupulously defends. We have not mentioned these things because what we are principally concerned with at the moment is to understand the political dynamics which disruption of the equilibrium of constitutional legitimation gives rise to. We will come back to the other effects later on.

For the moment then, let us return to the theoretical problem raised by the destructive potential of the nuclear energy capacity possessed by governments. It will be useful to make an immediate observation. The destructive potential of nuclear power which, by hypothesis, may characterize the legal exercise of violence and which in any case is in fact contained within it, does not manifest itself simply as the capacity for efficient destruction, but principally as the effect of the coercive overdetermination of the juridical order as a whole. From the point of view of the political constitution and its executive regulations and procedures, such destructive potential appears, then, as the power of overdetermination with regard to every alternative and antagonistic political movement (quite apart from behaviour which is unconstitutional or simply oppositional). The feeling of threat which so profoundly characterizes legality in general and the oppressive deterrent, brought to such a high level of repression, not only deform the abstract constitutive relationship of legitimacy, but also intervene in and overwhelm the multiplicity of concrete, historical-political relationships which the general relationship represents. By this I mean that the deterrent effect bears directly upon the exercise of political freedoms and the functioning of the constitution. Never in the history of political thought has the absoluteness of the sovereign power found such complete and total expression.

It consequently becomes a sheer theoretical absurdity to submit such absolute power to the traditional liberal-democratic analysis of checks on the exercise of power – even more so to assess it in terms of neo-contractualist or neo-utilitarian nonsense (whether they are replanted or transplanted, they remain planted). In the first instance, then, the nuclear state can be defined as a state which is entirely removed from the problematic concerning limits on the exercise of power and which is, therefore, entirely removed from the very definition of the legitimate state in the sense in which this has hitherto been understood. If democratic legitimacy is a constitutionally guaranteed relationship between the legal exercise of violence and the consensual formation of the organizations and directives by which such violence is exercised, then the 'linking' of nuclear power to the state annuls such a relationship

– inasmuch as the exercise of violence may lead to the destruction of the physical conditions of the relationship;

– inasmuch as the deterrent implicit in this threat may destroy the constitutional nature of the formation of the political will which such deterrent in any case overdetermines in totalitarian fashion;

– inasmuch as, at this level of the concentration of destructive power, the problem of constitutional checks is all but eliminated even in merely formal terms.

I should like to add (as a minor point) that the identification of a degenerative tendency in democratic legitimacy attendant upon the development of the nuclear state, has nothing in common with the usual critique of technocracy and the utopias of the technocratic state. In the case of nuclear power, the critique focuses not on its role, function or external appearance, but on the very meaning of power, its quality and substance – that is to say that analysis reveals how the very concept of sovereignty, as a result of this enormity of amassed power, tends to be reduced to pure materiality.

In saying all this, however, we are simply beginning to describe the form of the nuclear state. If in fact we shift our attention from normative analysis to political and constitutional science, then the breakdown of democratic relationships becomes even more apparent.

In fact, independently of the political form it takes (whether liberal-democratic or socialist), the nuclear state, besides tending to obstruct the formation of the political will (something which de-legitimates the state) tends also to bring about a series of complementary effects relating to the very form of government. When fixed social capital is embodied in constructions defined by the flow of nuclear energy, whether in production or in the policies governing reproduction and defence, the functions of social and political mediation not only begin to diverge, but to be organized separately. The logic of nuclear capital is logocentric, it is the logic of independent reproduction and autonomous organization. The political stratum of nuclear capital thus begins to take shape according to these functional necessities, and a new form of social stratification must, consequently, be brought about on this new social basis. The redistribution of national income is increasingly aimed at the construction of a new social hierarchy, first of all in order to realize separate goals, and then in order to establish separate structures. To the extent that the authorities extricate themselves from all dialectical relationships with the democratic formation of the political will, to the same extent do they tend to become isolated, to reproduce themselves in a state of separateness and to shape social reproduction in accordance with appropriate laws of stratification.

A second obstructing factor must at this point be emphasized – exactly as is done in the most recent democratic literature (Mary Kaldor, Cornelius Castoriadis etc.) which forcefully denounces the degeneration of the state-forms of the large imperialist powers (the U.S.A. and the U.S.S.R). Starting from the isolation of government from society, from the interruption of the flow of legitimation and from the formation of apparatuses which are ever more closely tied to an independent industrial-military-nuclear system, a block in general social productivity also becomes apparent. All this is immediately obvious if, at the level of social production, the concept of productivity implies internal forms of a participatory dialectic that are to a large extent common to political society; the shattering of these relationships on the political terrain spills over onto the terrain of the general productivity of the system.

The matter has also been extensively demonstrated in the economic sphere – where the sophistication of the nuclear-military industry – politically isolated as precisely happens – no longer contributes either to industrial innovation, or to economic growth. To an ever-increasing extent, nuclear-military development has been denounced as a grotesque excrescence having the sole capacity to reinforce the pure image of power, and in this absurd respect, to proliferate and to contaminate the world. In this connection, every third-world dictatorship could do with a small nuclear-military apparatus – not so much, clearly, for the purpose of combatting enemies, as for the purpose of reconstructing its reputation for power. Whoever would have thought that nuclear energy's legitimation of absolute power would have been in such close conformity with theological writings on the subject!

As to the democratic-corporatist countries of Europe, these latter are still rather backward in terms of this distorted development but it is beyond doubt that an appropriate solution to the problem of the disaggregation of agreements between interest groups (which these countries are today traumatically experiencing) could consist in a restructuring of corporatist stratification according to the framework of a nuclear-military project. In France, such projects are sometimes discernible both in decidedly reactionary political circles, and in social democratic/reformist groups.

In any event, it is entirely apparent that the awesome development of secret or clandestine power in the advanced industrialized countries is nothing other than the form in which the distorted rationality of the military-nuclear and industrial apparatuses is emerging. Through so-called industrial, financial and military 'scandals' we can thus begin to perceive how the forces that brought about the crisis of legitimacy are now attempting to reorganize a social project. As soon as this project becomes operative and as soon as it has been irresistibly shown to be necessary, then secret power will surface in the form of a new legality. Rather than being a deformation, secret power would seem to constitute the 'labour pains' of the transition to the nuclear state and its associated terror. In this sense, the 'mysterious empires' are nothing other than the illegal prefigurements and terroristic anticipations of a future whose realization is being forced by the governing strata. In Europe, we are effectively living through the pre-history of a developmental process which in countries such as the U.S.A. and the U.S.S.R. has already reached an extraordinarily advanced stage. The traditional France of Giscard or a future Germany under Strauss can be taken as indications of a capitalist trend which is also affecting Italy.

Having established these analytic points, to which many others could be added, we can thereby conclude that it is actually possible to speak of a 'nuclear state', that the concept is useful for explaining many phenomena and that it captures something specifically new about the normative and political structures of the contemporary state.

It may also be noted that with the nuclear state, the long process of historical development of the capitalist state seems to come to a conclusion. After a first, brutal, period of accumulation and its guarantee by the capitalist state, the latter cited market forces as the mystificatory 'proof' that society functioned democratically. But inasmuch as the smooth functioning of the market was impeded by the emergence of new forces which could not be assimilated to the market's logic and its 'liberal coercion', thus was born the necessity of reinvigorating the mechanisms of absolute coercion. What is at stake is the very form of control; the latter, in its nuclear guise, demonstrates that the absorption and exploitation of social time, on which capitalist accumulation is based, must at all costs be maintained, on pain of the annulment of the very time which nuclear power contains within itself as destructive capacity. The nuclear state is a historical-political formation which points to the zero-hour of human destruction, and which legitimizes its power on the basis of this threat. Within this framework, then, the relationship of democratic-constitutional legitimation is not only shattered by the nuclear state, but within the latter, new types of social exploitation – new forms of social stratification and new governmental apparatuses, which are special and separate – are consolidated. As a consequence, the very concept of power itself is thereby transformed.

Within this broad perspective, the watchword of peace has a conceptual importance which concerns not only the problems of life and its reproduction but, precisely because it bears upon them and defines them in opposition to a new form of totalitarian state, it has a significance which concerns the global interest of the proletariat in the transformation.

In the experience of the generations which fought for communism during the decades following the last great imperialist war, the watchword of peace was often distorted as a result of its involvement with international interests and also through more or less acknowledged or ambiguous utopian assurances. It was thereby despoiled and weakened by limiting and opportunistic ideas. Consequently, to some generations, to struggle for peace seemed to be to undermine the proletariat's capacity for struggle and to keep it within a negative, almost conservative wrapping.

If we have grasped the concept of the nuclear state, today we understand how, on the other hand, in the context of its mighty and brutal dimensions, the interest in the reproduction of life in opposition to death, and the urgency of social transformation, constitute a unity. It is not possible to think in terms of the reproduction of life without also thinking in terms of the destruction of the cancer with which the nuclear state has infected all the bonds of social production and collective existence. It is not possible to think in terms of one's own essential reproduction without struggling for a transformation which puts an end to fear as a basic feature of human association. But in order to eliminate this fear, it is necessary to transform the general conditions of collective existence and to destroy the destructive content which the constitutional organization of the nuclear state carries within itself and disperses everywhere. Peace is thus the basic watchword of our times. And it is positive, constructive, constitutional – in a word, alternative – in substance. In order to guarantee peace, we need to unblock political development and the development of social productivity. We need to overcome the subordination of free time to coerced labour-time and the destruction which is threatened by capital. We must restore hope to human existence.

One last point among the many that should be considered: in developed capitalism, the state has the function of the overall organization of society. The nuclear state regenerates and perfects this propensity. By assailing the whole of society, the development of nuclear energy not only instigates everywhere the new conditions of state legality but contaminates the world both through the substance and the overall conditions of production. At this point our analysis must revert to a descriptive mode. Between the extremes given by the destruction of the human biosphere and the administrative, police and military control of national territory, hundreds of areas of state intervention are laid out. The nuclear state assails and destroys these areas – no longer simply in terms of its potent normative activity or in formal terms, but in material terms – and in any case marshals them for its own ends. Resistance and the search for a new mode of existence are therefore necessary in all these fields – and the development of struggles cannot but be coextensive with the destructive impact, but at the same time coordinated, manifold and precisely adapted to the circumstances, the sectors and conjunctures of particular conflicts. This counter-attack will be very varied: its power will extend to the whole broad issue of the submission of society to the nuclear state and it will be intensified and spread to all aspects of its influence. At this juncture, the point to be grasped is that these widely diffused molecular struggles will require a real and effective coordinating centre – one which does not, however, under any circumstances imitate features drawn from capitalist development and from the structure of the nuclear state. It is not utopian to think that nowadays the centre of struggles for liberation consists in the multiplication of movements and in the daily, on-going effort to eliminate the fear which derives from the logic of nuclear power – and in the spontaneous proposal of new modes of existence, in the affirmation of a project of renewal and of transformation which is in no circumstance subordinated to a logocentric and instrumental logic. The complexity and extension of the struggle require not synthesis but diffusion. Peace is nowadays a watchword and a need which can push outwards this powerful liberation struggle.

13

Postmodern

To use the expression 'postmodern' is to imply that the old dispute concerning the concepts of the 'ancient' and the 'modern' – the topos running through European culture ever since the Renaissance – has been resolved. Affirmation of this resolution is even more important when it is remembered that, in the contemporary period, the concept of the modern has been closely tied to that of progress, and the concept of progress to that of the vanguard, so that in this way, a veritable historical theodicy has taken shape. Now the concept of the postmodern presents a forceful challenge to this progressive concatenation. The great frescos of history, whether speculative or religious, no longer have anything to tell us: 'Universality has collapsed', proclaims Jean-François Lyotard in *The Postmodern Condition: a Report on Knowledge* (University of Minnesota Press, Minneapolis, 1984), among others. But if postmodernism is a sign of the crisis of modern thought, it also shows how much there is that is new and undeniably innovative in present-day culture, both within and apart from the poverty of political and social analysis. In the more banal and pessimistic versions of the postmodern concept, the novel aspects of present-day culture lie in the total disintegration of the received language, of its meanings and expressions; it is the tectonic slippage of its foundation (J. Baudrillard, 'Symbolic Exchange and Death' trans. Charles Levin in *The Structural Allegory*, ed. John Fekete, Theory and History of Literature, vol. II, (University of Minnesota Press, Minneapolis, 1984)). By contrast, in conceptions which are more sophisticated but which stem from the same base, the postmodern is the pluralism of languages, the uncertain role of judgements, the becoming-ever-more-absolute of the horizon of communication (J.F. Lyotard, *Economie libidinale* (Minuit, Paris, 1974); *Le différend* (Minuit, Paris, 1984)). However, as far as novelty is concerned, the postmodern can be turned into a much richer concept.

It can be added that, somewhat paradoxically, negation of the modern together with affirmation of the novel features of our epoch, seems to imitate the romantics' negation of the revolution of the Enlightenment and their affirmation of the new cultural identities that were to emerge during the course of the nineteenth century. Perhaps belonging to the essence of the postmodern, then, is a relationship between the positive and negative. Can we then conclude that the postmodern is a new form of romanticism? In order to reply to this question, and more generally in order to flesh-out our definition, we will go over each of its aspects in turn.

First of all, then, there is a negative aspect which consists in the recognition of a crisis. This crisis is a political crisis: almost all the authors of the postmodern concept find their intellectual origins in that form of modernity and the representation of history as progress that was the 'culture of the Left'. Now it is the great values which constituted the framework of that culture which are in crisis. Their institutionalization has revealed their heteronomy. The claimed freedom has become despotism. Equality has been transformed into slavery. The real exchange of labour and value has become a symbolic exchange, the simulation of life and an image of death. In the circulation of values, every commodity has become money, every reference appears in a circuit of equivalent totalities and every singularity has thus lost all significance and the sense of being has become pure paranoia. We could continue cataloguing indefinitely the painful substance of this perception of the total insignificance of the being in which we are immersed: a being whose framework and directions we no longer perceive. Lying behind and sustaining the political crisis is an ideal, philosophical – I would even say, metaphysical – crisis. The lack of orientation which has been verified in the ethical-political world, is even more strongly felt in the ideal world of concepts and language. (J. Baudrillard, *For a Critique of the Political Economy of the Sign*, trans. Charles Levin (Telos Press, St. Louis, 1981).) Not without affectation – though with some justification – postmodernist philosophers consider,

then, that the most significant currents of contemporary thought
(from the phenomenological asceticism of Husserl to the linguistic
mysticism of Wittgenstein, and from the nihilism of Heidegger to
the latest versions of structuralism), offload their theoretical
difficulties onto, and to some extent converge in, the new
phenomenology which is described precisely by the postmodernists
(Vincent Descombes, *Le même et l'autre* (Minuit, Paris, 1979)).

Although postmodernism interprets the ideal crisis of our epoch
in eclectic terms, nevertheless, it has a high degree of descriptive
power. The frequent combining of areas of analysis, the breakdown
of disciplinary boundaries and the overlap of fields, all reinforce its
analytic power. And it is precisely through the contiguity between
the political and ideal crises that it indicates the chaos, inversion
and heteronomy of technological and productive values. Finally,
the crisis of modernism and the paradoxical postmodernist alternative are manifested, and prominently so, even in the realm of
aesthetics. If modernism consisted of style and constructiveness, if
it was the last form of artistic Prometheanism and a practical
synthesis of technologies, then all this too is finished. Now the
materials are so thoroughly evanescent and have been so impre-
cisely managed as to be able to be defined, rather, as 'immaterial'.
Postmodernism gathers *kitsch* and *pacht* as content, rejects every
selection, and places the author at the service of a series of utilities
without end. Moreover, the communications industry becomes the
preferred realm of postmodernism precisely through the lack of any
ontological reference point, the interchangeability of the real and
the imaginary and the apologia of the imaginary and its blind
vitality. Production and technology are no longer the roads to
progress. Too much time has now passed since the hegemony of
modernism and the illusion that 'socialism equalled Soviet power
plus electrification'! Today, production and technology can with
indifference be designated as life- or death-producing: it is
impossible to distinguish one from the other so that, for example, it
is not clear to what extent nuclear power serves creative rather than
destructive purposes. . . Postmodernism, then, lies in the awareness of this circularity of being, in this continuous circulation of
commodities (which is so fast as to become indescribable), in this
complete divorce between the sense and meaning of propositions
and actions, and finally in the absence of any possible way out of all
this. (Paul Virilio, *Speed and Politics*, trans. Mark Polizotti

(Semiotext[e] and Mark Polizotti, New York, 1986).) Postmodernism is a world made up of an infinity of atoms that contingently
form an existence (and they could equally well destroy it); it is a
symbolic, imaginary and simulated order: but as there is no reality
with which it can be compared, it itself is reality.

Alongside the definition of the crisis there is however, and not
only paradoxically, in postmodernism, the identification of a
positive moment. In fact, what is this world of political, ideal and
productive crisis, this world of sublimation and uncontrollable
circulation? What is it, then, if not an epoch-making leap beyond
everything humanity has hitherto experienced? The positive aspect
of the theoretical contribution made by postmodernism consists
precisely in registering this fundamental discontinuity: it pin-points
and emphasizes that moment in which the problem of human
society is posed in completely new terms – not only in the field of
production, but also, and above all, in the field of communication.
The vision of a human society (which is first of all a philosophical
vision, then the product of the world-wide circulation of commodities and of the subject that was subjected to it, and finally a
communicative concretization resulting from the great development of the means of information-dissemination), while destroying all progressive meaning, reveals, however, the enormous
potential of the human project that has been realized through this
process (G. Deleuze and Félix Guattari, *A Thousand Plateaus*,
trans. Brian Massumi (University of Minnesota Press, Minneapolis,
1987)). It constitutes simultaneously the ruin and the new potential
of all meaning. It is a circumstance so absolute as to become the
basis of all absolutes. This paradoxical character of the postmodernist perspective must be adapted to the subject and to the
subjects: the contingency of the relationship must be thrown onto
the terms of the proposition, of communication and of action.
Thereby, postmodernism presupposes not merely an enormous,
fluent universe of communication, but throughout every stretch of
this mass of communicative threads it identifies contradiction,
conflict and, above all, new power. These aspects of postmodernism have been tackled principally by those authors who, starting
from the crisis of the Frankfurt school and the philosophy of Krisis
have – in some way – tried to restore absoluteness to the linguistic
and communicative perspective, identifying and describing its
transcendental qualities (Habermas, Tugendhat, Apel).

It is appropriate, at this point, to refer to an important but little-studied text in the Marxian analysis of political economy. Both in the *Grundrisse* and in the unpublished sixth chapter of *Capital*, Marx distinguishes between the 'formal' and the 'real subsumption' of labour within capital. By 'formal subsumption' Marx means a situation in which a variety of different modes of production are subjected to capitalist relations of production. Such subjection comes about, not because labour-processes within each of these productive modes are organized on capitalist lines, but because capitalist relations of production exercise effective hegemony over society. Antiquated forms of production, of property and of the market may in this way have an orderly coexistence with capitalist hegemony. But capital then proceeds to penetrate and conquer the whole of society and there arrives a moment in which the old forms of production, of property and of circulation break down: in this situation, not only is the capitalist mode of production hegemonic, but the capitalist form of the labour-process becomes the only existing one. The entire society becomes one enormous factory, or rather, the factory spreads throughout the whole of society. In this situation, production is social and all activities are productive. However, since the old forms of production have been superseded, the contours of the totality become obscured and the specific sites of production seem to become dissolved throughout society. This allows capital, having itself become social, to disguise its hegemony over society and its interest in exploitation, and thus to pass its conquest off as being in the general interest. It is obvious that Marx's prediction concerning the course of events and the vision of communism that was possible in his day, cannot be reduced to and made indistinguishable from the postmodernist mystification of 'real subsumption' as an environment of indifference: it is, however, true that the first anticipates some of the basic descriptions of the second. (See my *Marx beyond Marx* (Bergin and Gervey, Massachusetts, 1984).) In postmodernism, the antagonistic framework, which in Marx constitutes the dynamic key to the construction of subsumption, is in effect eliminated. However, elimination of the antagonism cannot hide, even in postmodernism, the maturation of human society – i.e. of that society in which the paradox of the most complete abstraction of labour, together with its extraordinary productivity, is dissolved and becomes, according to Marx, a power of the collective individual, the liberation of singularity and the discovery and joy of free, communal activity.

This enormous contradiction is latent in postmodernism. It is for this reason that all its developments are in fact vicious circles. As an example, let us examine a current definition of the political proposed by postmodernism, namely the one appearing in systems theory, and, in particular, German systems theory as it has been elaborated by Niklas Luhmann (above all in the articles appearing in *Soziologische Aufklärung*). Through the elaboration of a social ideology of full circulation, of absolute flexibility and of radical simplification of the complex, in this theory an attempt is made to save the workings of the Western democracies from the conflict of organized interests and to ensure governability and the forging of instruments and strategies adapted to the attainment of these goals. In short, the theory is a phenomenology of postmodernism aimed at solving the political problems of the modern. The operation of reducing political and social complexity consists in abstracting the antinomies which have an ontological foundation, in incorporating them in a project of simulation, in short, in redefining them according to a schema which is substitutive of reality. In systems theory, the model of the simulated universe becomes a criterion of intervention, and, thereby, we witness a veritable process of the substitution of the real. The enormous complexity of inter-human relations must be reduced to simplifications which are adapted to the smooth functioning of the system. The administrative characteristics of this model do not detract from its power as a pertinent example. However, even in this sophisticated proposal we can verify the persistence, not so much of an ambiguity, as of a veritable contradiction. In fact, the systems theory model develops a postmodern framework in order to uncover a lack of contradictions, something which is supposedly peculiar to contemporary societies. However, the theory does not thereby prove that these societies are still governable. Rather, it merely ends up emphasizing the characteristics of fluidity, of circulation and of communication that are typical of human relationships in contemporary societies. This means that the contradiction between the development and maturation of capitalist society is not resolved in the postmodernist framework, but merely transformed into a vicious circle or even amplified in terms of substitution of the real. On the other hand, the aim of a richer, more amenable human society is hinted at in the administrative approaches and juridical definitions.

A second example of a political theory application of the postmodernist model, one which again reveals its contradictory nature, is given by the neo-liberal economic policies which have begun to be implemented during the last twenty years of the crisis. In this case too a postmodernist assertion serves to establish the theoretical framework, i.e. the assertion concerning the perfectly smooth working of the market and of the agents within it. According to this assertion, the only role of the state authorities is to facilitate this smooth working by removing market obstacles, lowering taxes, liberalizing the labour-market. . . and so on. Thereby, the goal of bringing about a greater level of social investment and a perfect functioning of the economic universe would supposedly be attained. The only problem is that extreme liberalization of the economy reveals its opposite, namely that the social and productive environment is not made up of atomized individuals and that where these exist, they represent marginal or residual phenomena (pertaining to the 'formality' as opposed to the 'reality' of subsumption) while the real environment is made up of collective individuals. In addition, new technology and the expansion of new productive forces increase the importance of this collective basis of production and highlight its new, rather than its old, contradictions. Thus we find ourselves once more confronted by a contradiction that has become a vicious circle, and the 'postmodernist' governments of economic neo-liberalism are so caught up in a game of heteronomies that when they try to beat inflation through regulation of the market, they find that inflation has become even worse, and when they try to increase investment through liberalization of the market, they find that investment falls, and so on.

To conclude, I would like to suggest that postmodernism be read as the mystified ideology of the new collectivities, or rather, as a primitive but effective allusion to the scientific determination of new subjects which in the Marxian phase of real subsumption (or more simply, in the phase of general circulation and communication) are being formed. The project is ambiguous, but it seems to me that the theorists of postmodernism have posed certain conditions, starting from which it is possible to construct the concept of new collective subjectivities. As always, the problem of the definition of subjectivity concerns the basic issues of space, time and the metaphysical quality of the substratum. In postmodernism, or rather, in the Marxian 'real subsumption', the spatial is characterized as absolute flexibility. Every social subject is as flexible as are the working day and the scannings of intersubjective communication. These qualifications concern and qualify the substratum. In postmodernism the subject is thus, by definition, completely mobile and flexible. Finally, the completely abstract substratum has been determined by production, consumption, knowledge and the desire for transformation and equality. None of this, as is obvious, creates equivalent and interchangeable individuals. On the contrary, these abstract qualities are linked within the universality of communicative potential, and this collective, human, communicative potential constitutes their substance *par excellence*. The real paradox is that the more mobile and flexible the human quality is, and the more abstract the productive capacity is, the more collective the world and the subject are. The 'primitive accumulation' of capital, as it is described by the classics, broke every natural and social tie and reduced the subject to a mere quantitative entity and a purely numerical existence in the market. On the contrary, the abstraction which is formed today is the one that permeates human intercommunicability and which, on this level, constructs the solidity of communitary relationships on the new reality of the subjects. (See K. Polanyi, *The Great Transformation* (Beacon Press, Boston Mass., 1957).)

Is postmodernism a romantic ideology, therefore? It seems to me that *mutatis mutandis*, postmodernism identifies, as the romantics had done, a period of crisis and of the subjection of society and work to capitalist domination. Bearing in mind the Marxian distinction between formal subsumption and real subsumption, what the romantics had documented and described in formal terms, postmodernism registers in real terms.

14

Towards new values?

Terminal: What relationship do you see as existing between information technology, the economy and social movements?

Toni Negri: In work which I undertook a number of years ago, I started from the hypothesis of a recomposition of the working class. However, with the appearance of automation, the potential of the 'mass labourer' became completely dissipated. In effect, we are confronted by a new form of production. This is not only because the mechanisms determining hierarchies have changed due to automation in and of itself, but because the productive process has taken on totally different forms. In terms of classical Marxism, it is almost impossible to define what is new about the totality of the relations of production. Automation can no longer be analysed as the perfection of the process of exploitation of productive labour, but rather it must be viewed as a modification of the totality of social relationships. The problem is to ascertain to what extent information technology is the means by which capital undertakes the real subsumption of all the social forces of production and reproduction. Through automation, the relationship between the production and circulation of commodities (including the labour force, which must be considered a commodity) is found to be totally integrated within capital. The socialization of production means that society is exploited by capital as such.

Interview conducted by M. Burnier, G. Lacroix, E. Braine and B. Pianta.

In the light of these hypotheses we have tried, through our activity in Italy, to establish a degree of potential to resist. In other words, accepting the new situation brought about by automation, we have tried to develop a political strategy aimed at the conquest of the social wage (i.e. a wage which is linked to people's needs, which has an egalitarian tendency, and – above all – which facilitates the breakdown of the division between the employed and the unemployed and any other social division). We also consider all forms of the welfare state to be a form of wage which is generalized throughout the whole of society. This is what has happened in Italy through multifarious and autonomous struggles – including such mistaken kinds as the theft of goods presented as wages struggles. The subjects of these movements were people who were involved in schools, factories, the application of information technology and the submerged economy – which was itself highly modernized owing to the fact that information technology had brought it to the highest possible levels of productivity and the production of value. I would like to mention the large automated factories. For example, the light engineering firm Bassani-Ticino, situated between Varese and Milan, employs 3,000 workers on the premises and 15,000, each with a computer and a lorry, on the outside. Each week, work-sheets are distributed and the previous week's work, produced using computerized machines, is collected. This is a traditional form of capitalism – but at a higher level. In the specific structural conditions (in particular the existence of peasant-workers and the absence of immigration) the workers' struggle is both traditional and advanced since on the social level it is aimed at both wage increases and schools for all citizens.

The same phenomenon is to be found more or less throughout the whole of northern Italy. Examining the situation closely, it is possible to see, for example, that child labour using old sewing machines is in fact regulated by a highly organized industrial process, one which is organized according to the regulations of the savings banks and of the Visentini law which gives fiscal benefits to large industry. Between Venice and Padua, in Marches and to the north of Milan etc. thousands of workers are employed in the 'dispersed factory' which, moreover, is tied to the needs of the international economy. In the footwear sector, for example, German firms provide the shoe designs, the machines and everything necessary for the 'great Italian territorial factory' which, in its turn, organizes extremely flexible working on the basis of centralized, information-based management.

All this poses a number of theoretical questions: workers' subjectivity takes on a new form because the economic value of production is no longer tied to specific technical capacities or to the skills of the worker. Class consciousness has been eliminated. The basic question is whether class consciousness will exist again, and to find an answer I am convinced that it is necessary to look among such subterranean phenomena as, for example, the duration of strikes of more than 200 hours, these being the manifestation of new solidarities and new social networks. I believe that there currently exists a 'clandestine' existence of the workers, a subterranean movement, through which workers' consciousness is in the process of being reconstructed.

Terminal: With automation, who is the opponent?

T.N.: The opponent consists in the organization of society. In Germany people say, 'We are neither on the left, nor on the right'. It is not simply the state or the bosses that are at issue, but the social structure which appropriates our culture and our work. . . This is a situation in which people are increasingly exploited – whereas they could possess a wealth of initiatives, freedoms and potentialities. Instead, capital has imposed on us a mechanism of displacement and of continuous movement devoid of meaning. The problem thus consists in identifying at what level the antagonism, the social conflict, takes place.

What is at issue is not simply the fact of the domination of the labour process and of hierarchy; there currently exist processes of the production of human subjectivity. From this a complete confusion arises. It becomes impossible to identify the antagonism and the directions which must be taken. I don't know how one is going to be able to redefine social values. The paradox is that even the choice of values which facilitates social control, necessitates antagonism.

In this respect the bosses, as they have always been, are more Marxist than we are. The collapse of politics, of the criteria of social orientation and the subsumption of society within capital, have brought about the crisis of Marxism. Marx believed that the triumph of industrialism would bring about (in a dialectical way) the liberation of humanity. On the contrary, the general orientation of values has totally collapsed. One can with justice say that power is value ('I have the opportunity to be richer than you'). To say this, however, is to declare the law of the jungle. All criteria of value have been blocked and nothing else has been liberated.

Terminal: Computerization, inasmuch as it intervenes in the new configuration of the general productive horizon, transforms labour processes through the elimination of a certain type of circulation of value. In these conditions, what is the value of the flow of production? What is productivity?

T.N.: Classically it is 'generically human labour power, at a certain level of organized knowledge, submitted to a mechanism for the utilization of labour'; but the calculation of value does not take place in these terms. There exists a contradiction in that, on the one hand, automation represents the establishment of two societies, one productive, the other unemployed. On the other hand, it also represents the establishment of a higher form of society in which time which is not spent working is nevertheless socially and productively useful.

The point, then, is not to say 'No' to unemployment, but to ask, 'What is social time?' If social time is useful in the transfer and production of the knowledge which today conditions production, then all of social time, whether it is idle or spent working, should be paid for. However, there has been controversy, and also a great deal of confusion, on this point!

In Germany, for example, the trade unions, in the face of increasing support for the Greens and the economic crisis, have proposed a thirty-five-hour week. Management, in order to retain control of the flows of production, agreed to negotiate. However, most of those located on the margins of production (such as apprentices and women etc.) refused to do battle over the thirty-five-hour week because they felt autonomous and preferred flexibility, the loss of which would for them have meant a loss of control. Therefore, to know who is on the left and who on the right has become secondary because the situation is of an almost irresolvable complexity. The Greens themselves are divided over this question.

Terminal: Computerization has been presented as making possible the realization of a whole number of new values such as autonomy, an increase in freedom and a diminution of fatigue. The self becomes a social value, whereas before, the group and the people were social values. Now it is the individual who says 'I can cope with my work'. This is, in effect, a very old value: the workers of the traditional factories were asked to be to a certain extent autonomous operatives. It will be said, in fact, that with the development of computerization people were invited to give a certain ideological assent to the new technology. They were made to see it as a positive horizon, the social road to change and new forms of communication etc.

T.N.: I believe that this is completely positive. In my opinion the contradiction lies not here but in the fact that capital, at this level of development, creates new needs which it suppresses at the same time. And this suppression is increasingly severe. I am convinced that a process of political reconstruction passes through protest against automation construed as a general social fact perhaps at state level. The autonomy which is claimed involves questioning the workings of the state. Above all, however, the autonomy which is claimed means more than community; it means the establishment of the 'social individual' and the integration of productive functions on a social plane. For example, I believe that instead of paying taxes for services, people could gradually try to organize alternative forms of solidarity, cooperatives etc.; and the likelihood of all this will be even greater the more they come to appropriate various financial, technical and productive resources etc.

Terminal: Does this not arouse a certain illusion of appropriation? For example, the citizens of certain French communes have been told to manage the municipal budget themselves, thus creating a new consensus.

T.N.: There was a time when the mystificatory imperative of capitalism was 'Enrich yourselves!' Now it is 'Computerize yourselves!' But to what end? – not in order to gain freedom. Destruction of the capitalist organization of technical resources is a difficult task which it will nevertheless be necessary to realize.

The most intense, anti-state contradiction is going to come about through this new, autonomous productive force – not in the sense of opposition to Mitterand or state institutions, but against the very form of social exploitation. I see less and less of a difference between social capital, the state and institutional forms of power.

Terminal: Do you think that we have entered a period of state capitalism?

T.N.: I would not say so. The proportion of state-owned capital is certainly enormous. In Italy state factories and holdings are responsible for more than half of gross production. If it is true that forms of production have today come to coincide with those of circulation, this means that the forms of production and reproduction tend to become assimilated one to the other. The real situation is more complex. For example: is social welfare a productive element in France? I do not know; but it is certain that the state tends to make it productive, or rather, that it tends to pass from forms of assistance to a general control over society. There no longer exists state monopoly capitalism, but something completely different: the forms have completely changed.

Terminal: Alternative mechanisms have been described as being possible values around which a reappropriation of labour and of forms of existence can be organized by people that are today oppressed. This idea is not very widespread in France where a great deal gets neglected because of the struggle over relative wages. How can these aspects of production and of alternative strategies constitute a form of resistance or appropriation in the face of the growth of a 'computerized capitalism'?

T.N.: This is *the* big problem to which thought must be given. One can give the Leninist reply which is to take power and smash the existing state machine. The only other response would be that one cannot do anything. Personally, I do not agree with the Leninist response: there exists neither a linear process of social integration, nor a simultaneous contradiction between the growth of working-class consciousness and the crisis of capitalism. Rather, the system tends towards disintegration. Social integration comes about through war – or rather, through the fear of war. Moreover, systems of domination are overdetermined by state violence.

Therefore, in order to re-establish a perspective, it is perhaps necessary to study the genealogy of these systems of domination. This means considering the elements of crisis which existed prior to current processes, and in particular, the contradiction between subjective needs and new potentialities.

Terminal: You talk about a complex and plural subject appropriating the new technological possibilities. Can you explain this idea?

T.N.: The conditions necessary for this to happen come about through capitalist development. Even the worker placed at the bottom of the hierarchy, having lost awareness of prior processes of production and not yet having awareness of the new, has the possibility of a confrontation at the level which is richest in values and where his or her position is still more important. In other words, in the organic composition of capital, the proportion of constant capital has become enormous, while the proportion of variable capital has become correspondingly small. Variable capital has thus become even more necessary than ever. Moreover, all innovation derives from variable capital.

Quantitatively, the yield is thus entirely negative, but qualitatively, the yield of productivity is immense: variable capital, in its precariousness, increases productivity enormously.

This productivity arises not simply by virtue of the position occupied by the worker in production, but in virtue of the totality of cultural values and mechanisms: the power of the individual who finds him/herself in that position (s/he is there but could be elsewhere) is totally bound up with this social relationship. This implies the freedom of the subject, or in other words, that this subject is no longer a slave of the machine.

Is this paradox perhaps productive? In order to discover the answer to this question it is necessary to act politically on these relationships, to seek confrontation and act. This is the only possible strategy. These problems will not be resolved simply with the help of theory. In this new reality it is necessary to take up the method of working-class investigation.

Terminal: From the classic perspective of workers' resistance, what is the role of the consciousness of those men or women working in the tertiary sector and who have traditionally been considered as belonging to the petty-bourgeoisie, and how can their consciousness be changed?

T.N.: To answer this question it is necessary to put aside all preconceptions and, with regard to such concepts as bourgeoisie, petty-bourgeoisie, etc. to start again from the beginning. Take the girl who comes to work in the centre of Paris, stays there fifteen hours a day to study, and who is obliged to work. Is she really 'petty bourgeois'?

Where I come from, employment in a bank once conferred considerable social status. In reality, however, the girl that typed away at a computer terminal was carrying out, at the bank, exactly the same tasks that she could equally have carried out in the nearby chemical factory. The only difference was that she had a fifteen-month annual salary as compared to the thirteen months' she would have earned working at the factory. However, not being a 'worker', the girl at the bank takes it for granted that she has a certain social status. What one is dealing with here is an extrinsic psychological attitude divorced from the reality of the situation. The point, then, is to analyse the form of the labour involved, the form of the working day (i.e. its time) and thirdly, the specific form of valorization which is set in motion.

What is the 'factory'? Owing to the evolution of capitalism and the working class, the walls of the 'factory' fell down long ago (so to speak) and it is now fifteen years since I last understood what the factory was. The enormous factory of the tertiary sector demands to be analysed as a 'society-factory'. However, because it encourages one to think only in terms of material products, the term 'factory' should be abandoned. Today, it is not only material products that are produced, but principally, information, and the components of domination (to which should be added the components of subjectivity).

Terminal: What is the nature of that society in which work continues and in which work no longer has value?

T.N.: It is a society in which there remains only the power of command and the coercive organization of society and which is controlled by the atomic bomb: 'If you do not work, you will all be destroyed'. There is total overdetermination. There no longer exists any value or work relations; there exists merely a relationship of domination. Such is the cultural stereotype of postmodernity.

Terminal: Is the political, as Lenin maintained, a concentrated form of the economic, and power a concentrated form of value?

T.N.: Exactly the opposite is true!

Terminal: Given that capital must be devalorized if it is to be valorized, is it not by the same token necessary to devalorize society in order to valorize capital?

T.N.: This phenomenon has been described by Schumpeter (creative destruction). The current crisis is a crisis of the devalorization of the social in order to revalorize capital. This is usually termed 'restructuration'. As far as capital is concerned, in the fields of computers and telecommunications there are currently a number of innovations underway which will soon determine value, or in other words, the substance of money. Money has never constituted general equivalence; rather, it is the carrier of power: not only political power but also 'revolutionary' economic power or 'avant garde' innovations. Therefore one might say that money has been, so to speak, the steam engine, then petroleum. . . and so on. Nowadays it is information technology and information as such. The point is not to say that the process of computerization brings about a general devalorization of other productive values, but rather, to note that beyond a certain point, computerization brings about a change in the quality of value: as a consequence one can no longer measure the processes of production by the yardstick of previously-considered value. We are no longer in the presence of labour-power as such, or labour-time as such, but rather, we exist in a universe constituted by a circulation of information, indeed a large quantity of information. Alternative units of measurement must therefore be adopted. Beyond the point at which it is no longer merely a means of transmission but has become the very essence of production, computerization is no longer simply the form by which quantities of commodities are transformed. Rather, it itself becomes a commodity.

Terminal: Will labour continue to be the 'tripalium'?

T.N.: At Fiat nowadays, work is much less arduous. Fiat is said to be the most automated car manufacturer in Europe. Cars can be assembled by one worker where previously thirty or forty would have been required. The tendency towards the considerable diminution in the variable proportion of capital, makes that proportion socially decisive.

Some will point out that production is being relocated in the non-industrialized countries. This does not constitute a particular objection. It is true that industry does not pay, or pays much less to the workers of Taiwan or South Korea; but these countries will themselves shortly be automated; in some cases they already are, and to a greater extent than the industrialized countries. Others place their faith in the development of liberation movements on the margins of automation. But this situation exists in the case of every transformation of the mode of production. The theory of the dual society is a mystification, or rather, a rigid classificatory ideology. Look at how the development of capitalism took place. A given capitalist industrial structure, itself limited, has the power to determine the whole of social evolution. As much was shown by Lenin in his study of capitalism in Russia around 1898/99. Technological innovation in agriculture released part of the labour force which was then re-engaged in industry. Automation having subsequently penetrated the factory, the workers so displaced moved into the tertiary sector. It is here that computerization, as a new form of technology, is intervening, thus placing in question the unity and the boundaries of the tertiary sector. Where, then, will the people of the tertiary sector go after they have been hounded out by computerization?

Terminal: Specialists of the tertiary sector say that in ten years more than half the labour force will be without work. Now the system does not have even the minimal appearance of being solid enough to support all this. Real valorization of working hours, something which society is not yet capable of doing, will therefore fail. Undoubtedly this is because employers still reason in terms of directly productive values, believing other social activities to be useless and serving solely to reproduce the labour force for the following day's work. And here a social explosion risks being produced: either it is acknowledged that 'non-productive' actvities are also value-producing, or there will be war.

T.N.: An attempt must be made to get the people to manage the crisis on their own. One must applaud the comrade who said, 'I currently earn two million; tomorrow I shall earn no more than one, but on the other hand I will produce models of boats'.

This accompanies a transformation that is not war. As has correctly been observed, new technology strains consensus. Nevertheless, I have the impression that the passage from the obligation to work to the right not to work, will be very violent. In effect, in the current transition, the relationship of valorization has been deprived of its human significance. We have reached a situation of production for production's sake, and this means that as a result of the crisis, certain of the ruling political and industrial strata have come to espouse racist and fanatical policies. They then find themselves caught in a series of vicious circles given by the fact that without the immigrants in France, it would be impossible to live. Racism is thus an element of the crisis of an authority which is tied to outdated policies.

By contrast, in Germany and the United States, for the first time, a crisis of values will be linked to the realization of radical alternatives; hence the reaction and the repression in the U.S.A., involving campaigns against abortion, Reaganism etc. In Germany, developments have been more positive even if still fragile; one has only to observe the composition of the Green movement with its old and traditional values such as forest-conservation on the one hand, and more modern values such as information technology, on the other. In Bade-Wurtemburg, there has been a general increase in support for the Greens among farmers (who were previously under the influence of Christian Democracy) and also among technicians and engineers. We are witnessing the paradoxical appearance of a conservative development (the restoration of roads to the country-side and the refusal of a certain form of industrialism) which could be called anti-capitalist neo-liberalism.

It is clear that unless there is a growth of struggles and alternatives, and unless we see the exercise of social countervailing powers, we will drift towards an increasingly reactionary situation – towards a veritable paranoia of power – tied to production for production's sake. In such circumstances war will surely be possible.

Appendix

The following quotations are taken from volumes in the Pelican Marx Library (Harmondsworth, Penguin, 1973 and 1976).

CAPITAL VOLUME I, TRANS. BEN FOWKES

All this notwithstanding, this change does not in itself imply a fundamental modification in the real nature of the labour process, the actual process of production. On the contrary, the fact is that capital subsumes the labour process as it finds it, that is to say, it takes over an *existing labour process*, developed by different and more archaic modes of production. And since that is the case it is evident that capital took over an *available, established labour process*. For example, handicraft, a mode of agriculture corresponding to a small, independent peasant economy. If changes occur in these traditional established *labour processes* after their takeover by capital, these are nothing but the gradual consequences of that subsumption. The work may become more intensive, its duration may be extended, it may become more continuous or orderly under the eye of the interested capitalist, but in themselves these changes do not affect the character of the actual labour process, the actual mode of working. This stands in striking contrast to the development of a *specifically capitalist mode of production* (large-scale industry, etc.); the latter not only transforms the situations of the various agents of production, it also *revolutionizes* their actual mode of labour and the real nature of the labour process as a whole. It is in contradistinction to this last that we come to designate as the *formal subsumption of labour under capital* what we have discussed earlier, viz. the takeover by capital of a mode of labour developed before the emergence of capitalist relations. The latter as a form of *compulsion* by which surplus labour is exacted by extending the duration of labour-time – a *mode of compulsion* not based on personal relations of domination and dependency, but simply on differing economic functions – this is common to both forms. However, the specifically capitalist mode of production has yet other methods of exacting surplus-value at its disposal. But given a pre-existing mode of labour, i.e. an *established* development of the productive power of labour and a mode of labour corresponding to this productive power, surplus-value can be created only by lengthening the working day, i.e. by increasing *absolute surplus-value*. In the *formal* subsumption of labour under capital, this is the *sole* manner of producing surplus-value. (p. 1021)

The *social* productive forces of labour, or the productive forces of directly social, *socialized* (i.e. collective) labour come into being through co-operation, division of labour within the workshop, the use of *machinery*, and in general the transformation of production by the conscious *use* of the sciences, of mechanics, chemistry, etc. for specific ends, technology, etc. and similarly, through the enormous increase of *scale* corresponding to such developments (for it is only socialized labour that is capable of applying the *general* products of human development, such as mathematics, to the immediate processes of production; and conversely, progress in these sciences presupposes a certain level of material production). This entire development of the productive forces of *socialized labour* (in contrast to the more or less isolated labour of individuals), and together with it the *use of science* (the *general* product of social development), in the *immediate process of production*, takes the form of the *productive power of capital*. It does not appear as the productive power of labour, or even that part of it that is identical with capital. And least of all does it appear as the productive power either of the individual worker or of the workers joined together in the process of production. The mystification implicit in the relations of capital as a whole is greatly intensified here, far beyond the point it had reached or could have reached in the merely formal subsumption of labour under capital. On the other hand, we here find a striking illustration of the historic significance of capitalist production in its specific form – the transmutation of the immediate process of production itself and the development of the social forces of production of labour.

It has been shown (Chapter III) how not merely at the level of ideas, but also in reality, the social character of his labour confronts the worker as something not merely alien, but hostile and antagonistic, when it appears before him objectified and personified in capital.

If the production of absolute surplus-value was the material expression of the formal subsumption of labour under capital, then the production of relative surplus-value may be viewed as its real subsumption. (p. 1024)

The real subsumption of labour under capital

The general features of the *formal subsumption* remain, viz. the direct *subordination of the labour process to capital*, irrespective of the state of its technological development. But on this foundation there now arises a technologically and otherwise *specific mode of production – capitalist production –* which transforms the nature *of the labour process and its actual conditions*. Only when that happens do we witness the *real subsumption of labour under capital*.

....

The real subsumption of labour under capital is developed in all the forms evolved by relative, as opposed to absolute surplus-value. With the real subsumption of labour under capital a complete (and constantly repeated) revolution takes place in the mode of production, in the productivity of the workers and in the relations between workers and capitalists.

With the real subsumption of labour under capital, all the changes in the labour process already discussed now become reality. The *social forces of production* of labour are now developed, and with large-scale production comes the direct application of science and technology. On the one hand, *capitalist production* now establishes itself as a mode of production *sui generis* and brings into being a new mode of material production. On the other hand, the latter itself forms the basis for the development of capitalist relations whose adequate form, therefore, presupposes a definite stage in the evolution of the productive forces of labour. (pp. 1034–5)

First, with the development of the *real subsumption of labour under capital*, or the *specifically capitalist mode of production*, the *real lever* of the overall labour process is increasingly not the individual worker. Instead, *labour-power socially combined* and the various competing labour-powers which together form the entire production machine participate in very different ways in the immediate process of making commodities, or, more accurately in this context, creating the product. Some work better with their hands, others with their heads, one as a manager, engineer, technologist, etc., the other as overseer, the third as manual labourer or even drudge. An ever increasing number of types of labour are included in the immediate concept of *productive labour*, and those who perform it are classed as *productive workers*, workers directly exploited by capital and *subordinated* to its process of production and expansion. If we consider the aggregate *worker*, i.e. if we take all the members comprising the workshop together, then we see that their *combined activity* results materially in an *aggregate* product which is at the same time a *quantity of goods*. And here it is quite immaterial whether the job of a particular worker, who is merely a limb of this aggregate worker, is at a greater or smaller distance from the actual manual labour. But then: the activity of this aggregate labour-power is its *immediate productive consumption by capital*, i.e. it is the self-valorization process of capital, and hence, as we shall demonstrate, the immediate production of surplus-value, the *immediate conversion of this latter into capital*. (pp. 1039–40)

GRUNDRISSE, TRANS. MARTIN NICOLAUS

As the basis on which large industry rests, the appropriation of alien labour time, ceases, with its development, to make up or to create wealth, so does *direct labour* as such cease to be the basis of production, since, in one respect, it is transformed more into a supervisory and regulatory activity; but then also because the product ceases to be the product of isolated direct labour, and the

combination of social activity appears, rather, as the producer. . . .
In direct exchange, individual direct labour appears as realized in a
particular product or part of the product, and its communal, social
character – its character as objectification of general labour and
satisfaction of the general need – as posited through exchange
alone. In the production process of large-scale industry, by
contrast, just as the conquest of the forces of nature by the social
intellect is the precondition of the productive power of the means of
labour as developed into the automatic process, on one side, so, on
the other, is the *labour of the individual in its direct presence posited as
suspended individual, i.e. as social, labour. Thus the other basis of this
mode of production falls away.* (p. 709)

But to the degree that large industry develops, the creation of real
wealth comes to depend less on labour time and on the amount of
labour employed than on the power of the agencies set in motion
during labour time, whose 'powerful effectiveness' is itself in turn
out of all proportion to the direct labour time spent on their
production, but depends rather on the general state of science and
on the progress of technology, or the application of this science to
production. (pp. 704–5)

Real wealth manifests itself, rather – and large industry reveals this
– in the monstrous disproportion between the labour time applied,
and its product, as well as in the qualitative imbalance between
labour, reduced to a pure abstraction, and the power of the
production process it superintends. Labour no longer appears so
much to be included within the production process; rather the
human being comes to relate more as watchman and regulator to
the production process itself. (What holds for machinery holds
likewise for the combination of human activities and the development of human intercourse.) No longer does the worker insert a
modified natural thing [*Naturgegenstand*] as middle link between
the object [*Objekt*] and himself; rather, he inserts the process of
nature, transformed into an industrial process, as a means between
himself and inorganic nature, mastering it. He steps to the side of
the production process, instead of being its chief actor. In this
transformation, it is neither the direct human labour he himself
performs, nor the time during which he works, but rather the
appropriation of his own general productive power, his understand-

ing of nature and his mastery over it by virtue of his presence as a social body – it is, in a word, the development of the social individual which appears as the great foundation-stone of production and of wealth. The *theft of alien labour time, on which the present wealth is based,* appears a miserable foundation in face of this new one, created by large-scale industry itself. As soon as labour in the direct form has ceased to be the great well-spring of wealth, labour time ceases and must cease to be its measure, and hence exchange-value [must cease to be the measure] of use value. The *surplus labour of the mass* has ceased to be the condition for the development of general wealth, just as the *non-labour of the few*, for the development of the general powers of the human head. With that, production based on exchange value breaks down, and the direct, material production process is stripped of the form of penury and antithesis. The free development of individualities, and hence not the reduction of necessary labour time so as to posit surplus labour, but rather the general reduction of the necessary labour of society to a minimum, which then corresponds to the artistic, scientific etc. development of the individuals in the time set free, and with the means created, for all of them. Capital itself is the moving contradiction, [in] that it presses to reduce labour time to a minimum, while it posits labour time, on the other side, as sole measure and source of wealth. Hence it diminishes labour time in the necessary form so as to increase it in the superfluous form; hence posits the superfluous in growing measure as a condition – question of life or death – for the necessary. On the one side, then, it calls to life all the powers of science and of nature, as of social combination and of social intercourse, in order to make the creation of wealth independent (relatively) of the labour time employed on it. On the other side, it wants to use labour time as the measuring rod for the giant social forces thereby created, and to confine them within the limits required to maintain the already created value as value. Forces of production and social relations – two different sides of the development of the social individual – appear to capital as mere means, and are merely means for it to produce on its limited foundation. In fact, however, they are the material conditions to blow this foundation sky-high. (pp. 705–6)

Index

Index by Jackie McDermott